Ad Hoc Arbitration in China

Arbitration is the dominant method in the world for resolving international commercial disputes. As compared with institutional arbitration, ad hoc arbitration has many advantages that make it a preferred way to resolve commercial disputes on many occasions. The Arbitration Law of the People's Republic of China, however, requires that parties appoint an arbitration institution in their arbitration agreement; otherwise an ad hoc arbitration agreement is invalid. This rule seems to preclude ad hoc arbitration under Chinese law and threatens the validity of many arbitration agreements that are imperfectly drafted. Fortunately, however, this does not mean Chinese courts will never enforce an ad hoc arbitration agreement or an ad hoc arbitration award. This book informs parties and practitioners of potential pitfalls related to ad hoc arbitration in China and offers practical guidance. It also conducts a comparative study of the history of arbitration in the Western world and in China, to identify the reasons for this hostility to ad hoc arbitration and calls for changes to this requirement under Chinese law.

Tietie "Frank" Zhang is a Lecturer in Corporate and Commercial Law at the University of Sheffield School of Law.

Ad Hoc Arbitration in China

Tietie Zhang

Routledge
Taylor & Francis Group
LONDON AND NEW YORK

First published 2019
by Routledge
2 Park Square, Milton Park, Abingdon, Oxon OX14 4RN

and by Routledge
52 Vanderbilt Avenue, New York, NY 10017

First issued in paperback 2020

Routledge is an imprint of the Taylor & Francis Group, an informa business

British Library Cataloguing-in-Publication Data
A catalogue record for this book is available from the British Library

Library of Congress Cataloging-in-Publication Data
Names: Zhang, Tietie, author.
Title: Ad hoc arbitration in China / by Tietie Zhang.
Description: Abingdon, Oxon [UK]; New York, NY: Routledge, 2018. | Includes index.
Identifiers: LCCN 2018027944 | ISBN 9780815394501 (hbk)
Subjects: LCSH: Arbitration and award—China. | Arbitration agreements, Commercial—China. | International commercial arbitration.
Classification: LCC KNQ1829 .Z43 2018 | DDC 347.951/09—dc23
LC record available at https://lccn.loc.gov/2018027944

ISBN 13: 978-0-367-58453-5 (pbk)
ISBN 13: 978-0-8153-9450-1 (hbk)

Typeset in Galliard
by codeMantra

Contents

Foreword ix
Acknowledgments xi

1 Introduction 1
I Overview and significance 1
II Background 4
A Arbitration vs. litigation 4
B Ad hoc vs. institutional arbitration 7
III The ad hoc problem under Chinese law 10

2 A history of legal transplant 14
I Arbitration's history in the Western world 14
II Arbitration's history in China 16
A The primitive stage: arbitration in Ancient and Imperial China 16
B The start of modernization: arbitration in the late Qing dynasty 17
C Continued modernization: arbitration in the Republic of China 21
D The current system: arbitration in the People's Republic of China 22
III The impact of history on the current Chinese arbitration law 30
IV A legal transplant story 32

3 Enforceability of ad hoc arbitration agreements in China 39
I Rejection of ad hoc arbitration agreements under Chinese law 39
II Different jurisdictions in the Greater China region 41
A Hong Kong and Macau 41
B Taiwan 44

III Enforcing ad hoc arbitration agreements under non-Chinese law 45

A Choice-of-law issues in international commercial arbitration 46

B The SPC's judicial interpretations 48

C The SPC's choice-of-law rule on an arbitration agreement's validity 49

IV Analyzing the SPC's choice-of-law rule 52

A Validity-preferring and pro-arbitration 52

B Potential issues 55

V Conclusion 57

4 Enforceability of ad hoc arbitration awards in China 58

I Foreign ad hoc arbitration awards are enforceable in China 58

II Seemingly dire prospects for Chinese ad hoc arbitration 63

A Successful operation seems impractical under Chinese law 63

B Awards unenforceable under Chinese law 69

C Awards' enforceability doubtful under the New York Convention 75

III Conclusion 80

5 Making ad hoc arbitration work in China under its current law 81

I A special drafting strategy 81

II Ad hoc arbitration in China will operate successfully 85

A External obstructions no longer possible 85

B Internal obstructions will not happen 86

III The ad hoc arbitration award will be enforceable 87

A More chances of being enforced inside China 88

B More likely to be enforced outside China 91

IV Conclusion 93

6 A system calling for change 94

I A broken system 94

II A vague and problematic standard 96

III Rationale behind the hostility no longer exists 98

A Reasons given by the Chinese lawmakers 99
B A more convincing explanation 100
C Changes in nowadays China 102
IV Conclusion 104

7 Re-thinking China's ad hoc arbitration legal framework 105
I China should have ad hoc arbitration 105
II China can have ad hoc arbitration 108
A Doubts are unnecessary 108
B Mediation offers a good example 109
III Towards a complete ad hoc arbitration system 114
A The SPC's role 114
B Legislative action is the only choice 119

8 Conclusion 121

Appendices 127
Appendix A: Arbitration Law of the People's Republic of China 127
Appendix B: Civil Procedure Law of the People's Republic of China (selected provisions) 144
Appendix C: The Supreme People's Court's interpretation on certain issues concerning the application of the "Arbitration Law of the People's Republic of China" 148

Index 155

Foreword

This work offers rich insights into both practical and historical-theoretical aspects of international arbitration in China. It focuses specifically on China's rejection of ad hoc arbitration—a form of dispute settlement universally accepted outside of China. Experienced arbitrators are unfailingly aware that China's arbitration law, taken at face value, will not enforce an arbitration agreement calling for ad hoc arbitration. On its face, Chinese law will also not enforce an arbitral award arising out of ad hoc arbitration. It insists that an arbitration institution—CIETAC or even possibly a foreign, non-governmental such institution like the ICC—must administer arbitration. To a Westerner, China's opposition to ad hoc arbitration is one of the most unusual—even baffling—aspects of its arbitration law. National arbitration law throughout the world—except in China—finds nothing amiss in the ad hoc form of dispute resolution. This option generally appeals to commercial parties wishing to avoid delays and constraints that an arbitral institution can impose and to reduce costs by avoiding institution fees. If in the rest of the world ad hoc arbitration is not infrequently chosen and offers a reasonable and desirable form of dispute resolution, one is impelled to ask: why is China opposed to it?

This book offers an answer to that question, and in doing so, introduces the reader to fundamental features of the Chinese legal system—in particular as it relates to arbitration. It also provides insight into the theory of legal transplants as a way of explaining how relatively new and developing legal systems borrow, adapt and sometimes transform legal concepts and institutions originating in more advanced legal systems.

The book remains loyal, however, to a pragmatic focus. Perhaps its major achievement is to explain how, through careful drafting, parties—presumably aided by legal counsel and somewhat paradoxically—can still avail themselves of ad hoc arbitration in a Chinese context. The author explains that by carefully choosing the arbitral seat, the law applicable to the arbitration agreement, the national arbitration law of the seat as the lex arbitri, and a good set of procedural rules for the arbitral proceedings, parties can achieve an enforceable agreement to arbitrate ad hoc and can be confident that a Chinese court will enforce the resulting award. This analysis will surely come as a revelation to practitioners who have consistently understood that ad hoc arbitration is forbidden in China.

The author is not content, however, to leave the analysis there. He goes on to argue persuasively that it would be in China's immediate and long-term self interest to simplify and modernize its arbitration law by openly abandoning its hostility to ad hoc arbitration.

The author is a young, highly talented legal scholar with a deep and practical understanding of the Chinese legal system and Western legal systems, especially in respect of international commercial arbitration. Practitioners and legal scholars keenly interested in international arbitration's role in the global economic system will learn from and prize this work and future work in this field authored by Dr. Zhang.

Professor John J. Barceló III
William N. Cromwell Professor of
International & Comparative Law
Cornell University Law School
Ithaca, NY
May, 2018

Acknowledgments

This book is based on my dissertation completed at Cornell University Law School for the degree of Doctor of Science of Law (J.S.D.). Pursuing this degree changed not only my career but also my life. I am deeply indebted to Cornell Law School, particularly its Graduate and International Program, for allowing me the opportunity and funding my study. I am also grateful to Cornell International Law Journal for giving me permission to reuse in this book some of the materials in my previously published article *Enforceability of Ad Hoc Arbitration Agreements in China: China's Incomplete Ad Hoc Arbitration System*, 46 CORNELL INT'L L. J. 361 (2013).

Individually, I first and foremost thank my J.S.D. advisor, Professor John J. Barceló III, William Nelson Cromwell Professor of International and Comparative Law at Cornell Law School, for his teaching, guidance, and support throughout the years. Without him, this book could not exist. I also thank Professor Xingzhong Yu, Anthony W. and Lulu C. Wang Professor in Chinese Law at Cornell Law School, for his mentoring and help both academically and personally. My heartfelt gratitude also goes to my colleagues at the University of Sheffield School of Law. Professors Robert Burrell, Tamara Hervey, and Andrew Johnston all offered me invaluable advice regarding the publication of this book. I am very grateful to them all.

Last but not least, I thank my parents, my wife, and my three daughters. They have always given me their full support, without which I can never accomplish anything. This book really belongs to them.

1 Introduction

I Overview and significance

This is the first book length study of ad hoc arbitration in China in either English or Chinese. This topic is of paramount importance. On the one hand, arbitration is the most favored dispute resolution mechanism for international business disputes.[1] On the other, China's economic power and influence are both fast increasing on the global stage. As a result, it is likely that the world will see more and more international arbitration cases in which at least one party is Chinese or where the parties want the arbitration to take place in China. Consequently, knowledge of Chinese arbitration law is essential for business entities and legal practitioners involved in international transactions.

Unfortunately, however, Chinese law is hostile towards ad hoc arbitration, despite its many advantages and popularity in most of the world. More precisely, the Arbitration Law of the People's Republic of China (the PRC Arbitration Law) appears to preclude ad hoc arbitration altogether by providing that an arbitration agreement is invalid unless it appoints an arbitration institution.[2] Furthermore, this hostility towards ad hoc arbitration is embedded at the very the heart of the Chinese arbitration legal framework. It defines many salient features of the Chinese legal system related to arbitration and reflects how Chinese lawmakers and legal elites understand arbitration fundamentally as a legal institution. Therefore, a thorough understanding of this central aspect of Chinese arbitration law is crucial to the successful resolution of existing disputes with a Chinese party or to any sufficient preparations for a business deal involving China.

Using ad hoc arbitration in China as an example, this book also brings forward a proactive and globally oriented Chinese judiciary waiting to be rediscovered by the West. Despite Chinese law's clear prohibition of ad hoc arbitration, the Supreme People's Court of China (the SPC) has done its best to

1 *See, e.g.*, Gary B. Born, International Commercial Arbitration 93–97 (2d ed. 2014); Fouchard, Gaillard, Goldman on International Commercial Arbitration 1 (Emmanuel Gaillard & John Savage eds., 1999).

2 *See* Zhongcai Fa (仲裁法) [Arbitration Law] (promulgated by the Standing Comm. Nat'l People's Cong., Aug. 31, 1994, effective Sept. 1, 1995, rev. Sept. 1, 2017), arts. 16, 18 (China).

minimize the prohibitive effect of the relevant legislation. It has taken a highly pro-arbitration stance and, directly or indirectly, via giving clear instructions to lower level Chinese courts, enforced many ad hoc arbitration agreements and awards. Among other things, the SPC has clearly aimed at ensuring that China meets its international obligations under the United Nations Convention on the Recognition and Enforcement of Foreign Arbitral Awards (the New York Convention). This runs contrary to the lazy caricature that is still too often used in Western discussions of the Chinese courts ignoring international legal norms. This picture is also frequently tied to the more general exploration of the existence, or non-existence, of rule-of-law in China, under which the Chinese judiciary is often depicted as politically subservient rather than independent. This book does not intend to resolve fully the myth of whether there is rule-of-law in China. This is not least because the scope of this book forbids it to encompass the otherwise necessary studies that would require a sophisticated analysis of, among other things, the nuanced and intricate definition of "rule-of-law" as well as the Chinese legal tradition and its role in Chinese society.[3] However, it does contribute to the existing literature on the subject by presenting a clear example of a Chinese judiciary that is tirelessly bending national legislative provisions to respect and comply with international norms. Therefore, this book does add valuable insights into that discourse.

This book also contributes to the discussions of Chinese arbitration law by providing historical and comparative perspectives, neither of which is frequently seen in the current literature. This book argues that the legislative preclusion of ad hoc arbitration must be understood as a product of Chinese legal history. Situated in a special historical stage of contemporary China, which includes the unfolding of Western legal imperialism, ad hoc arbitration's fate in China was closely connected with Chinese legal elites' struggle to revolutionize and modernize China. It was clearly a conscious legal transplant process. Understood against this background, the efforts that China devoted to establishing a modern arbitration system were evidently extraordinary and far removed from the story of passive legal reforms imposed by the West, as often portrayed in the English language literature. This historical account still has practical significance today. Through a comparative study with arbitration's historical development path in the West, this book is the first to show that the historical context in China directly shaped the conception, or misconception, of arbitration as a legal institution among Chinese lawmakers and legal elites. This historical context also has a deep impact on the Chinese legal system that has lasted to the present day. As a result, one can only have a complete and thorough understanding of the Chinese arbitration legal framework after familiarizing oneself with this historical background. Equally, any attempts to improve the Chinese arbitration system can only succeed after China overcomes and corrects this misconception.

3 *See* Teemu Ruskola, Legal Orientalism 11–16 (2013).

Moreover, this book is also the first to analyze Chinese arbitration law from the perspective of legal transplant theories. It demonstrates that arbitration's history in China is a story of legal transplant. This undoubtedly provides another lens through which to review and reflect on the current Chinese arbitration legal framework. By presenting the legal borrowing of arbitration in China as an example, this book first presents another successful example of legal transplants to endorse the relevant theories. It then enriches the existing literature by demonstrating that legal transplants can take place in different stages as a result of conscious choices made by legal elites in the receiving country. The incremental theory of legal transplant proposed by this book means that China can put the last piece into the puzzle when the time is right. China needs to complete the final stage in this legal transplant process by fully incorporating ad hoc arbitration into its legal system. This is also consistent with the doctrinal analyses that this book conducts simultaneously.

Supported by a series of doctrinal and historical analyses, this book takes the position that ad hoc arbitration is desirable and that China should now take necessary steps to end its hostility towards ad hoc arbitration. Ideally, Chinese lawmakers will amend and liberalize relevant Chinese laws to legitimize ad hoc arbitration completely. However, relevant groups, including most importantly the Chinese arbitration bar, need to mobilize enough political forces to push for the legislative move. Before this happens (hopefully in the near future), this book has carefully designed some useful and special drafting strategies for parties to adopt in practice so that they can take advantage of the pro-arbitration stance taken by the Chinese judiciary. In this way, the parties can successfully resolve their disputes in the way that they deem most suitable for their own cases.

This book is structured as follows. The rest of Chapter 1 will introduce the background to this book's main arguments. It will first discuss arbitration's advantages, particularly as compared with litigation, which explains its popularity as the preferred dispute resolution mechanism for international commercial disputes. It will also, in contrast to institutional arbitration, consider ad hoc arbitration's unique features that make it a welcome method to resolve certain disputes in arbitration practice. Chapter 1 will then bring forward the issues related to ad hoc arbitration under Chinese law. It will further point out that the ad hoc problem lies at the center of the Chinese arbitration legal framework and reflects many of its fundamental aspects. Chapter 2 will present a historical account of arbitration's development in China, in comparison with that in the West. This historical context directly shaped Chinese law's hostility towards ad hoc arbitration, and in many aspects still impacts on the current Chinese legal system today. Moreover, Chapter 2 will examine legal transplant theories and argue that the legal transplant of arbitration in China validates many of them and enriches this body of literature. Chapters 3, 4, and 5 will conduct a sophisticated doctrinal analysis of exactly how Chinese law's preclusion of ad hoc arbitration operates in practice, with a special focus on how it interacts with the international arbitration legal framework based upon the

New York Convention. These chapters will look at how Chinese courts enforce ad hoc arbitration agreements and awards, and will provide useful and practical advice to parties in practice regarding what they should do if they want to resolve their disputes in China via ad hoc arbitration. Building on both the doctrinal analysis and the historical study, Chapters 6 and 7 will try to project a way forward for arbitration legislation and judicial practice in China in the future. These chapters will carry out a cost-benefit analysis and argue that China should fully legitimize ad hoc arbitration. Chapter 8 will summarize the book's main arguments and reach a conclusion.

II Background

A Arbitration vs. litigation

Arbitration is the most popular dispute resolution mechanism for international commercial disputes in today's world.[4] Businesses all over the world prefer using arbitration to resolve their disputes rather than resorting to litigation, particularly in cases where two parties come from different jurisdictions. This is because arbitration offers a number of important advantages in an international setting, including mostly importantly:

i Neutrality. A neutral forum is perhaps what parties in international business dealings are most interested in when they contemplate how, or where, to resolve their disputes.[5] They would, first and foremost, want to avoid giving each other a home "court" advantage. This is understandable, because one side will always enjoy certain advantages in its home jurisdiction. Examples include familiarity with one's native legal system, easy access to local counsel, potential bias that judges may have against foreign parties, and so on. Therefore, choosing a forum in a third country would be a convenient compromise on the bargaining table. Unfortunately, litigating their dispute in a neutral country will not always be convenient, not least because courts in the agreed third country may not be willing to exercise jurisdiction over the dispute.[6] Parties can, however, easily find a neutral forum in arbitration. Arbitrators' jurisdiction over a dispute comes from the parties' agreement.[7] Parties can also freely choose the seat of their

4 *See, e.g.*, Christian Bühring-Uhle et al., Arbitration and Mediation in International Business 29 (2d ed. 2006); Gerald Aksen, *Arbitration and Other Means of Dispute Settlement*, *in* International Joint Ventures: A Practical Approach to Working with Foreign Investors in the U.S. and Abroad 287, 287–288 (David N. Goldsweig & Roger H. Cummings eds., 1990).

5 *See* Bühring-Uhle et al., *supra* note 4, at 17 & 109.

6 *See id.* at 15.

7 *See* Tibor Várady et al., International Commercial Arbitration: A Transnational Perspective 121 (6th ed. 2015).

arbitration.[8] Therefore, as long as parties agree to arbitrate their dispute in a certain place, the arbitrators will not hesitate to accept and decide the case. Another important fact is that, unlike in litigation, parties in arbitration proceedings choose their decision makers, namely the arbitrators. Consequently, parties can find a way to minimize any potential bias that arbitrators may have against either party. For example, parties can agree that the sole arbitrator, or the presiding arbitrator when there are three arbitrators in the tribunal, shall come from a country that is different from both parties.[9] As a result, by choosing arbitration, parties can ensure, to the greatest extent, that they can have their disputes resolved in a forum that is neutral to both parties, so that neither of them enjoys any advantages over the other during the proceedings.

ii Universal enforceability. In many disputes, winning a legal battle does not necessarily mean the triumphant party has crossed the finish line. When the losing party refuses to perform its obligations set out in a judgment or arbitration award, the winning party will need to request a local court, usually at the location of the losing party's assets, to enforce the decision. This can often become tricky in international litigation. There is no universal legal framework to enforce a foreign judgment. Doing so may be particularly difficult in some countries.[10] It can be a lengthy process, which may result in what essentially amounts to a "re-litigation" of the case.[11] In arbitration, however, the problem is solved by the New York Convention, one of the most successful treaties in the world.[12] Under the New York Convention, national courts will enforce a foreign arbitration award unless one of the seven grounds that it specifically provides for is met.[13] These seven grounds mostly cover procedural irregularities, so the national court's review of the arbitration award is largely limited to procedural aspects of the arbitration proceedings. This means that it is generally easier and faster to enforce a foreign arbitration award than a foreign judgment.[14] The fact that more than 150 countries and jurisdictions in the world have joined the New York Convention means at

8 *See* BORN, *supra* note 1, at 1541.

9 *See* VÁRADY ET AL., *supra* note 7, at 394.

10 *See* BÜHRING-UHLE ET AL., *supra* note 4, at 25–26.

11 *See* Arthur Anyuan Yuan, *Enforcing and Collecting Money Judgments in China from a U.S. Judgment Creditor's Perspective*, 36 GEO. WASH. INT'L L. REV. 757, 766–67 (2004).

12 *See* United Nations Convention on the Recognition and Enforcement of Foreign Arbitral Awards, June 10, 1958, 330 U.N.T.S. 38 [hereinafter New York Convention]; BÜHRING-UHLE ET AL., *supra* note 4, at 57; Kofi Annan, U.N. Sec'y Gen., Opening Address Commemorating the Successful Conclusion of the 1958 United Nations Conference on International Commercial Arbitration (June 10, 1998), *in* ENFORCING ARBITRATION AWARDS UNDER THE NEW YORK CONVENTION: EXPERIENCE AND PROSPECTS, U.N. Sales No. E.99.V.2, Mar. 1999, at 1, 2 *available at* http://www.uncitral.org/pdf/english/texts/arbitration/NY-conv/NYCDay-e.pdf.

13 *See* New York Convention, *supra* note 12, art. V.

14 *See* MARGARET L. MOSES, THE PRINCIPLES AND PRACTICE OF INTERNATIONAL COMMERCIAL ARBITRATION 3 (3d ed. 2017).

least two things: 1) parties in an international dealing have much freedom in choosing where they want to have their dispute resolved to achieve maximum neutrality, and 2) a winning party will very likely be able to successfully recover monetary compensation by requesting local courts all over the world, wherever the losing party has assets, to enforce the arbitration award.

iii Finality, efficiency, and lower cost. Unlike litigation which almost always guarantees an appeal process for a substantive decision, arbitration is once and for all.[15] Although the court at the seat of arbitration will have a chance to review the award if the losing party requests a set-aside of the award, this review usually only focuses on procedural aspects and will not touch the merits of the decision.[16] In other words, no courts will re-examine the substantive issues in the case. This increased efficiency means that parties will not be dragged into a painstaking and never-ending battle, and are able to move onto the next stage in their businesses no matter what the outcome is. Arbitration's efficiency as compared with litigation is also manifested by the much more flexible procedural rules in arbitration. Unlike the rigid procedural laws that parties and courts have to follow in litigation, the procedural rules in arbitration that parties choose are much more relaxed. Some arbitration rules offer parties chances to modify the procedures as they deem fit for their case.[17] This undoubtedly adds to the efficiency benefits that parties already enjoy in arbitration. Economic benefits may also come with high efficiency. By saving time, parties will save on legal costs. This is not to say that arbitration is always fast or cheap. It may not be. Some international arbitration cases, especially those involving multi-million dollar claims, can be very complex and therefore take a long time to complete. They may end up being very costly for both parties. However, it can reasonably be argued that these cases would have taken even longer and would have been even more costly if the parties had chosen to litigate them in a national court.

iv Confidentiality. Another benefit for parties resorting to arbitration is that they can enjoy the protection of their business information. Unlike litigation, in which the cases are usually made open to the public, arbitration is confidential.[18] Parties can keep the cases to themselves and do not need to worry about having sensitive business information released to the public. This can also be very appealing to business entities.

15 *See id.* at 2.

16 *See, e.g.*, Model Law on International Commercial Arbitration of the United Nations Commission on International Trade Law, G.A. Res. 61/33, U.N. Doc. A/61/453 (revising G.A. Res. 40/72), art. 34(2) (Dec. 4, 2006), ***available at*** http://www.uncitral.org/pdf/english/texts/arbitration/ml-arb/07-86998_Ebook.pdf [hereinafter Model Law].

17 See, e.g., Int'l Ctr. for Dispute Resolution, ***International Arbitration Rules*** in International Dispute Resolution Procedures (Including Mediation and Arbitration Rules), art. 1 (June 1, 2014), http://www.adr.org/sites/default/files/ICDR%20Rules_0.pdf [hereinafter ICDR Arbitration Rules].

18 *See* Moses, *supra* note 14, at 4.

Due to these advantages, arbitration has become increasingly popular among business entities all over the world.[19] At the same time, legal systems around the world have also grown more and more pro-arbitration. Many countries have passed arbitration "friendly" legislation. Judges are also more often in favor of supporting arbitration, in the sense that they are willing to enforce arbitration agreements and arbitration awards even when there are certain controversies over them. National courts throughout the world are respecting and are fulfilling their countries' obligations under the New York Convention.[20] In other words, the international commercial arbitration system based on the New York Convention has greatly facilitated resolution of cross-border disputes and, therefore, contributed to the world's continuing economic development.[21]

B Ad hoc vs. institutional arbitration

There are many ways to categorize arbitration. Judged by the subject matter involved in the disputes, arbitration can be divided into commercial arbitration, investor-state arbitration, labor arbitration, and so on. Determined by where the seat of arbitration is, or what law applies to the arbitration proceeding, there is domestic arbitration, foreign arbitration, non-domestic arbitration, and international arbitration. By the standard of whether or not the arbitration proceeding is administered by an established organization, an arbitration can be classified as either institutional or ad hoc. The concepts are rather straightforward. Institutional arbitration means the arbitration proceedings are "administered by an organization, usually in accordance with its own rules of arbitration."[22] Ad hoc arbitration, on the other hand, indicates that "there is no formal administration by any established arbitral agency; instead the parties have opted to create their own procedures for a given arbitration."[23]

Ad hoc is undoubtedly the original form of arbitration. Arbitration was ad hoc from the beginning of its very long history. Mankind had been practicing ad hoc arbitration for hundreds, or even thousands, of years before permanent arbitration institutions came into existence.[24] Those institutions only emerged in recent history when arbitration became so popular and frequent that a dedicated institution could profit from providing professional services that facilitate arbitration. Institutional arbitration, however, grew very fast from its inception.[25]

19 *See* Born, *supra* note 1, at 93–95.
20 *See id.* at 113–16.
21 *See* Bühring-Uhle et al., *supra* note 4, at 57–60; Annan, *supra* note 12, at 1–3.
22 Gerald Aksen, *Ad Hoc Versus Institutional Arbitration*, ICC Int'l Ct. Arb. Bull., June 1991, at 8, 8 [hereinafter Aksen, *Ad Hoc*].
23 *Id.*
24 *See* discussion *infra* Chapter 2.
25 In 2009, CIETAC decided 1,329 cases, and the ICC approved 415 awards. *2009 Statistical Report*, 21 ICC Int'l Ct. Arb. Bull., 5, 15 (2010); Zhang Wei (张维), *Maozhong Shouan Shuliang Chixu Zengzhang* (贸仲受案数量持续增长) [*Number of Cases Accepted by CIETAC Continues to Increase*]; Fazhi Ribao (法制日报) [Legal Daily], Feb. 5, 2010 (China).

Due to arbitration's decentralized nature and the confidentiality of its proceedings, it is difficult, if not entirely impossible, to accurately compare the numbers of cases resolved by ad hoc or institutional arbitration respectively, so as to conclude which of the two types is more popular.[26] However, today these two forms of arbitration operate side by side in most parts of the world. Although they share most of arbitration's common characteristics and benefits, each form has certain advantages over the other.[27]

Generally speaking, ad hoc arbitration has at least the following advantages:

- i Flexibility. In an ad hoc arbitration, parties have maximum freedom to make their own procedural rules as to how their arbitration should be conducted. They may tailor the proceeding to their own needs, depending on the circumstances of their own case.
- ii Efficiency. Because parties enjoy maximum flexibility in the procedure, they can achieve maximum efficiency. They do not need to follow any unnecessary internal procedures of any arbitration institution, and thus may resolve the dispute in the fastest way possible.
- iii Cost-effectiveness. At least for some cases, particularly those involving smaller amounts, ad hoc arbitration is cheaper. Parties do not need to pay any administration fee to an arbitration institution. They may also be able to cut down costs regarding attorney fees and arbitrator's fees, because of the time saved from adopting flexible procedures.
- iv Ad hoc arbitration may be an ideal choice when one party to the arbitration is a sovereign state. Because state governments often do not want to relinquish their sovereignty, they may be reluctant to submit their disputes to the control of an institution. Accordingly, ad hoc arbitration is more readily acceptable in this situation.

The promulgation of the UNCITRAL Arbitration Rules in 1976 has greatly facilitated ad hoc arbitration.[28] The biggest inconvenience for parties in an ad hoc arbitration is probably the need to draft, if they cannot find, a set of detailed rules to govern their arbitration proceeding. This, however, can be risky given the possibility of poor drafting or a failure to foresee pitfalls. Now, with the UNCITRAL Arbitration Rules, parties can easily incorporate this set of comprehensive and well-prepared rules by making a reference in their arbitration agreement.[29] This has made it much easier for the parties to gain the benefits of ad hoc arbitration.

26 *See* Julian D. M. Lew, Loukas A. Mistelis & Stefan M. Kröll, Comparative International Commercial Arbitration 33 (2003).

27 *See* Aksen, *Ad Hoc*, *supra* note 22, at 8.

28 The most recent version of the UNCITRAL Arbitration Rules was revised in 2010. UNCITRAL Arbitration Rules as Revised in 2010, G.A. Res. 65/22, U.N. Doc. A/65/465 (Dec. 6, 2010), *available at* http://www.uncitral.org/pdf/english/texts/arbitration/arb-rules-revised/arb-rules-revised-2010-e.pdf [hereinafter UNCITRAL Arbitration Rules].

29 *See* Aksen, *Ad Hoc*, *supra* note 22, at 9.

Institutional arbitration, on the other hand, can be said to offer:

i Professional services and breadth of experience.[30] By choosing institutional arbitration, parties may conveniently acquire assistance regarding issues such as appointment of an arbitrator, fixing arbitrator's fees, arranging a venue for a hearing, and so on. Arbitration institutions' rich experience also makes them a great resource for advice when parties or even tribunals are dealing with complex issues concerning jurisdiction or other procedural matters.

ii Very well-drafted arbitration rules that the arbitration institutions constantly amend to meet changes in practice.[31] The institutions also draft standard arbitration clauses for parties to incorporate into their contract.[32] By adopting these standard arbitration clauses, parties seldom need to worry about the arbitration agreement's validity, which is ultimately pivotal for a successful arbitration.

iii More deference and respect from courts in practice. Usually, because of the arbitration institutions' rich experience and good reputation, courts may be more willing to give weight to decisions made by the institutions or upon their advice, or to accept their opinion.[33] This, in the end, may help to resolve parties' disputes in a more efficient manner.

iv Better prospects for enforcing a default award. In cases where one party is absent, courts are usually more comfortable with enforcing a default institutional arbitration award, rather than an ad hoc award, because institutional rules usually have specific provisions as to how to proceed in such cases, and the institution's staff will usually supervise the process. As a result of the institution's involvement, courts are less worried about due process issues, because there is a neutral body to assure that the default party's rights have been well protected.[34]

Given their respective features and advantages, parties in most of the world have the freedom to choose either ad hoc or institutional arbitration to resolve their disputes, depending on what their needs are in a given case. Due to ad hoc arbitration's inherent advantages, including its efficiency, flexibility, and cost effectiveness, many parties want to use ad hoc arbitration to resolve their disputes, particularly when that dispute is less complicated or does not involve a very large amount at stake. At the same time, almost all legal systems in the world endorse ad hoc arbitration's legitimacy and recognize it as a private dispute resolution mechanism based on private parties' contractual freedom.

30 *See id.* at 10–11; Born, *supra* note 1, at 171.
31 *See* Aksen, *Ad Hoc*, *supra* note 22, at 9.
32 *See, e.g.*, *Standard ICC Arbitration Clause*, Int'l Chamber Com., https://iccwbo.org/dispute-resolution-services/arbitration/arbitration-clause/ (last visited Dec. 22, 2017).
33 *See* Born, *supra* note 1, at 171.
34 *See* Aksen, *Ad Hoc*, *supra* note 22, at 12.

III The ad hoc problem under Chinese law

The People's Republic of China (the PRC), as an economic superpower, has become an active player in the field of international arbitration. Its flagship arbitration institution, the China International Economic and Trade Arbitration Commission (CIETAC), is now hearing more cases than any other arbitration institution in the world.[35] As China becomes increasingly integrated into the globalization process, it is inevitable that the world will see a growing number of arbitration cases involving a Chinese party. More importantly, as the bargaining power of Chinese companies grows, it is likely that more international arbitration will actually take place in China. Therefore, it is essential that the rest of the world becomes familiar with the Chinese legal framework on arbitration.

Astonishingly, however, despite ad hoc arbitration's many unique features and inherent advantages that make it a preferred way for parties to resolve their disputes in many circumstances, Chinese law remains deeply hostile towards ad hoc arbitration. The PRC Arbitration Law requires that parties appoint an arbitration institution in their arbitration agreement.[36] An ad hoc arbitration agreement, therefore, is invalid per se under the PRC Arbitration Law. Arbitration's consensual nature dictates that an arbitration agreement is its cornerstone. A valid arbitration agreement is a necessary condition for a successful arbitration, because the agreement grants the arbitrators the authority to decide the case and divests jurisdiction from the courts.[37] The validity of an arbitration agreement will also affect the legal status of the ensuing arbitration award.[38] If an award is based on an invalid arbitration agreement, the court at the seat of arbitration may later set the award side.[39] Courts in other countries may also refuse to recognize and enforce the award based on the same reason under the New York Convention.[40] As a result, the PRC Arbitration Law's strict requirement that arbitration must be institutional seems to preclude ad hoc arbitration completely under Chinese law and also threatens the validity of an arbitration agreement that is not carefully drafted.

Fortunately, it would be difficult, if not entirely impossible, for China to delegitimize ad hoc arbitration unilaterally. This strict requirement that arbitration

35 *See* Markus Altenkirch & Jan Frohloff, *International Arbitration Statistics 2016 – Busy Times for Arbitral Institutions*, https://globalarbitrationnews.com/international-arbitration-statistics-2016-busy-times-for-arbitral-institutions/; Statistics – cietac Annual Caseload (Foreign-Related and Domestic), http://www.cietac.org/index.php?m=Page&a=index&id=40&l=en (last visited Dec. 22, 2017).

36 Zhongcai Fa (仲裁法) [Arbitration Law] (promulgated by the Standing Comm. Nat'l People's Cong., Aug. 31, 1994, effective Sept. 1, 1995, rev. Sept. 1, 2017), art. 16 (China).

37 *See* Várady et al., *supra* note 7, at 121.

38 *See id.*

39 *See, e.g.*, Model Law, *supra* note 16, art. 34(2)(a)(i); Zhongcai Fa (仲裁法) [Arbitration Law] (promulgated by the Standing Comm. Nat'l People's Cong., Aug. 31, 1994, effective Sept. 1, 1995, rev. Sept. 1, 2017), art. 58(1) (China).

40 *See* New York Convention, *supra* note 12, art. V(1)(a).

must be institutional does not mean Chinese courts will never enforce an ad hoc arbitration agreement or an ad hoc arbitration award. Instead, the consequences of this preclusion are much more complicated in practice, due to arbitration's international nature and the powerful and interconnected international arbitration legal framework based upon the New York Convention. First, as a contracting party to the New York Convention, China has an obligation to recognize and enforce an ad hoc arbitration award made in another New York Convention country. This is because the New York Convention makes no distinction between ad hoc arbitration awards and institutional awards, so Chinese courts cannot reject an award solely because it is ad hoc. Second, when a Chinese court is facing an ad hoc arbitration agreement in which the parties agree to arbitrate their dispute somewhere outside China, the Chinese court has no choice but to enforce that ad hoc arbitration agreement. This is because, among other reasons, ad hoc arbitration is presumably allowed at the seat of arbitration chosen by the parties and the ensuing ad hoc award will be enforceable in China under the New York Convention anyway. Third, the parties may choose a non-Chinese law to govern the validity of their arbitration agreement. The SPC has supported parties' contractual freedom on this issue in the past.[41]

At the same time, the SPC has consistently adopted many doctrines and approaches that are pro-arbitration. For example, the SPC established a "report system" for lower Chinese courts, under which, if a Chinese court decides to reject a foreign award's enforcement, it cannot do so unless and until it reports the case all the way up to the SPC and obtains the SPC's approval.[42] This has ensured that Chinese courts maintain a consistently pro-arbitration stance towards foreign arbitration. The SPC has, in a number of scenarios, also tried to relax the strict requirement under the PRC Arbitration Law that arbitration must be institutional.[43] That being said, it is nonetheless true that the rejection of ad hoc arbitration agreements under the PRC Arbitration Law has caused a great many complicated issues in arbitration practice in China. Moreover, Chinese law's stance towards ad hoc arbitration is not always clear or consistent. As a result, there is a considerable amount of uncertainty on this legal matter.

In light of Chinese law's hostility towards ad hoc arbitration, an important question is: what can, or should, parties do? Given the unique features and advantages of ad hoc arbitration, can parties still use it when one of them is

41 *See* discussion *infra* Chapter 3 Part III.

42 *See* Zuigao Renmin Fayuan Guanyu Zhongcai Sifa Shencha Anjian Baohe Wenti de Youguan Guiding (最高人民法院关于仲裁司法审查案件报核问题的有关规定) [Regulation on Certain Issues Concerning the Report and Examination of Cases on Judicial Review of Arbitration] (promulgated by the Sup. People's Ct., Nov. 20, 2017, effective Jan. 1, 2018), art. 2 (China); Zuigao Renmin Fayuan Guanyu Renmin Fayuan Chuli yu Shewai Zhongcai ji Waiguo Zhongcai Shixiang Youguan Wenti de Tongzhi (最高人民法院关于人民法院处理与涉外仲裁及外国仲裁事项有关问题的通知) [Notice on Certain Issues Concerning the People's Courts' Handling of Matters Involving Foreign-Related Arbitration and Foreign Arbitration] (promulgated by the Sup. People's Ct., Aug. 28, 1995, effective Aug. 28, 1995, rev. Dec. 16, 2008), art. 2 (China).

43 *See* discussion *infra* Chapter 3 Part III.

Chinese, or when the arbitration will take place in China? Is it still possible for an ad hoc arbitration to take place in China? These questions are becoming increasingly important. As China's market economy develops, Chinese business entities will continue searching for dispute resolution mechanisms that best suit their needs. As noted above, ad hoc arbitration's many intrinsic advantages—including flexibility, efficiency, and cost-effectiveness—often make it a preferred way to resolve commercial disputes. It is already not uncommon for Chinese parties to conclude ad hoc arbitration agreements in their international dealings. As Chinese companies' bargaining power increases, the world will likely see a growing number of international arbitrations seated in China. For the above-mentioned reasons, in many of these cases, parties may want to conduct an ad hoc arbitration. Given Chinese law's disfavoring of ad hoc arbitration, is ad hoc arbitration in China still a viable option for the parties?

The complex legal issues involved in this scenario mean that there are no simple or easy answers to these questions. Surprisingly, however, discussions among both academics and practitioners have evaded the key questions, suggesting instead that parties simply arbitrate elsewhere. Existing literature has failed to provide in-depth or comprehensive analysis of the issues in play. At the same time, the literature also failed to analyze ad hoc arbitration in China from the perspective of the interaction between the Chinese legal system and the New York Convention. This book, however, intends to fill this gap in the literature by carefully examining Chinese law's preclusion of ad hoc arbitration, bearing in mind the international commercial arbitration system based on the New York Convention. It will inform parties and legal practitioners of this complex situation, and give them a clear understanding of Chinese law's stance toward ad hoc arbitration. It will also advise them of potential pitfalls in practice and, perhaps most importantly, offer suggestions to them regarding alternative ways to cope with this mandatory rule. This will enable parties to resolve their disputes in the way that they desire, provided that they adopt some carefully designed drafting strategies.[44]

In addition, this book will answer an even more important question. To construe the nuances caused by Chinese law's hostility towards ad hoc arbitration fully, it is necessary to understand the reason why this hostility exists in the first place. Given the advantages of ad hoc arbitration as well as its popularity and legitimacy in most of the world, it is very puzzling why Chinese law is so hostile towards it. The Chinese legislators did offer some reasons, but they are far from convincing.[45] The existing literature has also failed to give a satisfactory explanation, or any explanation at all. In order to fill this gap, this book will conduct a comparative study of the history of arbitration in the Western world and in China, and will reveal that the reasons for this hostility are historically based and directly related to China's political, economic, and social structures at the

44 *See* discussion *infra* Chapter 5.

45 *See* discussion *infra* Chapter 6 Part III.A.

time of the PRC Arbitration Law's promulgation in 1994.[46] Furthermore, this hostility manifests a misguided conception of arbitration as a legal institution among Chinese lawmakers as well as judges and other lawyers. Chinese lawmakers have always viewed arbitration as a surrogate for a judicial system and as if arbitration institutions were parts of the country's state (public) apparatus. This is, however, at odds with the nature of arbitration as a *private* dispute resolution mechanism. This misconception has not only directly caused the preclusion of ad hoc arbitration under Chinese law, but infiltrates the entire Chinese arbitration legal framework. Therefore, the ad hoc arbitration problem lies at the center of Chinese arbitration law, practice, and tradition. It is a highly complex, and crucial, issue under Chinese law.

Finally, this book will argue that the hostility towards ad hoc arbitration runs against many doctrines and the spirit of the current Chinese arbitration legal framework. As a result, based on the doctrinal legal analysis as well as the comparative and historical rethinking, this book will argue that changes to the current law are necessary, and will discuss how to bring them about.

46 *See* discussion *infra* Chapter 6 Part III.B.

2 A history of legal transplant

I Arbitration's history in the Western world

Arbitration has a very long history. Its traces can be found in various myths and legends in Western cultures.[1] It is probably impossible to pinpoint the exact origins of arbitration, but one can assume that it appeared when people in ancient times had a dispute, needed a resolution, and turned to a knowledgeable, dignified, and impartial person for a decision.[2] Evidence shows that arbitration was already used in Egypt as early as 1500 B.C.[3] Of course, the "arbitration" at this stage was likely very primitive and different from what it is today. It might also be difficult to distinguish arbitration during this time from mediation or even litigation, because concepts such as state, government, or court, were non-existent.[4]

Arbitration developed as human societies became more complex. In both Greece and Rome, arbitration became a common method of dispute resolution.[5] Some of the principles and theories that are commonly accepted in modern arbitration practice were already adopted during these early times.[6] Even the arbitration proceedings were similar to those of today.[7] In Greece, for example,

1 *See generally* Larry E. Edmonson, Domke on Commercial Arbitration § 2:1 (3d ed. 2003, rev. ed. 2012); Frances Kellor, American Arbitration: Its History, Functions and Achievements 3–8 (1948); William Catron Jones, *History of Commercial Arbitration in England and the United States: A Summary View*, *in* International Trade Arbitration: A Road to World-Wide Cooperation 127, 127 (Martin Domke ed., 1958).

2 *See generally* Edmonson, *supra* note 1 § 2:1; Kellor, *supra* note 1, at 3–8; Jones, *supra* note 1, at 127.

3 *See* Thomas Oehmke, Commercial Arbitration 17 (1987).

4 *See* Michael John Mustill, *Arbitration: History and Background*, 6 J. Int'l. Arb. 43, 43 (1989); Christian Bühring-Uhle, Lars Kirchhoff & Gabriele Scherer, Arbitration and Mediation in International Business 31 (2d ed. 2006); Edmonson, *supra* note 1, § 2:1.

5 *See* Earl S. Wolaver, *The Historical Background of Commercial Arbitration*, 83 U. Pa. L. Rev. 132, 132 (1934–1935); J. Martin Hunter, *Arbitration Procedure in England: Past, Present and Future*, 1 Arb. Int'l 82, 82 (1985); Nicholas Geoffrey Lemprière Hammond, *Arbitration in Ancient Greece*, 1 Arb. Int'l 188, 188 (1985); Oehmke *supra* note 98, at 17; Edmonson, *supra* note 1, §§ 2:2–2:3.

6 *See* Edmonson, *supra* note 1, §§ 2:2–2:3.

7 *See id.*

parties would choose a person considered wise and impartial to hear their case.[8] If there was more than one arbitrator, the case would be decided by a majority.[9] In Rome, it was established that an arbitrator's authority came from the contract between the parties and himself.[10] Moreover, arbitration during the Greek and Roman eras had two important developments. First, arbitration became international. In Greece, arbitration was not only used to resolve disputes between different cities, but also between citizens of different cities.[11] Later, because of Rome's crucial position, arbitration spread to other parts of Europe.[12] Second, commercial arbitration arose. Greek merchants adopted arbitration in their business practice and their Roman colleagues enjoyed sufficient autonomy by having their own arbitration procedure.[13]

Arbitration later survived the Medieval Period. During that period, arbitration was still in operation in Italy, France, Germany, and England.[14] Later, as international trading and other commercial activities developed, arbitration's advantages over litigation made it increasingly favored by merchants.[15] With arbitration, merchants were able to avoid the costly intricacies of different national court systems and have their disputes resolved with maximum neutrality, efficiency, and commercial expertise.[16] As a result, arbitration became well established in commercial and maritime fields and spread to other corners of the world, including the United States.[17] In the meantime, arbitration practice developed into a very sophisticated procedure which, in most instances, survives to this day.[18]

The rest of the story is relatively well-known. For quite some time, courts were generally hostile towards arbitration.[19] But as time went by, arbitration's advantages in privately resolving parties' disputes, particularly international commercial disputes, became indisputable. Nowadays, arbitration has achieved widespread respect and recognition in jurisdictions worldwide and has become the dominant method for resolving international commercial disputes. In modern times, permanent arbitration institutions were founded. They began to provide professional services to parties and arbitrators to facilitate the arbitration process.[20]

8 *See* Edmonson, *supra* note 1, § 2:2.
9 *See id.*
10 *See* Arthur Engelmann, A History of Continental Civil Procedure 259 (1927).
11 *See* Kellor, *supra* note 1 at 4; Edmonson, *supra* note 1, § 2:2.
12 *See* Edmonson, *supra* note 1, § 2:3.
13 *See id.* §§ 2:2–2:3.
14 *See id.* § 2:4.
15 *See id.* § 2:4.
16 *See id.* § 2:4.
17 *See id.* § 2:6.
18 *See id.* § 2:4.
19 *See* Kellor, *supra* note 1, at 5–6; Oehmke *supra* note 3, at 19.
20 For example, the ICC International Court of Arbitration was established in 1923. For a brief introduction to its history and development, see *ICC International Court of Arbitration*, Int'l

II Arbitration's history in China

Overall, the history of arbitration in China went through two stages of development: the primitive stage and the modernization stage. The primitive stage started thousands of years ago and lasted throughout the history of ancient and imperial China. However, arbitration in China underwent very few and largely insignificant changes in this stage. The modernization stage, on the other hand, has seen many drastic changes in a relatively short space of time. The modernization stage can be further divided into three important sub-stages, covering respectively the eras of the late Qing dynasty, the Republic of China, and the People's Republic of China.

A The primitive stage: arbitration in Ancient and Imperial China

Similar to the way arbitration originated in the Western world, in ancient China, or even at a time before China emerged as a country, when two parties wanted to resolve a dispute in a peaceful manner, they most likely had to resort to a third person who they both considered knowledgeable, dignified, and impartial. Understandably, there might not have been a clear distinction between arbitration and litigation at that time, because it was doubtful that any formal "courts" existed. It would also be equally difficult to distinguish arbitration from mediation or conciliation at the time. This is because the main difference between them, as per our understanding at the present day, is that decisions made by arbitrators are legally binding upon the parties and are directly enforceable by law, while a settlement reached by parties after a successful mediation or conciliation only has contractual value.[21] Given that there were no clear concepts of law, legal bindingness, or legal enforcement at this early stage, it would have been impossible to separate arbitration from mediation and conciliation. In any event, historical records show that the Chinese government adopted mediation as a legal institution during the Zhou dynasty (1046–256 B.C).[22] In 587 B.C., it was recorded that two states in China submitted their dispute to a third party for determination.[23]

Although sharing a similar story of origin with its Western counterpart, arbitration in China unfortunately remained in its primitive form for an excessively long time. Starting from 221 B.C. until at least 1840 A.D., China was an imperial state, comprising dozens of successive dynasties. In more than 2,000 years, arbitration in China remained largely unchanged. There were at least two obstacles that hampered the possible development of arbitration in imperial China.

Chamber Com., https://iccwbo.org/dispute-resolution-services/arbitration/icc-international-court-arbitration/ (last visited Dec. 22, 2017).

21 *See* Tibor Várady et al., International Commercial Arbitration: A Transnational Perspective 29–30 (6th ed. 2015).

22 *See* Deng Ruiping (邓瑞平) & Sun Zhiyu (孙志煜), *Lun Guoji Shangshi Zhongcai de Lishi Yanjin* (论国际商事仲裁的历史演进) [*Historical Progress of International Commercial Arbitration*], 6 Jinan Xuebao (Zhexue Shehui Kexue Ban) (暨南学报(哲学社会科学版)) [J. Jinan Univ. (Phil. & Soc. Sci.)] 92, 93 (2009) (China).

23 *See id.* at 92–93.

First, under Confucianism, which was the mainstream ideology for Chinese society throughout Imperial China, people should live in harmony and try their best to avoid disputes.[24] Even when there was a dispute, parties should try to resolve it by way of settlement, rather than through a confrontational process like litigation or arbitration.[25] From this perspective, mediation was the preferred dispute resolution method; arbitration was not.

Second, commercial activities were not free or vibrant in Imperial China. During this long historical period, different Chinese governments, almost without exception, emphasized agriculture as a national policy and adopted measures oppressing commercial activities.[26] Merchants were heavily controlled and disadvantaged.[27] Because of the underdevelopment of commerce, commercial disputes were relatively rare in China. As a result, arbitration did not have much room to grow. Any disputes relating to property or economic interests, if any, were resolved by the state.[28]

Moreover, commercial activities between ancient China and other countries were inactive due to factors including distance, lack of efficient transportation, and national policies. This lack of international trade also did not favor arbitration's potential growth. To make matters worse, during the Ming dynasty (1368–1644 A.D.) and the Qing dynasty (1644–1912 A.D.), the Chinese government imposed strict control over Chinese national borders and foreign trade.[29] This further diminished chances of having commercial disputes in the first place, which, in turn, reduced the need for arbitration.

B The start of modernization: arbitration in the late Qing dynasty

China began to experience drastic economic and social changes in the second half of the nineteenth century. After China had suffered grave losses in the two Opium Wars,[30] Western powers forced the rulers of the Qing dynasty[31] to open

24 *See id.* at 94; JOHN KING FAIRBANK, THE UNITED STATES AND CHINA 118–20 (4th ed. 1979).

25 *See* Deng & Sun, *supra* note 22, at 94.

26 *See id.*

27 *See* JOHN KING FAIRBANK & MERLE GOLDMAN, CHINA: A NEW HISTORY 179–82 (2d ed. 2006).

28 In imperial China, there was no separation of powers. As a result, there were no separate courts. The functions of courts were carried out by executive officials. *See* ESTHER LAM, CHINA AND THE WTO: A LONG MARCH TOWARDS THE RULE OF LAW 13 (2009); Hayden Windrow, *A Short History of Law, Norms, and Social Control in Imperial China*, 7 ASIAN-PAC. L. & POL'Y J. 244, 246 (2006) (referring to the absence of a separation of powers tradition).

29 *See* FAIRBANK & GOLDMAN, *supra* note 27, at 139, 194–97; HAROLD TANNER, CHINA: A HISTORY 312, 372–75 (2009).

30 *See Opium Wars*, ENCYCLOPÆDIA BRITANNICA, http://www.britannica.com/EBchecked/topic/430163/Opium-Wars (last visited Oct. 20, 2017) (discussing Wars between China and the British Empire after China sought to restrict illegal British opium trafficking, which consisted of the First Opium War (1839–1842) and the Second Opium War (1856–1860)).

31 The last ruling imperial dynasty of China (1644–1911/12), also known as the Manchu Dynasty. *Qing Dynasty*, ENCYCLOPÆDIA BRITANNICA, http://www.britannica.com/EBchecked/topic/112846/Qing-dynasty (last visited Dec. 23, 2017).

China to the world and to allow Chinese parties to engage in commercial activities with foreign businesses. In the meantime, realizing its own weakness and facing serious internal problems, the Qing government initiated various reforms for the purpose of self-strengthening. Among them, promotion of commerce was an important initiative. Consequently, economic activities in China became much more vigorous than before, and conditions for arbitration to develop as a legal institution finally emerged.

Under the traditional legal regime of the Qing dynasty, state governments, or courts, heard and resolved all commercial disputes, together with all other kinds of disputes that arose in Chinese society. As commercial activities developed, Chinese merchants became extremely reluctant to resolve their disputes through Chinese courts for a number of reasons. First, in Imperial China, there was no distinction between commercial cases, civil cases, and criminal cases. The same set of procedural and substantive laws applied to all types of disputes.[32] As a result, Chinese judges, or government officials, heard commercial cases in the same way as they heard criminal cases. This led to some very undesirable results for the merchants. For example, torture, which was then commonly used in criminal proceedings as a fact-finding method, might also be used in commercial cases for the same purpose. This inappropriate measure was not only extremely humiliating for merchants, but could also adversely affect their reputation in their business circles and make it difficult for parties to cooperate again in the future.[33] Second, Chinese imperial governments emphasized agriculture and oppressed commerce, as both a tradition and a national policy.[34] Under this mindset, judges predominantly considered commercial disputes as trivial matters. Thus, commercial cases were usually severely delayed in courts, sometimes for years. Merchants loathed this low efficiency.[35] Third, at the time, Chinese judges seldom knew anything whatsoever about business or commerce. It was, therefore, very difficult for them to make a correct or even reasonable decision in a commercial dispute.[36] All these reasons led to serious alienation and estrangement between merchants and courts in China.[37]

As illustrated above, it was obvious that the traditional legal system of Imperial China was not fit for the changing and growing economic situation that the country

32 *See* Albert Hung-yee Chen, An Introduction to the Legal System of the People's Republic of China 18 (4th ed. 2011).

33 *See* Ren Yunlan (任云兰), *Lun Jindai Zhongguo Shanghui de Shangshi Zhongcai Gongneng* (论近代中国商会的商事仲裁功能) [*Chambers of Commerce's Function of Commercial Arbitration in Modern China*], 4 Zhongguo Jingji Shi Yanjiu (中国经济史研究) [Chinese Econ. Hist. Res.] 117, 117 (1995) (China).

34 *See* Deng & Sun, *supra* note 22, at 94.

35 *See* Ma Min (马敏), *Shangshi Caipan yu Shanghui Lun Wanqing Suzhou Shangshi Jiufen de Tiaochu* (商事裁判与商会——论晚清苏州商事纠纷的调处) [*Commercial Arbitration and Chamber of Commerce: Mediation of Commercial Disputes in Suzhou in Late Qing Dynasty*], 1 Lishi Yanjiu (历史研究) [Hist. Res.] 30, 30 (1996) (China).

36 *See* Ren, *supra* note 33, at 117.

37 *See id.*

was facing. As a result, the Qing government initiated various reforms to its legal system.[38] During this process, the government actively studied the legal systems of the Western powers and borrowed many laws and legal institutions from them.[39] This includes attempts to establish a whole new arbitration system in China.

As a start, the Qing rulers established Offices of Commerce on the provincial level towards the end of the nineteenth century.[40] They endowed these new governmental bodies with the authority to adjudicate commercial disputes, with the hope of building a better mechanism for the resolution of commercial disputes.[41] Unfortunately however, this did not significantly resolve the merchants' practical difficulties. The offices, at least at the beginning, were only willing to hire standby public officials[42] instead of people with expertise or experience in commerce. As a result, they became not too dissimilar to ordinary courts.[43]

At the beginning of the twentieth century, the Qing government had clearly realized the increasing importance of commerce as well as China's underdevelopment in that respect.[44] At the same time, there was also a strong call from Chinese merchants seeking more substantial support from the government regarding dispute solution of commercial disputes.[45] In 1904, in order to further promote commerce and protect merchants' interests, the Qing government promulgated the Concise Chamber of Commerce Act.[46] Through this legislation, the government encouraged the establishment of chambers of commerce across China.[47] At the same time, realizing government bodies' incompetence to resolve commercial disputes, Article 15 of the Act provided that, when disputes arose between Chinese merchants, the merchants could notify the chairman of the local chamber of commerce, who would invite members to justly debate the case in due course, and arbitrate it in public.[48] If either party later disagreed with the outcome of the award, it could file the case in court.[49] Based on this

38 *See* Jerome Cohen, *Keynote: An Introduction to Law in China,* 8 Vt. J. Envtl. L. 393, 194–95 (2007).

39 *See id.*

40 See Zhu Ying (朱英), *Lun Waiqiing de Shangwuju Nonggongshangju* (论晚清的商务局、农工商局) [Departments of Commerce and Departments of Agriculture and Industry in Late Qing Dynasty], 4 Jindaishi Yanjiu (近代史研究) [Mod. Chinese Hist. Stud.] 73, 74–79 (1994) (China).

41 *See* Ma, *supra* note 35, at 30; Zhu *supra* note 40, at 81.

42 Qing Dynasty had a system under which a person might be admitted as a public official but needed to wait for a certain period of time before being officially placed at a certain position.

43 *See* Ma, *supra* note 35, at 30.

44 *See* Feng Mingming (冯铭明), *Wanqing Shagnhui dui Shewai Shangshi Jiufen de Sifa Ganyu* (晚清商会对涉外商事纠纷的司法干预) [*Chambers of Commerce's Judicial Involvement in Foreign-related Commercial Disputes in Late Qing Dynasty*], 22 Fazhi yu Shehui (法制与社会) [Legal Sys. & Soc'y] 42, 42 (2006) (China).

45 *See id.*

46 *See* Ma, *supra* note 35, at 31; Ren, *supra* note 33, at 117.

47 *See* Ma, *supra* note 35, at 31; Ren, *supra* note 33, at 117–18.

48 *See* Ma, *supra* note 35, at 31; Ren, *supra* note 33, at 117.

49 *See* Ma, *supra* note 35, at 31; Ren, *supra* note 33, at 117.

provision, many local chambers of commerce, at the time of or shortly after their establishment, set up a division or a department that was specifically in charge of conducting arbitration.[50]

Despite being a huge step forward, arbitration conducted by a chamber of commerce in the late Qing dynasty was clearly not arbitration in the modern sense. As specified in the Concise Chamber of Commerce Act, an arbitration award issued by a chamber of commerce was only binding upon the parties if they both agreed with it. A party still had the chance to file the already arbitrated case in court. Should this happen, the arbitration award would not become binding. This is fundamentally different from a modern arbitration award that is legally binding upon both parties.

Moreover, during this period, the Chinese chambers of commerce frequently conducted mediation when hearing commercial cases.[51] This is not surprising given mediation's traditional popularity in Chinese society, particularly for internal disputes within a close community. Because chambers of commerce were considered organizations for merchants, businessmen understandably favored mediation to promote harmony within their own circle.[52] Another reason for mediation's popularity was that China had very few commercial laws for arbitrators to apply in their decisions at the time. As a result, they relied heavily on business customs and morality, which makes mediation a logical and reasonable option.[53]

Another significant feature of the Concise Chamber of Commerce Act is that it distinguished between domestic and international arbitration.[54] For example, Article 16 of the Act provided for a set of special procedures to govern disputes between a Chinese and a non-Chinese party.[55] This special procedure differed from the normal arbitration procedure between two Chinese parties. Under this provision, when disputes arose between a Chinese and a foreign merchant, the chamber of commerce should order each party to appoint one person to hear and decide the case.[56] If the two appointed people could not agree to a decision, they should together appoint a third person to make a decision.[57] Where the two parties had already had their case decided by a Chinese court or a foreign consul, if the Chinese party felt that the decision was wrongful, it could notify the chamber of commerce, which would appeal the case on its behalf.[58] If the case was serious, the chairman of the chamber of commerce should report it to the Department of Commerce which would handle the case together with the Department of Foreign Affairs.[59]

50 *See* Ma, *supra* note 35, at 31; Ren, *supra* note 33, at 117–18.
51 *See* Ma, *supra* note 35, at 31–32.
52 *See id.*
53 *See* Ren, *supra* note 33, at 119.
54 *See* Feng Mingming, *supra* note 44, at 42.
55 *See id.*
56 *See id.*
57 *See id.*
58 *See id.*
59 *See id.*

C Continued modernization: arbitration in the Republic of China

Chinese history entered into a new chapter with the revolution in 1911.[60] Imperial China came to an end with the abdication of the last Qing Emperor and the founding of the Republic of China in 1912. The new republican government made huge efforts to modernize China. It continued learning from Western legal systems and promulgated a large number of new laws for China. Among these efforts, the government tried to improve the late Qing arbitration legal framework. In 1913, the Republic of China's Department of Justice and Department of Industry and Commerce jointly promulgated the Division of Commercial Arbitration Act.[61] The General Provisions section of the Act provided that chambers of commerce should establish divisions of commercial arbitration, which would arbitrate commercial disputes between merchants with the main purpose of ending disputes and reaching settlement.[62]

According to the Division of Commercial Arbitration Act, divisions of commercial arbitration could hear disputes in two scenarios. First, the two parties to a dispute might voluntarily submit their case to a division of commercial arbitration before they filed the case in court.[63] Second, after a case was filed in court, the court might entrust the case to a division of commercial arbitration for resolution.[64] After the division heard a dispute and rendered an award, the award was only legally binding if both parties agreed with it. A party might still file the case in court if it found the outcome unsatisfactory.[65] This is perhaps a major difference that distinguishes the arbitration system during this era from arbitration in the modern sense. Furthermore, the Act also provided for other detailed rules related to a division of commercial arbitration's internal operation mechanism, number of personnel, and payment of arbitration fees.[66]

60 *See* Fairbank & Goldman, *supra* note 27, at 250–53; Tanner, *supra* note 29, at 419–20.

61 *See* Fu Haiyan (付海晏), *Qingmo Minchu Shangshi Caipan Zuzhi de Yanbian* (清末民初商事裁判组织的演变) [*The Evolutionary Changes of Commercial Adjudication Organ During the Late Qing and Early Republic of China*], 41–2 Huazhong Shifan Daxue Xuebao (Renwen Shehui Kexue Ban) (华中师范大学学报(人文社会科学版)) [J. Cent. China Normal U. (Human. & Soc. Sci.)] 88, 91 (2002) (China); Ren, *supra* note 33, at 119; Zhang Song (张松), *Minchu Shangshi Gongduanchu Tanxi yi Jingshi Gongduanchu wei Zhongxin* (民初商事公断处探析——以京师商事公断处为中心) [*A Study of Divisions of Commercial Arbitration in Early Republic of China: Centering Beijing Division of Commercial Arbitration*], 28–3 Zhengfa Luntan (政法论坛) [Trib. Pol. Sci. & L.] 31, 31 (2010) (China).

62 *See* Fu, *supra* note 61, at 91; Ren, *supra* note 33, at 119; Zhang, *supra* note 61, at 31.

63 *See* Ren, *supra* note 33, at 119; Zhang, *supra* note 61, at 31.

64 *See* Ren, *supra* note 33, at 119; Zhang, *supra* note 61, at 31.

65 *See* Ren, *supra* note 33, at 119; Zhang, *supra* note 61, at 31.

66 *See* Fu, *supra* note 61, at 91; Ren, *supra* note 33, at 119; Zhang, *supra* note 61, at 31.

Unfortunately, Chinese society experienced significant instability and chaos throughout the entire Republic of China era.[67] It was filled with constant state-building attempts and frequent regional and national wars. Therefore, during this period, China's social, economic, and legal orders were very unstable nationwide. Organizations of government also went through multiple and significant changes. Consequently, operation of divisions of commercial arbitration, later renamed as "commissions of commercial arbitration," and chambers of commerce were also constantly interrupted. As a result, although many commercial disputes were indeed resolved by arbitration during the Republic of China era, arbitration as a legal institution remained immature overall.

D *The current system: arbitration in the People's Republic of China*

A brutal civil war broke out in China soon after the end of the Second World War. It ended with a victory by the Communist Party of China and the founding of the People's Republic of China (the PRC) in 1949.[68] Between the start of the PRC and the present day, however, China has experienced multiple rounds of drastic changes in almost every aspect of its society.[69] Together with complete restructuring of the country's economic system, its legal regime has also undergone significant alterations. At its beginning, the PRC built its legal system almost entirely based on the Soviet Union model.[70] However, this Soviet legal system did not last very long, and China soon lapsed into a state of "lawlessness," particularly during the Culture Revolution (1966–1976).[71] Starting from 1978, China entered into a new phase of "reform and opening up," and very actively built a new legal system by borrowing laws from many parts of the world.[72] In this historical context, the PRC's legal framework of arbitration also went through profound changes during different periods in its history.

Despite the radical changes, PRC law has always kept a distinction between domestic and foreign-related arbitration. Under PRC law, domestic arbitration means arbitration seated in Chinese territory between two Chinese parties. Foreign- related arbitration means although the seat of arbitration is in China, one party to the dispute is non-Chinese, or the dispute relates to properties located outside China or some other foreign elements. It is worth noting that these two types of arbitration are both considered domestic as per internationally accepted conceptions, because the seats of arbitration in both cases are within

67 *See* Fairbank & Goldman, *supra* note 27, at 255–56; Tanner, *supra* note 29, at 419–20, 457.

68 *See* Fairbank & Goldman, *supra* note 27, at 331–37; Tanner, *supra* note 29, at 492–95.

69 *See* Fairbank & Goldman, *supra* note 27, at 343–44. *See generally* Tanner, *supra* note 29, at 501–77 (discussing the different historical phases in the PRC era).

70 See Cohen, *supra* note 38, at 397.

71 *See id.* at 397–98.

72 *See id.* at 399–400.

Chinese territory. That said, PRC law has always treated them differently by adopting a bifurcated system. Moreover, PRC law always treated foreign arbitration, which is seated outside China, differently from domestic awards ever since it acceded to the New York Convention in 1987.

1 Domestic Arbitration in the PRC

a 1949–mid-1970s

After founding the PRC in 1949, the communist government abolished the legal system of the "old China" in its entirety, including its arbitration system. From 1957 on, China adopted a highly centralized planned economy system. Under this system, business entities did not make independent decisions regarding their own business operations. Instead, they had to follow government orders or directives to produce, supply, purchase, or sell. Under such circumstances, disputes between business entities became rare, because there were seldom any commercial transactions between them that would normally occur in a market economy. Any disputes that did arise would be resolved by administrative bodies of the government rather than through arbitration or litigation.

In 1961, the Central Committee of the Communist Party of China (CPC) promulgated and circulated the Regulation on State-run Industrial Enterprises. Article 46 of the Regulation provided that "disputes relating to economic contracts between enterprises or other entities shall be adjudicated and resolved by special departments established by the Economic Committees at various levels."[73] In 1962, the CPC Central Committee, together with the State Council, promulgated the Notice on Strictly Performing Basic Construction Procedure and Economic Contract, which provided that:

> [A]ny disputes arising from performing a contract shall be arbitrated by the Economic Committees at various levels. Local People's Banks or Construction Banks shall enforce decisions made by the Economic Committees at various levels and further seize and make payment.[74]

73 Quanguo Renda Changweihui Fazhi Gongzuo Weiyuanhui (全国人大常委会法制工作委员会) [The Legislative Affairs Commission of the Standing Committee of the National People's Congress], Zhonghua Renmin Gongheguo Zhongcai Falü Shiping (中华人民共和国仲裁法律释评) [Commentaries on Arbitration Laws of China] 2 (1997) [hereinafter The Legislative Affairs Commission of the Standing Committee of the National People's Congress, Commentaries]; *See also* Arbitration Laws of China 18 (The Legislative Affairs Commission of the Standing Committee of the National People's Congress of the People's Republic of China ed., 1997) (translation modified by author).

74 Zhonghua Renmin Gongheguo Zhongcai Fa Quanshu (中华人民共和国仲裁法全书) [Pandects of Arbitration Laws of the People's Republic of China] 9 (Quanguo Renda Changweihui Fazhi Gongzuo Weiyuanhui Minfa Shi (全国人大常委会法制工作委员会民法室) [Civil Law Office of the Legislative Affairs Comm'n of the Standing Comm. of the Nat'l People's Congress] & Zhongguo Guoji Jingji Maoyi Zhongcai Weiyuanhui Mishu Ju (中国国际经济贸易仲裁委员会秘书局) [Secretariat of China Int'l Econ. & Trade Arbitration Comm'n] eds, 1995).

The Economic Committees that these two regulations referred to were departments in the executive branch of the Chinese government. These committees were responsible for planning the economy and directing enterprises' operations. Moreover, the "economic contracts" referred to in these regulations were fundamentally different from commercial contracts in a market economy, or contracts under modern contract law principles.[75] Under the then-existing Chinese law, "economic contracts" were based on governmental orders and functioned as methods to implement such orders.

Under the highly-centralized planned economy, the commercial dispute resolution mechanism in China was fundamentally different from what market economy countries had. In practice, commercial disputes as normally understood mostly did not exist. Any disputes that occurred in the process of economic operations would be resolved by the administrative bodies of the PRC government.[76] Arbitration, and even litigation, were marginalized because they were no longer needed. Although some regulations occasionally mentioned "arbitration," it was obvious that the word was merely borrowed to refer to certain administrative proceedings.

b late 1970s–1994

Starting in the late 1970s, the Chinese government began to adopt a "reform and opening-up policy."[77] This created a major turn in China's economic system, under which the highly centralized planned economy was gradually dismantled, and a transition toward a market economy began. During this process, business entities were given more freedom to operate their own businesses, and therefore, they were able to enter into commercial contracts with other parties based on their free will. Under this economic policy, commercial activities became vibrant. Understandably, commercial disputes also became frequent. Just as in the late Qing dynasty, changing economic circumstances once again called for a new dispute resolution mechanism.

While undertaking numerous reforms in its judicial system, the Chinese government in the early 1980s established an "arbitration" system for the resolution of domestic commercial disputes.[78] Many of the laws and regulations that the government promulgated during this period provided for arbitration

75 See Shi Jichun (史际春) and Deng Feng (邓峰), *Hetong de Yihua yu Yihua de Hetong Guanyu Jingji Hetong de Chongxin Dingwei* (合同的异化与异化的合同——关于经济合同的重新定位) [*Dissimilation of Contracts and Dissimilated Contracts: On Repositioning Economic Contracts*], 3 Faxue Yanjiu (法学研究) [CASS J. L.] 39, 46 (1997) (China).

76 *See* The Legislative Affairs Commission of the Standing Committee of the National People's Congress, Commentaries, *supra* note 73, at 2.

77 *See* Vai Io Lo, *Arbitration of Commercial Disputes in China*, Md. Series in Contemp. Asian Stud., no. 5, 2001 at 1, 2-3, *available at* http://digitalcommons.law.umaryland.edu/cgi/viewcontent.cgi?article=1165&context=mscas.

78 *See* Zhonghua Renmin Gongheguo Zhongcai Fa Quanshu, *supra* note 74, at 9–10.

as a dispute resolution mechanism.[79] These laws covered a variety of disputes, including economic contract disputes, labor disputes, copyright disputes, real estate disputes, and consumer rights disputes. As promising as the new laws appeared, it is perhaps understandable that the Chinese legislators would inevitably carry over some of their mindset and models from the old planned economy era. In these laws, they continued to enable the administrative bodies of the government to act as the authority under this "arbitration" system.[80] Various "arbitration" laws and regulations endowed certain government offices with the power to "arbitrate" disputes.[81] In addition, these laws established some "arbitration institutions" as subsidiaries of government bodies to hear commercial disputes.[82] Proceedings to be followed in these institutions were similar to those adopted by either the administrative bodies or the courts. Awards rendered by these institutions were usually not final, unless both parties agreed to it. A party not happy with the "arbitration" result usually had the option to challenge the award by filing a request to court.

For example, both the Economic Contract Law of the People's Republic of China and the Regulation on Economic Contract Arbitration of the People's Republic of China provided that any party to an economic contract may have two choices to have its dispute resolved. It may apply for "arbitration" at a local Economic Contract Arbitration Commission. This Commission is established by the local Administration for Industry and Commerce, a department in the executive branch of the local government. Alternatively, the party may choose to file a lawsuit at a court. The State Administration for Industry and Commerce specified that these "arbitration" commissions were "different from arbitration institutions in capitalist countries,"[83] because they were "executing authority to arbitrate on behalf the country,"[84] and "their awards represent[ed] the country's will."[85] Moreover, after an "arbitration" commission renders an award, a party that does not agree with the award may file the case in court within fifteen days. If no such lawsuit is filed after fifteen days, the award becomes legally binding.[86]

79 *See, e.g.*, Jingji Hetong Fa (经济合同法) [Economic Contract Law] (promulgated by the Nat'l People's Cong., Dec. 13, 1981, effective July 1, 1982), art. 48 (China).

80 *See* Zhonghua Renmin Gongheguo Zhongcai Fa Quanshu, *supra* note 74, at 9–10.

81 *See, e.g.*, Jingji Hetong Fa (经济合同法) [Economic Contract Law] (promulgated by the Nat'l People's Cong., Dec. 13, 1981, effective July 1, 1982), art. 48 (China).

82 *See, e.g.*, Jingji Hetong Zhongcai Tiaoli (经济合同仲裁条例) [Regulation on Economic Contract Arbitration] (promulgated by the St. Council, Aug. 22, 1983, effective Aug. 22, 1983), art. 2 (China).

83 *See* Guojia Gongshang Xingzheng Guanli Ju Jingji Hetong Si Guanyu Guanche Zhixing "Jingji Hetong Zhongcai Tiaoli" de Jidian Yijian (国家工商行政管理局经济合同司关于贯彻执行《经济合同仲裁条例》的几点意见) [Several Opinions on Implementing "Regulation on Economic Contract Arbitration"] (promulgated by the State Administration for Industry and Commerce, Office of Economic Contracts, Nov. 3, 1983, effective Nov. 3, 1983), art. 2 (China).

84 *See id.*

85 *See id.*

86 *See* Zhonghua Renmin Gongheguo Zhongcai Fa Quanshu, *supra* note 74, at 9.

Similar provisions can also be found in many other national and local laws and regulations.[87]

As of 1994, in China, there were fourteen national legislative acts, more than eighty administrative regulations, and almost two hundred local regulations that contained provisions related to "arbitration."[88] There are at least two possible explanations for why the Chinese legislators wanted to establish this type of "arbitration" system. First, in a planned economy, government departments are in charge of all the economic operations in the society and the dispute resolution process. In the transition towards a market economy, it was probably easy and practical to transfer the old dispute resolution function of the government to these "arbitration institutions." Second, some administrative bodies might have preferred this "arbitration" mechanism because it could reduce their chances of being sued in court as defendants in an administrative lawsuit. This is because, under the PRC law, if a government body makes an administrative decision, the party bound by this decision may challenge the decision in court. The government body may make the same decision via "arbitration," and if one of the parties involved is not happy with the outcome, it may file the case in a court. The litigation, however, will center on the merits of the case, instead of the decision made by the government body. In this lawsuit, the government will not become the defendant.[89]

This complex "arbitration" system had many problems that made it hard to qualify as an arbitration system in the modern sense. First, the "arbitration" institutions in China during this period were highly administratively oriented. They were either established by the administrative bodies of the government, or in some cases, they were the administrative bodies of the government themselves. In any event, these "arbitration" institutions were subordinate to the government. Staff of the arbitration institutions were basically public officials, with many of them working in the government concurrently. As a result, "arbitrations" administered by these institutions were not privately organized, but were very similar to, if not essentially the same as, administrative proceedings. Second, parties were able to initiate "arbitration" without an arbitration agreement. This is because these "arbitration" institutions enjoyed an official or quasi- official status under many then-existing laws and regulations. Therefore, these institutions acquired jurisdiction to hear those disputes by law, instead of by party consent. From this perspective, these "arbitration" proceedings were similar to court proceedings or administrative proceedings. Third, awards rendered by these "arbitration" institutions were usually not final. A party that was not happy with the outcome of the case had the right to challenge the award's merits by filing the case in court.

87 *See id.* at 9–11.

88 *See* The Legislative Affairs Commission of the Standing Committee of the National People's Congress, Commentaries, *supra* note 73, at 4; Zhonghua Renmin Gongheguo Zhongcai Fa Quanshu, *supra* note 74, at 12.

89 *See* Zhonghua Renmin Gongheguo Zhongcai Fa Quanshu, *supra* note 74, at 13.

Because of these problems, some scholars argue that the "arbitration" in China during this period of time was not true arbitration properly understood, but simply a kind of administrative proceeding.[90] It was effectively an administrative body's way to resolve disputes, and only the word "arbitration" was borrowed.

The late 1980s and early 1990s nevertheless witnessed a deeper reform in China's arbitration legal framework. Some laws and regulations began to provide that an arbitration award was final, which meant that the parties were bound by the award once it was rendered, and would not be able to later request the court to hear its merits again.[91] Unfortunately, however, these laws only applied to certain special types of disputes. Despite these promising new rules, China's arbitration system during this period remained confusing, and even chaotic, in the aggregate.

c 1995–present

In 1994, the Chinese legislature promulgated the current *Arbitration Law of the People's Republic of China* in response to the problems of China's then-existing arbitration system. The Law, which took effect in 1995, aimed to bring the Chinese arbitration system closer to modern principles and practices as well as to safeguard the smooth operation of a market economy and the economic development resulting from it.[92]

Although far from being perfect, the PRC Arbitration Law largely followed the major principles and doctrines of arbitration that are internationally accepted. Under the Law, a valid arbitration agreement establishes an arbitrator's jurisdiction to hear and decide the merits of a case, and will be enforced by Chinese courts. An arbitration award is final and binding upon both parties. Arbitration institutions are independent from government. Parties are free to choose their arbitrators. Accordingly, the PRC Arbitration Law became China's first ever arbitration law in the modern sense.[93]

2 Foreign-related arbitration in the PRC

Compared to domestic arbitration, the PRC's legal framework for foreign-related arbitration remained much more stable. Not too long after its founding, and following in the footsteps of other socialist countries, the PRC established its own foreign-related arbitration institutions in the 1950s.

90 *See id.*

91 *See id.* at 10.

92 *See* The Legislative Affairs Commission of the Standing Committee of the National People's Congress, Commentaries, *supra* note 73, at 1; Zhonghua Renmin Gongheguo Zhongcai Fa Quanshu, *supra* note 74, at 13.

93 *See generally* Zhongcai Fa (仲裁法) [Arbitration Law] (promulgated by the Standing Comm. Nat'l People's Cong., Aug. 31, 1994, effective Sept. 1, 1995, rev. Sept. 1, 2017) (China).

Aiming to "resolve disputes that may possibly arise in foreign trade contracts and transactions,"[94] the Chinese government founded the Foreign Trade Arbitration Commission in April 1956 under the China Council for the Promotion of International Trade (CCPIT).[95] The Commission was later renamed several times and is now known as the China International Economic and Trade Arbitration Commission (CIETAC), or the Arbitration Court of the China Chamber of International Commerce (CCOIC). Through a similar process, the CCPIT Maritime Arbitration Commission was founded in 1958,[96] and was later renamed as the China Maritime Arbitration Commission (CMAC).

The reason for establishing these two institutions was obvious and practical. At the time when China was adopting a highly centralized planned economy, some Chinese enterprises, including specialized import and export companies, had to engage in business transactions with the outside world on international trade. Although there was essentially no functioning market within China during the time, these Chinese enterprises conducting international trade still needed to participate in the world market. Commercial disputes between Chinese enterprises and foreign business entities still had to be resolved. Arbitration was a logical option for that purpose given its advantages. In 1950, for example, the PRC and the Soviet Union concluded the *Protocol for General Conditions of Delivery of Goods*.[97] This bilateral treaty provided that contractual disputes between companies from the two countries should generally not be filed in court, but rather be resolved by arbitration that would take place in either China or the Soviet Union, determined by the nationality of the respondent.[98]

There are huge differences between the two Chinese foreign-related arbitration institutions and Western international arbitration institutions in the 1950s. The most obvious one is the institution's relationship with the government. Chinese institutions were under the leadership and supervision of the PRC government. This is hugely at odds with Western institutions' private and independent nature. Arbitrators serving in the Chinese institutions at the time were essentially civil servants of the PRC, while arbitrators appointed in a Western institution were

94 Zhongyang Renmin Zhengfu Zhengwuyuan Guanyu Zai Zhongguo Guoji Maoyi Cujin Weiyuanhui Nei Sheli Duiwai Maoyi Zhongcai Weiyuanhui de Jueding (中央人民政府政务院关于在中国国际贸易促进委员会内设立对外贸易仲裁委员会的决定) [Decision to Establish Foreign Trade Arbitration Commission within the China Council for the Promotion of International Trade] (promulgated by the Government Administration Council of the Cent. People's Gov't, May 6, 1954, effective May 6, 1954) (China).

95 *See id.*

96 *See* Zhonghua Renmin Gongheguo Guowuyuan Guanyu Zai Zhongguo Guoji Maoyi Cujin Weiyuanhui Nei Sheli Haishi Zhongcai Weiyuanhui de Jueding (中华人民共和国国务院关于在中国国际贸易促进委员会内设立海事仲裁委员会的决定) [Decision to Establish Maritime Arbitration Commission within the China Council for the Promotion of International Trade] (promulgated by the St. Council, Nov. 21, 1958, effective Nov. 21, 1958) (China).

97 *See* Zhonghua Renmin Gongheguo Zhongcai Fa Quanshu, *supra* note 74, at 8; Jingzhou Tao, Arbitration Law and Practice in China 8 (3d ed. 2012).

98 *See* Zhonghua Renmin Gongheguo Zhongcai Fa Quanshu, *supra* note 74, at 8; Tao, *supra* note 97, at 8.

independent and did not work for their government. Despite the differences in nature, the PRC's foreign-related arbitration legal framework tried to conform to international standards regarding the arbitration proceeding itself.[99]

In the late 1970s when China began to adopt the reform and opening-up policy, more Chinese companies were allowed to engage in international trade and foreign companies began to arrive in China for purposes of trade and investment. Therefore, more foreign-related disputes arose. Many Chinese laws and regulations began to provide for arbitration as a dispute resolution method in foreign-related commercial activities. Prior to the birth of the PRC Arbitration Law in 1994, provisions for foreign-related arbitration were frequent in Chinese laws, and they tried to follow standard international practices in arbitration.[100] When the PRC Arbitration Law was promulgated in 1994, it included a separate chapter on foreign-related arbitration.[101] This chapter provides considerably more favorable treatment for foreign-related arbitration, as compared with ordinary domestic arbitration in China, and largely follows international practice.[102]

3 Foreign Arbitration in the PRC

The Chinese government and courts have always shown much respect towards foreign awards, namely arbitration awards seated outside China. China ratified the New York Convention in 1986 and began to recognize and enforce foreign arbitration awards according to the New York Convention even before having its own arbitration legislation.[103] So far, Chinese courts have been very pro-arbitration when it comes to recognition and enforcement of foreign awards.[104]

99 *See* Zhonghua Renmin Gongheguo Zhongcai Fa Quanshu, *supra* note 74, at 9.

100 *See e.g.* Minshi Susong Fa (Shixing) (民事诉讼法(试行)) [Civil Procedure Law (For Trial Implementation)] (promulgated by the Standing Comm. Nat'l People's Cong., Mar. 8, 1982, effective Oct. 1, 1982), arts. 192–95 (China); Shewai Jingji Hetong Fa (涉外经济合同法) [Foreign-related Economic Contract Law] (promulgated by the Standing Comm. Nat'l People's Cong., Mar. 21, 1985, effective July 1, 1985), arts. 31, 37 & 38 (China).

101 *See* Zhongcai Fa (仲裁法) [Arbitration Law] (promulgated by the Standing Comm. Nat'l People's Cong., Aug. 31, 1994, effective Sept. 1, 1995, rev. Sept. 1, 2017), ch. 7 (China).

102 *See id.*

103 *See* Quanguo Renmin Daibiao Dahui Changwu Weiyuanhui Guanyu Woguo Jiaru "Chengren ji Zhixing Waiguo Zhongcai Caijue Gongyue" de Jueding (全国人民代表大会常务委员会关于我国加入《承认及执行外国仲裁裁决公约》的决定) [Decision on Accession Into the "Convention on the Recognition and Enforcement of Foreign Arbitral Awards"] (promulgated by the Standing Comm. Nat'l People's Cong., Dec. 2, 1986, effective Dec. 2, 1986) (China); Zuigao Renmin Fayuan Guanyu Zhixing Woguo Jiaru de "Chengren ji Zhixing Waiguo Zhongcai Caijue Gongyue" de Tongzhi (最高人民法院关于执行我国加入的《承认及执行外国仲裁裁决公约》的通知) [Notice on Executing the "Convention on the Recognition and Enforcement of Foreign Arbitral Awards" that Our Country has Acceded Into] (promulgated by the Sup. People's Ct., Apr. 10, 1987, effective Apr. 10, 1987) (China).

104 *See* Tao, *supra* note 97, at 18–19.

III The impact of history on the current Chinese arbitration law

From a comparative perspective, arbitration followed distinct paths of development in the West and in China. In the Western world, arbitration arose and developed from the bottom up. It originated from parties' needs to have their dispute resolved by a third party in an amicable and non-forcible way. Later, arbitration evolved to meet parties', most importantly merchants', desires to resolve their dispute outside a country's judicial system so that they could enjoy maximum neutrality, flexibility, efficiency, and confidentiality. Later, national laws and courts recognized and respected these wishes and further conceptualized and implemented a legal framework to support and facilitate the operation of this private dispute resolution mechanism. In this process, ad hoc was the original form of arbitration, and it still represents the authentic features of arbitration. Institutional arbitration, on the other hand, came into existence only in modern times.

On the other hand, despite having as ancient an origin as its Western counterpart, arbitration in China stayed in its primitive stage for an excessively long time. Arbitration in traditional China was never exposed to the appropriate circumstances that would allow it to grow in a bottom-up fashion, namely developing among merchants in a private manner and later being recognized by law. Instead, it was adopted by the Chinese government in a top-down manner, as an alternative or substitute for an incompetent and dysfunctional court system. At least at the beginning, parties in China did not choose to resolve their dispute by arbitration out of concerns like efficiency, neutrality, or party autonomy. Instead, they "chose" arbitration largely because it was the only reasonable dispute resolution mechanism available to them. Understandably, when the Chinese government established the arbitration system in this top-down manner, it could only institutionalize it. Choosing institutional arbitration over ad hoc arbitration was the only logical option for the Chinese lawmakers. This is because it was much more practical, efficient, and effective to create a national arbitration system by establishing a number of arbitration institutions all around the country, than to slowly cultivate a culture of ad hoc arbitration when there were no existing practices of it at the time. Therefore, ad hoc arbitration became negligible in this lawmaking process. As a result, China never had ad hoc arbitration as a modern legal institution. Arbitration in China has been institutional from the very beginning.

Arbitration's unique development history in China has led to significant consequences today. Many features of today's PRC Arbitration Law, including its hostility towards ad hoc arbitration, can be traced back to this historical background. First, Chinese parties and even legal elites share a misconception of arbitration's nature. They do not fully appreciate arbitration's nature as a private dispute resolution mechanism built on party autonomy. Instead, they view arbitration as a quasi-public dispute resolution system complementary to the judicial system. As a result, arbitration institutions themselves play a larger and more important role under Chinese arbitration laws. For example, the current PRC

Arbitration Law gives arbitration institutions, not the arbitration tribunals, the power to decide on arbitrability, or jurisdiction, matters.[105] This is different from what the internationally accepted Kompetenz-Kompetenz doctrine, as embodied in many national arbitration laws around the world, would normally call for, i.e. empowering arbitrators themselves to decide on their own jurisdiction.[106] This suggests that the Chinese lawmakers conceptualize the relationship between arbitrators and arbitration institutions as similar to the relationship between judges and courts. This misconception has directly caused Chinese law's hostility towards ad hoc arbitration, because ad hoc arbitration represents party autonomy, not state power, and therefore does not have any place in this quasi-judicial system.

Second, due to their misconception of arbitration as a quasi-public dispute resolution system, it was likely that Chinese lawmakers wrongfully assumed that arbitration institutions will only function within a country's territory, like courts do. Therefore, they neglected the possibility that international arbitration institutions may well operate and administer arbitration within Chinese territory and that Chinese arbitration institutions may do the same outside China, although it is absolutely normal and common for the world's arbitration institutions to conduct cross-border operation due to arbitration's private and international nature. This may at least help to explain why the PRC Arbitration Law does not incorporate the concept of "seat of arbitration" as most of the world's jurisdictions do, but instead determines an award's nationality in accordance with the nationality of the arbitration institution.[107] This wrongful assumption has resulted in Chinese law's difficulties in dealing with an arbitration award that is seated in a different country from where the arbitration institution's headquarter is located, and has in particular caused very complex issues under Chinese law related to arbitrations administered in China by an international arbitration institution such as the ICC. Although there have been a few cases where Chinese courts held these awards as non-domestic under Chinese law, this issue has not been definitively resolved under Chinese law.[108]

105 *See* Zhongcai Fa (仲裁法) [Arbitration Law] (promulgated by the Standing Comm. Nat'l People's Cong., Aug. 31, 1994, effective Sept. 1, 1995, rev. Sept. 1, 2017), art. 20 (China).

106 *See, e.g.*, Model Law on International Commercial Arbitration of the United Nations Commission on International Trade Law, G.A. Res. 61/33, U.N. Doc. A/61/453 (revising G.A. Res. 40/72), art. 16 (Dec. 4, 2006), *available at* http://www.uncitral.org/pdf/english/texts/arbitration/ml-arb/07-86998_Ebook.pdf [hereinafter Model Law].

107 *Compare* Zhongcai Fa (仲裁法) [Arbitration Law] (promulgated by the Standing Comm. Nat'l People's Cong., Aug. 31, 1994, effective Sept. 1, 1995, rev. Sept. 1, 2017) (China) (not mentioning seat of arbitration at all), *with* Model Law, *supra* note 106, art. 1(2), 35–36 (using place of arbitration as the basis for the application of the relevant provisions).

108 *See, e.g.*, Deguo Xupulin Guoji Youxian Zeren Gongsi Shenqing Chengren he Zhixing Guowai Zhongcai Caijue An (德国旭普林国际有限责任公司申请承认和执行国外仲裁裁决案) [Application by Züblin International GmbH for Recognition and Enforcement of Foreign Arbitration Award] (Wuxi Interm. People's Ct., July 19, 2006) (pku.cn) (holding the ICC award in this case is a non-domestic award under Chinese law)

Third, because ad hoc arbitration has never been part of the Chinese legal system, all Chinese laws share the common ground that all arbitration in China is institutional.[109] Sometimes they even assume, problematically or even wrongfully, that the same is true for arbitration outside China. For example, in the relevant parts of the PRC Civil Procedure Law that provides for the recognition and enforcement of foreign arbitral awards, the Law only mentioned "awards made by foreign arbitration institutions," while remaining silent on foreign ad hoc awards.[110] Moreover, the judiciary occasionally made the same mistake. The SPC once referred to ad hoc arbitration tribunals outside China as "ad hoc arbitration institutions." [111] This indicates a wrongful presumption that all arbitration is institutional, and a lack of knowledge regarding the basic concepts of ad hoc arbitration. The non-recognition of ad hoc arbitration among Chinese laws has not only created a systematic problem for ad hoc arbitration's operation in China, but also means that any attempt to legitimize ad hoc arbitration under Chinese law would have to encompass a systematic rewriting of many Chinese laws, besides the PRC Arbitration Law, that relate to arbitration.

IV A legal transplant story

The historical discussion above shows that arbitration as a legal institution is not a Chinese invention. Instead, it was borrowed, or transplanted, from the Western world. Therefore, it is very helpful to examine the Chinese arbitration legal framework from the perspective of legal transplant. The ideas and practices of legal transplant are not unfamiliar for China. It has always been an important part of China's legal reform in its contemporary history.[112] Even today, Chinese lawmakers frequently look to foreign legal systems for inspirations on Chinese legal reform, particularly in the areas of commercial and business law.[113] Therefore, reflecting on the legal transplant of arbitration in China may not only help us fully understand ad hoc arbitration's current status under Chinese law, but also provide a successfully example and many useful insights for the rest of the world.

109 *See generally* Minshi Susong Fa (民事诉讼法) [Civil Procedure Law] (promulgated by the Nat'l People's Cong., Apr. 9, 1991, effective Apr. 9, 1991, rev. June. 27, 2017) (China).

110 *See id.*, art. 283.

111 *See* Zuigao Renmin Fayuan Guanyu Fujian Sheng Shengchan Ziliao Zong Gongsi yu Jinge Hangyun Youxian Gongsi Guoji Haiyun Jiufen Yi'an Zhong Tidan Zhongcai Tiaokuan Xiaoli Wenti de Fuhan (最高人民法院关于福建省生产资料总公司与金鸽航运有限公司国际海运纠纷一案中提单仲裁条款效力问题的复函) [Reply Letter Concerning the Validity of the Bill of Lading's Arbitration Clause in the International Shipping Dispute Case Between Fujian Province Production Material Corporation and Jinge Shipping Co., Ltd.] (promulgated by the Sup. People's Ct., Oct. 20, 1995, effective Oct. 20, 1995) (China).

112 *See* Pitman B. Potter, The Chinese Legal System: Globalization and Local Legal Culture 4–5 (2001).

113 *See, e.g.*, Shuangge Wen, *The Ideals and Reality of a Legal Transplant – The Veil-Piercing Doctrine in China*, 50 Stan. J. Int'l L. 319 (2014); Ling Zhou, *The Independent Director System and Its Legal Transplant into China*, 6 J. Comp. L. 262 (2011).

Over the decades, comparative law scholars have built up a rich body of theories on the borrowing or transplant of legal rules and legal institutions. The debates first started with the idea of whether legal transplant is possible. To answer this question, scholars discussed the relationship between a country's law and its social, economic, and political contexts. Two opposing camps, described as "transferists" and "culturalists" by Nicholas Foster, put forward very contrasting opinions.[114]

Alan Watson, or at least the "strong version" of Watson,[115] argues that legal transplant is not only possible, but also extremely common and easy to accomplish.[116] For Watson, law is merely an idea that lawmakers can easily borrow from others.[117] Watson also emphasizes the legal profession's role in lawmaking as well as their habit of relying on precedents and authorities as an explanation of legal transplant's popularity and success.[118] In his opinion, law develops by transplanting, not because any certain rule is decided by the social structure, but because lawmakers, or the legal elites, think a foreign rule can be beneficial.[119] The "strong version" of Watson goes on to argue that law is thus autonomous and insulated from social or other factors,[120] so the main differences between legal systems are the result of history and not of social contexts.[121] The "weak version" of Watson takes a step back from this extreme position and acknowledges the relation between law and society,[122] but insists that this relation is not "extremely close, natural, or inevitable."[123] This weaker version argues that law possesses a life of its own and does not accurately reflect its social contexts.[124] Therefore, law is not a "mirror" of society.[125] The "weak version" of Watson also acknowledges that laws frequently, and maybe always, undergo transformations and modifications after being transplanted, and that these modifications can even be substantial.[126]

114 *See* Nicholas Foster, *Transmigration and Transferability of Commercial law in a Globalized World*, in COMPARATIVE LAW IN THE 21ST CENTURY 55, 59 (Adrew Harding & Esin Örücü eds., 2002).

115 *See* William Ewald, *Comparative Jurisprudence (II): The Logic of Legal Transplants*, 43 AM. J. OF COMP. L. 489, 491 (1995).

116 *See* ALAN WATSON, LEGAL TRANSPLANTS: AN APPROACH TO COMPARATIVE LAW 95 (Second Edition, 1993) [hereinafter WATSON, LEGAL TRANSPLANTS].

117 *See* Alan Watson, *Legal Transplants and Law Reform*, 92 L. Q. REV. 79, 79 (1976); Alan Watson, *Comparative Law and Legal Change*, 37 CAMBRIDGE L.J. 313, 315 (1978) [hereinafter Watson, *Comparative Law and Legal Change*].

118 *See* WATSON, LEGAL TRANSPLANTS, *supra* note 116, at 117–18.

119 *See* Watson, *Comparative Law and Legal Change*, *supra* note 117, at 315.

120 *See* ALAN WATSON, ROMAN LAW & COMPARATIVE LAW 97–98 (1991); Ewald, *supra* note 115, at 500–01.

121 *See* ALAN WATSON, THE MAKING OF THE CIVIL LAW 38 (1981).

122 *See* Watson, *Comparative Law and Legal Change*, *supra* note 117, at 321.

123 *See id.* at 315.

124 *See id.* at 321.

125 *See* Ewald, *supra* note 115, at 501–02.

126 *See* WATSON, LEGAL TRANSPLANTS, *supra* note 116, at 116; Watson, *Comparative Law and Legal Change*, *supra* note 117, at 314.

On the opposing side, Otto Kahn-Freund thinks that legal transplant is possible, but there are chances of rejection.[127] In his opinion, the transplant of a law is more of an organic process than a mechanical insertion.[128] Moreover, different laws have different degrees of transferability, decided by, most importantly, political factors in the receiving country.[129] Kahn-Freund's conclusion is, therefore, that the transplantability of rules or institutions should not be taken for granted, and legal transplant "requires a knowledge not only of the foreign law, but also of its social, and above all its political, context."[130] Pierre Legrand goes even further in this direction and claims that legal transplant is impossible.[131] According to Legrand, "law" means much more than simply "rules," which usually take the form of statutes and judicial decisions.[132] He argues that because a rule needs to be interpreted, the meaning of a rule, which forms an essential component of the rule, is not entirely supplied by the rule itself, but is largely dependent on the interpreter's historical and cultural background.[133] Therefore, even though a rule may be borrowed, its meaning cannot be.[134] As a result, the borrowed rule is no longer the same rule, so legal transplant does not happen.[135]

Many comparative law scholars since then have rejected the absolutist theories proposed in the "strong version" of Watson and by Legrand, but instead chosen to build their theories' foundations on middle grounds.[136] They have largely accepted that legal transplant is possible, but is subject to, or can be influenced by, a law's cultural or social contexts.[137]

For example, Gunther Teubner proposes that, in contrast to an organ transplant which will lead to only two outcomes, repulsion or integration, a borrowed legal rule will work as an "irritation" in the receiving system.[138] These "legal irritants" will lead to fundamental reconstruction and transformation of both themselves and the receiving legal systems, creating complex outcomes while unable to bring different legal orders together.[139] Máximo Langer and Esin Örücü each, to a certain extent, share a view similar to Teubner's. Langer believes when a law is transferred, both the legal idea or practice and the

127 *See* Otto Kahn-Freund, *On Uses and Misuses of Comparative Law*, 37 Mod. L. Rev. 1, 6 (1974).
128 *See id.* at 6–7.
129 *See id.* at 8.
130 *See id.* at 27.
131 *See* Pierre Legrand, *The Impossibility of "Legal Transplants"*, 4 Maastricht J. Eur. & Comp. L. 111 (1997).
132 *See id.* at 111–12.
133 *See id.* at 114–15.
134 *See id.* at 117.
135 *See id.* at 117–18.
136 *See* Margit Cohn, *Legal Transplant Chronicles: The Evolution of Unreasonableness and Proportionality Review of the Administration in the United Kingdom*, 58 Am. J. of Comp. L. 583, 587 (2010).
137 *See id.* at 587–88.
138 *See* Gunther Teubner, *Legal Irritants: Good Faith in British Law or How Unifying Law Ends Up in New Divergences*, 61 Mod. L. Rev. 11, 12 (1998).
139 *See id.* at 12–13, 32.

receiving legal system will be transformed.[140] Therefore, he proposes "legal translation" as a new metaphor for legal borrowing.[141] Örücü prefers using "transposition" and "tuning," as used in music, to describe respectively the legal borrowing process and the work conducted by those who move the law, usually domestic judges.[142] She also believes that a legal transplant's potential success is built on multiple conditions, such as the size and characteristics of the transplant, whether the tuning is successful, whether the transplant is forced or voluntary, and the social culture of the receiving country.[143] Daniel Berkowitz, Katharina Pistor, and Jean-Francois Richard focus their analysis on the effectiveness of a legal transplant, or the "transplant effect."[144] They propose that the process of transplant is more decisive for the transplant's effectiveness than the contents of the transplanted legal rules.[145] In their conclusion, elements that may decide whether the legal transplant is successful include: whether the legal evolution is internal and thus the transplant is voluntary; whether the appropriateness of the transplanted rules has been considered so that modifications have been made in order for the rules to adapt to the receiving country; and whether the receiving country and its population are already familiar with the transplanted rules and the legal system from which they come.[146] Richard Small makes a further distinction between "culture," a society's entire background, and "context," circumstances that specifically drive the development of a particular rule.[147] He proposes a scenario where the "context," rather than just the law itself, is transplanted.[148] In this situation, Small claims that the new context will demand a new law, while the culture of the receiving country will shape the law.[149] He concludes that law also needs to adapt to the changes in contexts.[150] Finally, Jonathan Miller and Margit Cohn analyze legal transplants by using typology.[151] This sociological methodology helps them identify multiple factors and consequences of legal transplant.[152]

140 *See* Máximo Langer, *From Legal Transplant to Legal Translation: The Globalization of Plea Bargaining and the Americanization Thesis in Criminal Procedure*, 45 Harv. Int'l L.J. 1, 31–32 (2004).
141 *See id.* at 32–35.
142 *See* Esin Örücü, *Law as Transposition*, 51 Int'l & Comp. L.Q. 205, 207–08 (2002).
143 *See id.* at 212.
144 *See* Daniel Berkowitz, Katharina Pistor, Jean-Francois Richard, *The Transplant Effect*, 51 Am. J. of Comp. L. 163, 171 (2003).
145 *See id.* at 189.
146 *See id.* at 189–90.
147 *See* Richard G. Small, *Towards a Theory of Contextual Transplants*, 19 Emory Int'l L. Rev. 1431, 1437–38 (2005).
148 *See id.* at 1438.
149 *See id.*
150 *See id.* at 1455.
151 *See* Jonathan M. Miller, *A Typology of Legal Transplants: Using Sociology, Legal History and Argentine Examples to Explain the Transplant Process*, 51 Am. J. of Comp. L. 839 (2003); Cohn, *supra* note 136.
152 *See* Miller, *supra* note 151; Cohn, *supra* note 136.

This new perspective rejects an extreme and binary distinction of the possibility of legal transplant and, in fact, reflects the theories proposed by various scholars in the middle ground.[153]

The history of arbitration in China undoubtedly supplies another example of legal transplant. Borrowed from the Western world, arbitration as a legal institution was transplanted to China. China's relatively mature arbitration legal framework and fast-growing arbitration industry in the present day proves that legal transplant is definitely possible. That said, arbitration's legal transplant process in China clearly indicated a strong tie between the legal institution and China's social contexts.

First, the legal transplant of arbitration in China supports Otto Kahn-Freund's theory in the sense that it indeed depended heavily on China's social, and particularly political, contexts at different times in history. The Chinese political system and culture of the early 1990s had a direct impact on the content of the current PRC Arbitration Law. The legal transplant of arbitration in China also supports theories proposed by Gunther Teubner and Máximo Langer, in the sense that during the transplant process, both the transplanted law, namely the arbitration legal framework, and the existing Chinese legal system were transformed so that the new law could blend in. Moreover, Chinese legal elites, including lawmakers and judges, did not stop after transplanting the arbitration law, but continued fitting it into the Chinese legal system, by e.g. ensuring that it is consistent with Chinese Civil Procedure Law and other legislations. This is in line with the "tuning" process suggested by Örücü. Also, the legal transplant of arbitration in China was the result of the country's changing economic structure, so the law was borrowed when the context changed, as suggested by Small, and was indeed shaped by China's culture.

Apart from supporting these various theories, certain features of arbitration's legal transplant in China also provide a number of opportunities for further reflection. First, the legal transplant of arbitration in China shows that in the process of legal transplant, the receiving country does not always borrow the law in its totality, but may instead choose to reshape the legal rule or institution and tailor it to the country's needs, or fit its social, political, and economic contexts. The Chinese government in the late 1970s, for example, intentionally removed ad hoc arbitration from the complete legal institution of arbitration and only transplanted institutional arbitration as a dispute resolution method to safeguard the operation of China's transition economy. The government realized that ad hoc arbitration was not suitable for that purpose, nor could it fit into the then existing political, social, or economical contexts of Chinese society. As a result, it chose to remove the ad hoc portion from a legal institution that is otherwise whole. Not surprisingly, this strategy proved to be highly successful. Although Chinese lawmakers and judges still needed to fine-tune the curtailed,

153 *See* Cohn, *supra* note 136, at 590–96.

and institutional only, arbitration system to make it fit into the Chinese legal system, the transplant occurred quite smoothly. This was because institutional arbitration was a very good fit for the Chinese legal system at the time, while ad hoc arbitration would have conflicted radically with it. As a result, this conscious cherry-picking ensured that the legal transplant process ran smoothly and ended in success.

Of course, this strategy comes with the cost of having only part of a borrowed law but not the full package. Although the strategy of cherry-picking can be helpful at the time when the transplant initially takes place, having only a curtailed legal rule or institution may not be ideal when, years later, the receiving country's economic, social, and political contexts have changed and become ready to receive the part that was abandoned initially. Moreover, a curtailed system can sometimes become misleading and lose certain important features that are not always easily perceivable, particularly to lawmakers in the receiving country who might not be completely familiar with all the hidden issues. In the case of arbitration in China, the removal of ad hoc arbitration directly resulted in the misguided perception and conception of arbitration as a legal institution by the Chinese government, and arguably among Chinese lawyers generally. Because of this, the Chinese government and lawyers view arbitration as a quasi-judicial system that is not too much different from the *public* litigation system. This is, however, fundamentally at odds with the nature of arbitration as a *private* dispute resolution mechanism. This misconception has given rise to many difficult and complex legal issues in practice.

This, however, can suggest that a legal transplant does not always have to happen all at once, but may instead take place in multiple or gradual stages. This is one of the reasons why this book will call for the legitimization of ad hoc arbitration under Chinese law. China chose to establish an incomplete arbitration system from the beginning, but it may be open to supplementing it with ad hoc arbitration in the future. More than two decades after the initial legal transplant, China has undergone rapid economic development as well as significant changes in its political, social, and economic structures. It has become increasingly clear that maintaining this preclusion of ad hoc arbitration is no longer necessary for China, nor is it in China's or anyone's interest. Perhaps more importantly, Chinese legislators have indeed expressed willingness to legitimize ad hoc arbitration once the time is right.[154] As a result, it is entirely possible that Chinese lawmakers may decide to incorporate ad hoc arbitration into its existing laws in the future. This indicates that legal transplant does not have to happen all at once. Based on the receiving country's strategy, the transplant process may be intentionally divided into different phases. Whether and exactly when the later phases will happen likely depends on the receiving country's perception of the

154 *See* Hu Kangsheng (胡康生), *Zhongcai de Benzhi Shi Minjian Xing* (仲裁的本质是民间性) [*The Nature of Arbitration is Private*], Fazhi Ribao (法制日报) [Legal Daily], Sept. 8, 2004 (China).

first phase's level of success and probably also on changes in the political, economic, and social contexts of the receiving country's society that take place after the first phase. This strategy may particularly be useful for transition economies in which a society's economic, social, and political structures undergo rapid and drastic changes throughout a certain period of time. China's experience with arbitration offers an excellent example in this regard.

3 Enforceability of ad hoc arbitration agreements in China

I Rejection of ad hoc arbitration agreements under Chinese law

After looking at the historical development of the Chinese arbitration system from a comparative perspective, we now turn our focus to the current legal framework of ad hoc arbitration under Chinese law. While it is true that lawyers, judges, and legal scholars frequently categorize arbitration into ad hoc and institutional, this distinction has little legal significance in most jurisdictions in the world. Parties in practice will surely choose either ad hoc or institutional arbitration depending on which best suits their needs in a particular case. However, whether their arbitration agreement calls for submission of the dispute to an ad hoc tribunal or to a tribunal working with an arbitration institution would normally make no difference legally. As long as the agreement clearly demonstrates their intent to arbitrate, it will be a valid arbitration agreement under most of the world's arbitration laws. Moreover, awards rendered by ad hoc tribunals and by tribunals working with arbitration institutions enjoy the same legal status. They are equally binding upon the parties and equally enforceable by courts. In any case, the New York Convention does not distinguish between ad hoc or institutional awards. An ad hoc arbitration award will certainly fall under the scope of Article I(2) of the New York Convention, which reads, "the term 'arbitral awards' shall include . . . awards made by arbitrators appointed for each case . . . " and therefore will be enforceable under the Convention.[1]

In China, however, this distinction does make a legal difference. Relevant parts of Article 16 and Article 18 of the PRC Arbitration Law read as follows:

> Article 16
>
> . . . .
>
> An arbitration agreement shall contain the following particulars:
>
> . . . .
>
> (3) a designated *arbitration commission*.[2]

1 United Nations Convention on the Recognition and Enforcement of Foreign Arbitral Awards art. I(2), June 10, 1958, 330 U.N.T.S. 38 [hereinafter New York Convention].

2 Zhongcai Fa (仲裁法) [Arbitration Law] (promulgated by the Standing Comm. Nat'l People's Cong., Aug. 31, 1994, effective Sept. 1, 1995, rev. Sept. 1, 2017), art. 16 (China) (English

> Article 18
>
> If an arbitration agreement contains no or unclear provisions concerning . . . *the arbitration commission*, the parties may reach a supplementary agreement. If no such supplementary agreement can be reached, the arbitration agreement shall be null and void.[3]

As these provisions make clear, an arbitration agreement must specify an arbitration institution to administer the arbitration so as to be valid under the PRC Arbitration Law.[4] Accordingly, an ad hoc arbitration agreement is invalid under the PRC Arbitration Law. Because an arbitration agreement is the cornerstone of an arbitration process, this provision under the PRC Arbitration Law obviously creates a major obstacle to anyone wishing to arbitrate in China on an ad hoc basis. Moreover, the SPC has strictly interpreted this institutional arbitration requirement. If, in an arbitration agreement, the parties only choose an institution's rules rather than the institution itself, the agreement may be held invalid.[5] Similarly, if the parties agree on two possible arbitration institutions in an arbitration agreement, that agreement is invalid unless they reach a valid supplementary agreement choosing one of the two institutions and eliminating the other.[6]

The PRC Arbitration Law's rejection of ad hoc arbitration agreements has grave consequences. First, this means no ad hoc arbitration agreement will be enforced under the PRC Arbitration Law. As a result, an arbitrator who is appointed by a party to an ad hoc arbitration agreement does not have jurisdiction or power to hear the case under Chinese law. The case should instead be heard and decided by a judge. Second, even if the two parties who concluded an ad hoc arbitration agreement both wanted to move forward with their arbitration proceeding and in fact did so, the final award issued by their appointed arbitrator would nonetheless be unenforceable under Chinese law.

These seemingly straightforward conclusions, however, are over-simplified and need qualifications. Because China is a contracting state to the New York Convention, under which ad hoc arbitration is undoubtedly supported, Chinese courts

---

translation provided by the Nati'l People's Cong., available at http://www.npc.gov.cn/english npc/Law/2007-12/12/content_1383756.htm) (emphasis added).

3 *Id.* art. 18 (emphasis added). Here, however, "invalid" may be a better translation than "null and void."

4 *See* Zhongcai Fa (仲裁法) [Arbitration Law] (promulgated by the Standing Comm. Nat'l People's Cong., Aug. 31, 1994, effective Sept. 1, 1995, rev. Sept. 1, 2017), art. 16 (China).

5 *See* Zuigao Renmin Fayuan Guanyu Shiyong "Zhonghua Renmin Gongheguo Zhongcai Fa" Ruogan Wenti de Jieshi (最高人民法院关于适用《中华人民共和国仲裁法》若干问题的解释) [Interpretation on Certain Issues Concerning the Application of the "Arbitration Law of the People's Republic of China"] (promulgated by the Sup. People's Ct., Aug. 23, 2006, effective Sept. 8, 2006), art. 4 (China).

6 *See id.* art. 5.

have the obligation to enforce ad hoc awards made outside China in another contracting state.[7] Of course, if the seat of an arbitration is in China, the New York Convention will not apply to this arbitration award. Chinese law will govern issues related to its enforcement. Accordingly, the prospect of having a Chinese court enforce an ad hoc arbitration award seated in China is, although not entirely absent, slight. Moreover, international commercial arbitration is a highly sophisticated system sometimes referred to by scholars as autonomous.[8] Under this framework, all contracting states to the New York Convention may potentially be involved and no single country can control the whole process. As a result, this extremely rare preclusion of ad hoc arbitration under the PRC Arbitration Law may also cause complicated consequences on the international level. For example, if the parties place the seat of arbitration in China and choose ad hoc arbitration, will other contracting states to the New York Convention enforce the award?[9]

With respect to enforcement of ad hoc arbitration agreements by Chinese courts, the picture is still rather complicated. Although Chinese courts will likely strike down an ad hoc arbitration agreement when Chinese law applies, the PRC Arbitration Law will not apply to all the arbitration agreements entered into by Chinese parties or presented before Chinese courts. This is because when concluding an arbitration agreement in an international commercial transaction, parties are free to agree on the seat of arbitration and the law that will govern the validity of the arbitration agreement. Therefore, it is important to know in what situations a Chinese court will apply the PRC Arbitration Law and strike down an ad hoc arbitration agreement.

II Different jurisdictions in the Greater China region

Before turning to the complicated choice-of-law issues that Chinese courts have adopted to deal with arbitration related cases, it is important to point out that there are multiple jurisdictions within the PRC, and the so-called "Greater China Region." This, to a certain extent, shapes the structure of the Chinese arbitration legal framework.

A Hong Kong and Macau

Under the current Chinese constitutional and legal system, Hong Kong and Macau are separate jurisdictions from mainland China, despite being parts of

7 *See* New York Convention, *supra* note 1, art. I(2).

8 *See* Gary B. Born, International Commercial Arbitration 214, 216 (2d ed. 2014); Fouchard, Gaillard, Goldman on International Commercial Arbitration 50 (Emmanuel Gaillard and John Savage eds, 1999); Julian D. M. Lew, Loukas A. Mistelis & Stefan M. Kröll, Comparative International Commercial Arbitration 81 (2003).

9 *See* discussion *infra* Chapter 4.

the PRC.[10] The two territories were ceded from China by treaties in the nineteenth century to the UK and Portugal respectively.[11] As a result, the PRC was not exercising sovereignty over Hong Kong or Macau until their handovers back to China in 1997 and 1999 respectively. During negotiations between China and the UK as well as Portugal before the handovers, China was still adopting a highly centralized planned economy in addition to its socialist political ideology. Both of them were radically different from the economic and political systems in Hong Kong and Macau at the time. To accommodate the handovers under these circumstances, the Chinese central government designed and implemented a legal regime commonly known as "One Country, Two Systems."

"One Country, Two Systems" essentially means that mainland China's socialist system will not be implemented in Hong Kong or Macau. Instead, the economic, political, and legal systems effective in Hong Kong and Macau prior to their handovers will in general be kept intact.[12] The constitutional basis of this legal framework has its roots in Article 31 of the Constitution of the People's Republic of China (PRC Constitution), which provides that

> [t]he State may establish special administrative regions when necessary. The systems to be instituted in special administrative regions shall be prescribed by law enacted by the National People's Congress in the light of specific conditions.[13]

Pursuant to this constitutional provision, the National People's Congress of China (NPC) enacted the Basic Law of the Hong Kong Special Administrative Region of the People's Republic of China (Hong Kong Basic Law) and the Basic Law of the Macau Special Administrative Region of the People's Republic of China (Macau Basic Law). As the name of the two acts suggest, Hong Kong and

10 *See* Xianggang Tebie Xingzhengqu Jiben Fa (香港特别行政区基本法) [The Basic Law of the Hong Kong Special Administrative Region] (promulgated by the Nat'l People's Cong., Apr. 4, 1990, effective July 1, 1997), chs. 1–2 (China); Aomen Tebie Xingzhengqu Jiben Fa (澳门特别行政区基本法) [The Basic Law of the Macau Special Administrative Region] (promulgated by the Nat'l People's Cong., Mar. 31, 1993, effective Dec. 20, 1999), chs. 1–2 (China).

11 *See* Harold Tanner, China: A History 386 (2009); Rosmarie Wank-Nolasco Lamas, History of Macau: A Student's Manual § 8.4.2. (1998).

12 *See generally* Joint Declaration of the Government of the United Kingdom of Great Britain and Northern Ireland and the Government of the People's Republic of China on the Question of Hong Kong with Annexes, Dec. 19, 1984, Gr. Brit.-P.R.C., Gr. Brit. T.S. No. 26 (1985), (Cd. 9543), available at http://treaties.fco.gov.uk/docs/fullnames/pdf/1985/TS0026%20(1985)%20CMND-9543%201984%2019%20DEC,%20BEIJING%3B%20JOINT%20DECLARATION%20OF%20UK%20&%20CHINA%20ON%20THE%20QUESTION%20OF%20HONG-KONG%20WITH%20ANNEXES.pdf; Joint Declaration of the Government of the People's Republic of China and the Government of the Portuguese Republic on the question of Macao (with annexes), Mar. 26, 1987, P.R.C.-Port., 1498 U.N.T.S. 195, available at https://treaties.un.org/doc/Publication/UNTS/Volume%201498/v1498.pdf.

13 Xianfa art. 31 (1982) (China).

Macau are now officially known as Hong Kong Special Administrative Region of China and Macau Special Administrative Region of China.

Under this legal framework, PRC laws, with very few exceptions, do not apply in Hong Kong or Macau.[14] Instead, Hong Kong and Macau, have kept in force the majority of their laws in place before their change in sovereignty,[15] They also enjoy independent executive power, legislative power, and judicial power.[16] The fact that Hong Kong and Macau each have their own distinct legal and judicial systems is clear evidence that they are two separate jurisdictions within China. In other words, Hong Kong and Macau are essentially given a "quasi-foreign" status under the regime of "One Country, Two Systems," although they are nonetheless recognized as Chinese territories.

Regarding the PRC arbitration legal framework, the PRC Arbitration Law does not apply in Hong Kong or Macau. They both have their own arbitration laws.[17] Accordingly, arbitration awards seated in Hong Kong and Macau are not made under the PRC Arbitration Law and are therefore "quasi-foreign." What this means is, if a party wants to enforce a Hong Kong or Macau award in China, it needs to apply to a Chinese court and seek recognition and enforcement of the award, just as it would otherwise do with a foreign award. That said, because Hong Kong and Macau are indeed Chinese territories, these awards cannot be considered "foreign" under Chinese law. Accordingly, Chinese courts will not apply the New York Convention to these awards. To ensure the mutual recognition and enforcement of arbitration awards, the Chinese central government and governments in Hong Kong and Macau concluded specific agreements in this regard. The SPC promulgated the Arrangement on Mutual Enforcement of Arbitration Awards Between Mainland and Hong Kong Special Administrative Region in 2000 and the Arrangement on Mutual Recognition and Enforcement of Arbitration Awards Between Mainland and Macau Special Administrative

14 *See* Xianggang Tebie Xingzhengqu Jiben Fa (香港特别行政区基本法) [The Basic Law of the Hong Kong Special Administrative Region] (promulgated by the Nat'l People's Cong., Apr. 4, 1990, effective July 1, 1997), art. 18, para. 2 (China); Aomen Tebie Xingzhengqu Jiben Fa (澳门特别行政区基本法) [The Basic Law of the Macau Special Administrative Region] (promulgated by the Nat'l People's Cong., Mar. 31, 1993, effective Dec. 20, 1999), art. 18, para. 2 (China).

15 *See* Xianggang Tebie Xingzhengqu Jiben Fa (香港特别行政区基本法) [The Basic Law of the Hong Kong Special Administrative Region] (promulgated by the Nat'l People's Cong., Apr. 4, 1990, effective July 1, 1997), art. 8 (China); Aomen Tebie Xingzhengqu Jiben Fa (澳门特别行政区基本法) [The Basic Law of the Macau Special Administrative Region] (promulgated by the Nat'l People's Cong., Mar. 31, 1993, effective Dec. 20, 1999), art. 8 (China).

16 *See* Xianggang Tebie Xingzhengqu Jiben Fa (香港特别行政区基本法) [The Basic Law of the Hong Kong Special Administrative Region] (promulgated by the Nat'l People's Cong., Apr. 4, 1990, effective July 1, 1997), arts. 16, 17, 19 (China); Aomen Tebie Xingzhengqu Jiben Fa (澳门特别行政区基本法) [The Basic Law of the Macau Special Administrative Region] (promulgated by the Nat'l People's Cong., Mar. 31, 1993, effective Dec. 20, 1999), arts. 16, 17, 19 (China).

17 *See* Arbitration Ordinance, (2014) Cap. 609. (H.K.); Decree-Law no. 55/98/M, 23 November. (Macau).

Region in 2008.[18] These documents contain a set of standards and procedures for enforcement of Hong Kong and Macau awards that are virtually identical to those under the New York Convention.[19] From this perspective, Hong Kong and Macau awards are indeed "quasi-foreign" under Chinese law.

B Taiwan

Taiwan's legal status is unique under Chinese law. As a political issue, the PRC always maintains that Taiwan is an integral part of Chinese territory. As a legal issue, the PRC Constitution takes the same stance.[20] However, because the Chinese central government does not exercise any actual control over Taiwan, Taiwan undoubtedly remains a separate jurisdiction from mainland China. Taiwan has its own laws and judicial system, while laws in mainland China are obviously not applicable in Taiwan.

In the field of arbitration, Taiwan enjoys a "quasi-foreign" status similar to Hong Kong and Macau under Chinese law. Arbitration awards seated in Taiwan are not considered domestic under the PRC Arbitration Law. However, the New York Convention does not apply to Taiwan awards for at least two reasons. First, as said, the PRC maintains that Taiwan is part of China, therefore Chinese courts will not apply any international treaty to Taiwanese awards. Second, Taiwan is not a contracting party to the New York Convention. Because the PRC made a reciprocity reservation, which means that it will only apply the New York Convention to an award made in another contracting party's territory, the PRC

18 *See* Zuigao Renmin Fayuan Guanyu Neidi yu Xianggang Tebie Xingzhengqu Xianghu Zhixing Zhongcai Caijue de Anpai (最高人民法院关于内地与香港特别行政区相互执行仲裁裁决的安排) [Arrangement on Mutual Enforcement of Arbitration Awards Between Mainland and Hong Kong Special Administrative Region] (promulgated by the Sup. People's Ct., Jan. 24, 2000, effective Feb. 1, 2000) (China); Zuigao Renmin Fayuan Guanyu Neidi yu Aomen Tebie Xingzhengqu Xianghu Renke he Zhixing Zhongcai Caijue de Anpai (最高人民法院关于内地与澳门特别行政区相互认可和执行仲裁裁决的安排) [Arrangement on Mutual Recognition and Enforcement of Arbitration Awards Between Mainland and Macau Special Administrative Region] (promulgated by the Sup. People's Ct., Dec. 12, 2007, effective Jan. 1, 2008) (China).

19 *Compare* Zuigao Renmin Fayuan Guanyu Neidi yu Xianggang Tebie Xingzhengqu Xianghu Zhixing Zhongcai Caijue de Anpai (最高人民法院关于内地与香港特别行政区相互执行仲裁裁决的安排) [Arrangement on Mutual Enforcement of Arbitration Awards Between Mainland and Hong Kong Special Administrative Region] (promulgated by the Sup. People's Ct., Jan. 24, 2000, effective Feb. 1, 2000) (China), and Zuigao Renmin Fayuan Guanyu Neidi yu Aomen Tebie Xingzhengqu Xianghu Renke he Zhixing Zhongcai Caijue de Anpai (最高人民法院关于内地与澳门特别行政区相互认可和执行仲裁裁决的安排) [Arrangement on Mutual Recognition and Enforcement of Arbitration Awards Between Mainland and Macau Special Administrative Region] (promulgated by the Sup. People's Ct., Dec. 12, 2007, effective Jan. 1, 2008) (China), with Zuigao Renmin Fayuan Guanyu Zhixing Woguo Jiaru de "Chengren ji Zhixing Waiguo Zhongcai Caijue Gongyue" de Tongzhi (最高人民法院关于执行我国加入的《承认及执行外国仲裁裁决公约》的通知) [Notice on Implementing the "Convention on the Recognition and Enforcement of Foreign Arbitral Awards" that Our Country has Acceded Into] (promulgated by the Sup. People's Ct., Apr. 10, 1987, effective Apr. 10, 1987) (China).

20 *See* Xianfa pmbl. (1982) (China).

would not have applied the Convention to a Taiwanese award even if it considered Taiwan as an independent country.[21] In any case, the SPC formulated special rules for the recognition and enforcement of Taiwanese awards as they did for Hong Kong and Macau awards.

In the past, the standards and procedures for the recognition and enforcement of Taiwanese arbitration awards in mainland China were the same as those for recognition and enforcement of Taiwanese court judgments in mainland China.[22] Grounds for refusing enforcement under those rules were different from those under the New York Convention and could hardly be seen as pro-arbitration.[23] In 2015, the SPC promulgated a new judicial interpretation that specifically applies to recognition and enforcement of arbitration awards made in Taiwan.[24] This new set of rules contains standards and procedures very similar to those under the New York Convention and those that the SPC set forth for Hong Kong and Macau awards.[25] It, therefore, provides for a set of pro-arbitration rules towards Taiwanese awards.

In conclusion, there are indeed different jurisdictions in the PRC or the so-called Greater China Region. When it comes to arbitration, Chinese law treats awards made in Hong Kong, Macau, and Taiwan as "quasi-foreign" awards and provides specific and pro-arbitration rules regarding their recognition and enforcement in mainland China. In this book, whenever Chinese laws or PRC laws are mentioned, they refer to national laws applicable to mainland China, while laws of Hong Kong, Macau, and Taiwan are excluded. Similarly, when China or Chinese territory is mentioned in relevant parts of this book, the reference is to mainland China only, not including Hong Kong, Macau, or Taiwan, unless otherwise specified.

III Enforcing ad hoc arbitration agreements under non-Chinese law

Chinese courts have indeed enforced many ad hoc arbitration agreements in practice, despite the PRC Arbitration Law's compulsory provision that an ad hoc

21 *See* Quanguo Renmin Daibiao Dahui Changwu Weiyuanhui Guanyu Woguo Jiaru "Chengren ji Zhixing Waiguo Zhongcai Caijue Gongyue" de Jueding (全国人民代表大会常务委员会关于我国加入《承认及执行外国仲裁裁决公约》的决定) [Decision on Accession Into the "Convention on the Recognition and Enforcement of Foreign Arbitral Awards"] (promulgated by the Standing Comm. Nat'l People's Cong., Dec. 2, 1986, effective Dec. 2, 1986) (China).

22 *See* Zuigao Renmin Fayuan Guanyu Renmin Fayuan Renke Taiwan Diqu Youguan Fayuan Minshi Panjue de Guiding (最高人民法院关于人民法院认可台湾地区有关法院民事判决的规定) [Regulation on the People's Courts' Recognition of Civil Judgments Made by Relevant Courts in Taiwan] (promulgated by the Sup. People's Ct., May 22, 1998, effective May 26, 1998) (China).

23 *See id.*

24 *See* Zuigao Renmin Fayuan Guanyu Renke he Zhixing Taiwan Diqu Zhongcai Caijue de Guiding (最高人民法院关于认可和执行台湾地区仲裁裁决的规定) [Regulation on the Recognition and Enforcement of Arbitration Awards Made in Taiwan] (promulgated by the Sup. People's Ct., June 29, 2015, effective July 1, 2015) (China).

25 *See id.* art. 14.

arbitration agreement is invalid. This is because Chinese law does not necessarily apply to all the cases before Chinese courts, due to arbitration's international nature. The SPC adopted a choice-of-law rule that reduces the chance for Chinese law's potential application.[26]

A Choice-of-law issues in international commercial arbitration

Choice-of-law issues play a very important role in international commercial arbitration. They can also become highly complicated because there could be multiple applicable laws governing different legal issues within one arbitration case. Generally speaking, the person who hears the case, either an arbitrator or a judge, needs to decide what law applies to three fundamental issues. First, what law governs the substance or merits of the dispute? Second, what law governs the validity of the arbitration agreement? Based on the doctrine of separability, an arbitration agreement is treated as a separate agreement in itself, even when it takes the form of a clause within a larger container agreement.[27] As a result, two different laws can potentially govern these two different contracts. Third, what law governs the arbitration proceeding? This third law is also commonly known as the "curial law" or the "*lex arbitri*."[28] Although in practice the parties may choose one law to govern all of these issues or, depending on the facts in the case, the arbitrator or judge may decide that one law applies to all of these issues, there is a significant chance that multiple laws become applicable in one arbitration case. Even though the same law may apply to all these issues, for the purpose of legal analysis, it is nonetheless necessary to carefully distinguish between these different applicable laws within the same arbitration case.

When a Chinese court decides whether it shall enforce or strike down an ad hoc arbitration agreement, it first needs to determine the law governing the validity of the arbitration agreement. In international practice, judges and arbitrators around the world adopt different approaches on this issue. Some use traditional conflict-of-laws approaches, under which they will identify the conflict-of-law (private international law) rules and select the governing law after considering all the connecting factors.[29] Some, represented by Swiss Law, establish a validity-preferring rule, which means that they will choose from a number

26 *See, e.g.*, Zuigao Renmin Fayuan Guanyu Shiyong "Zhonghua Renmin Gongheguo Zhongcai Fa" Ruogan Wenti de Jieshi (最高人民法院关于适用《中华人民共和国仲裁法》若干问题的解释) [Interpretation on Certain Issues Concerning the Application of the "Arbitration Law of the People's Republic of China"] (promulgated by the Sup. People's Ct., Aug. 23, 2006, effective Sept. 8, 2006), art. 16 (China).

27 *See* Tibor Várady et al., International Commercial Arbitration: A Transnational Perspective 179 (6th ed. 2015).

28 *See id.* at 807.

29 *See* Fouchard, Gaillard, Goldman On International Commercial Arbitration, *supra* note 8, at 218–28; Lew et al., *supra* note 8, at 118–22.

of potentially applicable laws a law that will validate the arbitration agreement.[30] French courts, conceptualizing the international arbitration system as autonomous, rest the validity of an arbitration agreement solely on the common intention between the parties, limited only by public policy reasons.[31] As long as the parties expressed an intention to have their dispute resolved by arbitration, their arbitration agreement is valid, unless it violates international public policy or a mandatory rule of French law.[32]

As a result, except for the French courts, when a tribunal or a national court tries to decide what law applies to an arbitration agreement, it will need to select a law from a number of alternatives, unless parties explicitly agree on the law governing the validity of their arbitration agreement, which is a rather rare occasion. At least theoretically, options for selection usually include: (i) the law governing the merits of the dispute; (ii) the law at the seat of arbitration; or (iii) the law at the forum where judicial enforcement of the arbitration agreement is sought.[33] In practice, there is no uniformity among arbitral tribunals or national courts regarding how they will make their choices.[34] One popular choice is the law governing the merits of the dispute. This is most reasonable when the arbitration agreement takes the form of a clause within the larger contract (the container contract), which is the most common situation in reality. The rationale is that the law parties choose to govern the whole contract should also logically govern the arbitration clause in it, absent any specific indication from the parties otherwise.[35] Another popular choice is the law at the seat of arbitration. This is because arbitrators and judges consider the seat of arbitration as the strongest connecting factor to this choice-of-law issue, and presume that parties want to take advantage of a jurisdiction's arbitration law when they put the seat of their arbitration there.[36] Some courts, including Swiss and French courts, may validate the arbitration agreement by relying on forum law or a special body of transnational rules on international arbitration agreements which focus on parties' intent and not on any national law.[37]

30 *See* Fouchard, Gaillard, Goldman On International Commercial Arbitration, *supra* note 8, at 236–38; Lew et al., *supra* note 8, at 122.

31 *See* Fouchard, Gaillard, Goldman On International Commercial Arbitration, *supra* note 8, at 228–30; Lew et al., *supra* note 8, at 123.

32 *See* Fouchard, Gaillard, Goldman On International Commercial Arbitration, *supra* note 8, at 228–30; Lew et al., *supra* note 8, at 123.

33 *See* Lew et al., *supra* note 8, at 118–22.

34 *See* Born, *supra* note 8, at 95.

35 *See* Fouchard, Gaillard, Goldman On International Commercial Arbitration, *supra* note 8, at 222–23; Lew et al., *supra* note 8, at 120.

36 *See* Fouchard, Gaillard, Goldman On International Commercial Arbitration, *supra* note 8, at 225–27; Lew et al., *supra* note 8, at 124–26.

37 *See* Fouchard, Gaillard, Goldman On International Commercial Arbitration, *supra* note 8, at 228–30, 237–38; Lew et al., *supra* note 8, at 122–23.

B The SPC's judicial interpretations

The SPC has adopted a clear and straightforward choice-of-law rule to determine the law governing the validity of an arbitration agreement by issuing a number of judicial interpretations. In order to fully understand the relevant rules, it is necessary to discuss how the SPC interprets Chinese law and ensures the uniform interpretation of Chinese law. China is a country with a civil law tradition. Unlike courts in common law tradition countries, decisions made by Chinese courts are not binding upon later cases. However, there is always a need for all Chinese courts to interpret Chinese law in a uniform way to ensure the law's stability. As a result, the SPC routinely issues legal documents known as "judicial interpretations" to lower level Chinese courts to maintain consistency in the interpretation of Chinese law.

The PRC Constitution endows the National People's Congress (the NPC), the national legislature of China, with the power to interpret Chinese law.[38] This is commonly known as "legislative interpretation." However, the NPC Standing Committee[39] has in turn authorized the SPC to interpret laws in the process of adjudication.[40] Based on this authority, the SPC formulated a series of rules on how it would promulgate judicial interpretations in judicial practices.[41] According to these rules, there are four forms of judicial interpretations, which include *Interpretations*, *Regulations*, *Replies*, and *Interpretative Revisions.*[42] *Interpretations* and *Regulations* are free-standing and comprehensive documents related to certain Chinese legislations. They usually supply detailed rules, procedural or substantive, to fill the gaps in the often generalized and abstract legislations. These sophisticated documents can sometimes be even longer than the laws being interpreted themselves. Due to their sophistication and practicality, *Interpretations* and *Regulations* are the primary authorities that lower level Chinese courts heavily rely on when they hear and decide actual cases, although some scholars criticize the SPC for illegitimately playing the

38 *See* Xianfa art. 67, §. 4 (1982) (China).

39 The National People's Congress Standing Committee is the permanent body of the National People's Congress. *See id*. art. 57.

40 Quanguo Renmin Daibiao Dahui Changwu Weiyuanhui Guanyu Jiaqiang Falü Jieshi Gongzuo de Jueyi (全国人民代表大会常务委员会关于加强法律解释工作的决议) [Resolution on Improving the Work on the Interpretation of Law] (promulgated by the Standing Comm. Nat'l People's Cong., June lo, 1981, effective June 10, 1981), art. 2 (China); Renmin Fayuan Zuzhi Fa (人民法院组织法) [Organizational Law of the People's Courts] (promulgated by Nat'l People's Cong., July 1, 1979, effective Jan. 1, 1980, rev. Oct. 31, 2006), art. 32 (China).

41 *See, e.g.*, Zuigao Renmin Fayuan Guanyu Sifa Jieshi Gongzuo de Guiding (最高人民法院关于司法解释工作的规定) [Regulation on Judicial Interpretation] (promulgated by the Sup. People's Ct., Mar. 9, 2007, effective Apr. 1, 2007) (China).

42 *See id*. art. 6. A literal translation for "Interpretive Revision" is "Decision". The author intentionally avoids using this term so as not to mislead readers into understanding it as a court decision in a litigated case.

role of the legislature by issuing documents like these.[43] *Replies*, on the other hand, are used to answer lower level courts' questions in a specific case, and are therefore much shorter and usually confined to the particular issues in that specific case. *Interpretative Revisions* are used to amend or rescind existing judicial interpretations. Apart from these four formal types of judicial interpretations, the SPC also uses other types of documents to interpret laws and provide guidance to lower level Chinese courts. These include, for example, *Opinions*, *Notices*, *Measures*, *Conference Minutes*, *Reply Letters*, *Answers*, and so on. Although these documents are not formally categorized as judicial interpretations in the SPC's Regulation on Judicial Interpretation, lower level Chinese courts usually treat them in the same way.[44]

Lower level Chinese courts see all kinds of judicial interpretations made by the SPC as decisive authorities and always rely on them when deciding cases. As a result, the SPC's judicial interpretations are highly relevant and very important when analyzing issues under Chinese law.

C The SPC's choice-of-law rule on an arbitration agreement's validity

The SPC has explicitly stated, in both cases and judicial interpretations, that if the parties have specifically chosen a governing law for the validity of the arbitration agreement itself, which is distinguished from the substantive law that the parties have chosen to govern the merits of the container contract,[45] then that chosen law shall apply.[46] If they failed to choose any such law, but have agreed

43 *See* Ronald C. Brown, Understanding Chinese Courts and Legal Process: Law with Chinese Characteristics 67–70 (1997); Albert HY Chen, An Introduction to the Legal System of the People's Republic of China 118–28 (3d Ed. 2004).

44 *See* Kong Xiaohong, *Legal Interpretation in China*, 6 Conn. J. Int'l L. 491, 498–503 (1991).

45 *See* Zuigao Renmin Fayuan Guanyu Shenli Zhongcai Sifa Shencha Anjian Ruogan Wenti de Guiding (最高人民法院关于审理仲裁司法审查案件若干问题的规定) [Regulation on Certain Issues Concerning the Adjudication of Cases Involving Judicial Review of Arbitration] (promulgated by the Sup. People's Ct., Dec. 26, 2017, effective Jan. 1, 2018), art. 13 (China); Di'erci Quanguo Shewai Shangshi Haishi Shenpan Gongzuo Huiyi Jiyao (第二次全国涉外商事海事审判工作会议纪要) [Minutes of the Second National Working Conference on Adjudication of Foreign-related Commercial and Maritime Cases] (promulgated by the Sup. People's Ct., Dec. 26, 2005, effective Dec. 26, 2005), art. 58 (China) (providing that the substantive law chosen by parties to govern the merits of the container contract cannot be used to determine the validity of the arbitration clause within the container contract).

46 *See* Zuigao Renmin Fayuan Guanyu Shiyong "Zhonghua Renmin Gongheguo Zhongcai Fa" Ruogan Wenti de Jieshi (最高人民法院关于适用《中华人民共和国仲裁法》若干问题的解释) [Interpretation on Certain Issues Concerning the Application of the "Arbitration Law of the People's Republic of China"] (promulgated by the Sup. People's Ct., Aug. 23, 2006, effective Sept. 8, 2006), art. 16 (China); Di'erci Quanguo Shewai Shangshi Haishi Shenpan Gongzuo Huiyi Jiyao (第二次全国涉外商事海事审判工作会议纪要) [Minutes of the Second National Working Conference on Adjudication of Foreign-related Commercial and Maritime Cases] (promulgated by the Sup. People's Ct., Dec. 26, 2005, effective Dec. 26, 2005), art. 58; Zuigao Renmin Fayuan Guanyu Sichuan Huahong Guoji Jingji Jishu Touzi Youxian Gongsi Su Hanguo Hanhua

on the seat of arbitration, the law at the seat of arbitration shall apply to the validity of the arbitration agreement.[47] If they failed to choose both the governing law for the arbitration agreement's validity and the seat of arbitration, then the forum law, i.e. Chinese law, shall apply.[48]

In 2010, the NPC Standing Committee enacted the PRC Law on Application of Law in Foreign-related Civil Relations, which adopted the SPC's choice-of-law rule in general. This statute allows parties to choose the law governing the validity of their arbitration agreement, and when parties fail to identify the governing law, the statute provides that the law of the place where the arbitration institution resides or the seat of arbitration shall govern.[49] Although the choice-of-law rule provided in the statute slightly differs from the SPC's rule in that it mentions "the law at the place where the arbitration institution resides,"[50] the SPC's rule is not inconsistent with the statute.

As a result of this choice-of-law rule, the PRC Arbitration Law does not always apply in a case where the validity of an arbitration agreement is being challenged before a Chinese court. It will only apply where (i) the parties have agreed that Chinese law shall govern the validity of their arbitration agreement; (ii) the parties have not agreed on the law governing the validity of their arbitration agreement but nevertheless have agreed to put the seat of their arbitration in China; or (iii) the parties failed to agree on either of these two issues. Therefore, one can reasonably infer that in many cases before a Chinese court in which the validity of an ad hoc arbitration agreement is being challenged, the Chinese court will not invalidate the arbitration agreement solely because it is ad hoc and thus invalid under Chinese law. It will instead enforce the ad hoc arbitration agreement either when the parties have specifically chosen a law, which allows for ad hoc arbitration, to govern the arbitration agreement's validity, or when the parties have agreed to put the seat of the arbitration in a jurisdiction whose law allows for ad hoc arbitration.

The SPC has in fact kept a consistent approach on this issue over time. Even before producing this choice-of-law rule, the SPC did enforce arbitration agreements calling for ad hoc arbitration outside China. In October 1995, for example, the SPC enforced an ad hoc arbitration agreement only two months after the PRC Arbitration Law took effect. In its Reply Letter to the Higher

Zhushihuishe Maimai Hetong Jiufen Yi'an Zhongcai Tiaokuan Xiaoli Wenti de Qingshi de Fuhan (最高人民法院关于四川华宏国际经济技术投资有限公司诉韩国韩华株式会社买卖合同纠纷一案仲裁条款效力问题的请示的复函) [Reply Letter to the Request for Instructions Concerning the Validity of the Arbitration Clause in the Sales Contract Dispute Case Between Sichuan Huahong International Economic and Technical Investment Co., Ltd and Hanwha Corporation (Korea)] (promulgated by the Sup. People's Ct., Aug. 24, 2007, effective Aug. 24, 2007) (China).

47 *See* sources cited, *supra* note 46.

48 *See id.*

49 *See* Shewai Minshi Guanxi Falü Shiyong Fa (涉外民事关系法律适用法) [Law on Application of Law in Foreign-related Civil Relations] (promulgated by the Standing Comm. Nat'l People's Cong., Oct. 28, 2010, effective Apr. 1, 2011) art. 18 (China).

50 *See id.*

People's Court of Guangdong Province, the SPC stated the following, in literal translation:

> In foreign-related cases where parties have agreed in the contract in advance or reached an agreement after the dispute occurred that the dispute should be arbitrated by a foreign ad hoc arbitration institution or non-permanent arbitration institution, the validity of such an arbitration agreement should be recognized in principle. The court shall not accept the case.[51]

The term "ad hoc arbitration institution" as used by the SPC is incoherent, perplexing, and unintelligible. It indicated a misunderstanding of the SPC, at least at the time, that all arbitrations are institutional. This is a typical example of the misconception of arbitration in Chinese legal culture, shaped by historical and ideological reasons.[52] It would only make sense to interpret that the SPC was in fact referring to an "ad hoc arbitration tribunal" when it used the term "ad hoc arbitration institution." Furthermore, the SPC was not explicit on what it meant by a "foreign" tribunal. Presumably, the SPC was considering a situation in which the seat of arbitration was outside Chinese territory. Given that most jurisdictions in the world allow ad hoc arbitration, it was only logical for the SPC to decide that Chinese courts should enforce an ad hoc arbitration agreement calling for arbitration seated outside China.

As a result, an alternative translation that better captures the SPC's intended meaning would be as follows:

> In foreign-related cases where parties have agreed in the contract in advance or reached an agreement after the dispute occurred that the dispute should be arbitrated by an ad hoc arbitration tribunal or non-permanent arbitration tribunal having its seat outside China, the validity of such an arbitration agreement should be recognized in principle. The court shall not hear the case on its merits.

In conclusion, despite the PRC Arbitration Law's requirement that parties specify an institution in their arbitration agreement and therefore by implication an ad hoc arbitration agreement is invalid per se, the SPC has consistently narrowed the Law's scope of application. The SPC has adopted a choice-of-law rule that the Chinese lawmakers later enacted into legislation, under which a Chinese

51 Zuigao Renmin Fayuan Guanyu Fujian Sheng Shengchan Ziliao Zong Gongsi yu Jinge Hangyun Youxian Gongsi Guoji Haiyun Jiufen Yi'an Zhong Tidan Zhongcai Tiaokuan Xiaoli Wenti de Fuhan (最高人民法院关于福建省生产资料总公司与金鸽航运有限公司国际海运纠纷一案中提单仲裁条款效力问题的复函) [Reply Letter Concerning the Validity of the Bill of Lading's Arbitration Clause in the International Shipping Dispute Case Between Fujian Province Production Material Corporation and Jinge Shipping Co., Ltd.] (promulgated by the Sup. People's Ct., Oct. 20, 1995, effective Oct. 20, 1995) (China).

52 *See* discussion *supra* Chapter 1, Part III.

court will enforce an ad hoc arbitration agreement as long as the parties have chosen a non-Chinese law to govern the validity of the arbitration agreement or placed the seat of arbitration outside China.

IV Analyzing the SPC's choice-of-law rule

A Validity-preferring and pro-arbitration

This choice-of-law rule on the law governing an arbitration agreement's validity is an example of the many pro-arbitration approaches that the SPC has adopted in recent years. It is a validity-preferring rule. First, the SPC has limited the situations in which the PRC Arbitration Law applies to an ad hoc arbitration agreement and increased the chance that a non-Chinese law will apply. Second, a careful analysis will indicate that the choice-of-law rule adopted by the SPC may, in effect, ensure that Chinese courts end up enforcing ad hoc arbitration agreements to the largest extent.

As previously mentioned, when an arbitration agreement's validity is being challenged before a Chinese court, the court may, in theory, choose to apply one of the following laws: (i) the law that the parties have explicitly chosen to govern the validity of their arbitration agreement; (ii) the law governing the substance of the container contract; (iii) the law at the seat of arbitration; or (iv) the forum, i.e. Chinese, law. First, because of arbitration's consensual nature, it is logical for a court to apply the law explicitly chosen by the parties to govern the validity of the arbitration agreement, if they have indeed made such a choice. Also, explicitly choosing the law to govern the validity of an arbitration agreement is a highly technical and detailed matter that parties often neglected in practice.[53] When parties consciously make such a choice regarding an ad hoc arbitration agreement, it is very likely that they are taking advantage of this mechanism purposefully to ensure that their ad hoc arbitration agreement stays away from the PRC Arbitration Law's hostility towards ad hoc arbitration. Therefore, they will for sure choose a non-Chinese law that allows for ad hoc arbitration. Second, because of the PRC Arbitration Law's bizarre requirement that arbitration must be institutional, if a Chinese court wants to adopt a validity-preferring approach to ad hoc arbitration agreements and enforce them as much as it can, then the forum law, i.e. Chinese law, should be avoided whenever possible. Consequently, when the SPC was contemplating a sequence of different laws that Chinese courts will apply, in order to be validity preferring, it should place the law specifically chosen by the parties at the top of the list and the forum law at the bottom of it. The more difficult choice is, however, between (ii) and (iii)—the substantive law of the container contract and the seat law.

53 *See* Albert Jan van den Berg, The New York Arbitration Convention of 1958: Towards a Uniform Judicial Interpretation 291–92 (1981); Fouchard, Gaillard, Goldman On International Commercial Arbitration, *supra* note 8, at 222; Lew et al., *supra* note 8, at 120.

There are four possible scenarios based on different combinations of the location of the seat of arbitration and the substantive law of the container contract: (a) the seat is China, and the substantive law is also Chinese law; (b) the seat is China, and the substantive law is a non-Chinese law; (c) the seat is outside China, and the substantive law is Chinese law; and (d) the seat is outside China, and the substantive law is a non-Chinese law. As far as the author has been able to determine, no other country's law mandates institutional arbitration. Thus, for purposes of analysis, we shall assume in relevant parts of this book that no non-Chinese law will invalidate an ad hoc arbitration agreement solely because it is ad hoc. In scenarios (a) and (d), the choice between the substantive law of the container contract and the seat law makes no difference regarding the validity of an ad hoc arbitration agreement, because they both point to the same law. A choice between the substantive law of the contract and the law of the seat will only lead to a different result in scenarios (b) and (c).

Overall, it is reasonable and practical for the SPC to give preference to seat law over substantive law of the contract in its choice-of-law rule. First, in scenario (b), the hypothetical ad hoc arbitration will take place in China. In this situation, even if the arbitration agreement were valid under the non-Chinese law, the ad hoc arbitration would likely still be inoperative, unless the parties could fully cooperate on all aspects in the arbitration proceeding.[54] This is because the PRC Arbitration Law is silent on ad hoc arbitration, and contains no provision authorizing Chinese courts to assist parties in an ad hoc arbitration proceeding. Due to their civil law tradition, Chinese courts usually interpret their authority narrowly and are reluctant to take action absent explicit statutory authorization.[55] As a result, an ad hoc arbitration seated in China likely would not receive support from either the PRC Arbitration Law or a Chinese court regarding important issues throughout the arbitration proceeding.[56]

For example, in case the parties unfortunately fail to reach a specific agreement on how to appoint their arbitrators, if one party wants to obstruct arbitration, it may simply refuse to make the appointment or cooperate with the other party regarding the appointment. Under these circumstances, the arbitration proceeding will be at a deadlock because no Chinese court will assist the other party in appointing the arbitrators. As a result, successful operation of an ad hoc arbitration seated in China could potentially be very difficult because a party could very easily obstruct the arbitration proceeding.[57] Of course, the parties may choose a set of sophisticated arbitration rules, such as the UNCITRAL Arbitration Rules, for their ad hoc arbitration. These rules will likely eliminate

54 *See* discussion *infra* Chapter 4 Part II.A.

55 *See* John Henry Merryman and Rogelio Pérez-Perdomo, The Civil Law Tradition: An Introduction to the Legal Systems of Europe and Latin America 34–38 (3d ed. 2007); *Key Features of Common Law or Civil Law Systems*, World Bank, http://ppp.worldbank.org/public-private-partnership/legislation-regulation/framework-assessment/legal-systems/common-vs-civil-law (last visited Jan. 24, 2018).

56 *See* discussion *infra* Chapter 4 Part II.A.

57 *See id.*

most of the potential pitfalls in the arbitration proceeding for the parties. However, the parties will still run into considerable difficulties at the stage of enforcing the arbitration award, because Chinese law does not provide for ad hoc arbitration. Therefore, if a Chinese court does enforce the ad hoc arbitration agreement calling for an arbitration seated in China, it will likely lead to an inoperative arbitration or an unenforceable award at its best. Consequently, to avoid this unwanted result, it is perhaps practical or realistic for the Chinese court to apply the seat law, namely Chinese law, in this scenario to invalidate the ad hoc arbitration agreement in the first place.

In scenario (c), on the other hand, it will also be desirable for the Chinese court to apply the seat law. This is because arbitration will take place outside of China where ad hoc arbitration is allowed, so applying the seat law rather than the substantive law, i.e. Chinese law, would be validity-preferring and pro-arbitration. Moreover, Chinese law mandatorily applies to certain types of contracts that are to be performed within Chinese territory, including Sino-foreign joint-venture contracts and Sino-foreign joint-exploration of natural resources contracts.[58] These contracts concern areas where a vast quantity of business activities occur between Chinese and foreign entities. Parties to these types of contract may not specifically agree on the law governing the validity of their arbitration agreement, which is completely normal in practice, but have agreed to put the seat of arbitration, which could be ad hoc, outside China. In this situation, if Chinese courts apply the substantive contract law, i.e. Chinese law, rather than the seat law, it would invalidate the ad hoc arbitration agreement. This result will obviously be against the parties' intent, as manifested by their decision to place the seat of arbitration in a country whose law allows for ad hoc arbitration. As a result, taking into consideration the parties' likely intent to take advantage of the seat law's support of ad hoc arbitration, as well as the possible application of Chinese mandatory law on contracts' substantive issues, it is validity-preferring to apply the seat law instead of the substantive law of the container contract under these circumstances.

Based on the analysis above, if Chinese courts, as a general rule, apply the seat law rather than the substantive law of the container contract, the courts will enforce ad hoc arbitration agreements more often than not. As a result, the choice-of-law rule that the SPC adopted when deciding the law applicable to the validity of an arbitration agreement is validity-preferring and pro-arbitration. With this rule, the SPC ensures that Chinese courts will enforce as many ad hoc arbitration agreements as possible.

58 *See* Shewai Minshi Guanxi Falü Shiyong Fa (涉外民事关系法律适用法) [Law on Application of Law in Foreign-related Civil Relations] (promulgated by the Standing Comm. Nat'l People's Cong., Oct. 28, 2010, effective Apr. 1, 2011), art. 4 (China); Hetong Fa (合同法) [Contract Law] (promulgated by the Nat'l People's Cong., Mar. 15, 1999, effective Oct. 1, 1999), art. 126, para. 2 (China); Zuigao Renmin Fayuan Guanyu Shenli Shewai Minshi Huo Shangshi Hetong Jiufen Anjian Falü Shiyong Ruogan Wenti de Guiding (最高人民法院关于审理涉外民事或商事合同纠纷案件法律适用若干问题的规定) [Provisions on Relevant Issues Concerning the Application of Law in Hearing Foreign-related Civil and Commercial Contractual Disputes Cases] (promulgated by the Sup. People's Ct., July 23, 2007, effective Aug. 8, 2007), art. 8 (China).

B Potential issues

1 Will the SPC support the party choice of a non-Chinese lex arbitri?

Despite being validity-preferring and pro-arbitration in general, the SPC's choice-of-law rule is by no means perfect.

For example, parties in practice seldom explicitly specify the law governing the validity of their arbitration agreement when they conclude a container contract. According to the SPC's rule, however, in order for courts to rely on the law specified by the parties, the parties must clearly state that their chosen law governs the arbitration agreement's validity rather than the substance of the container contract.[59] Sometimes, however, parties may choose a law different from the seat law to govern the arbitration proceeding and provide a legal framework for the whole arbitration. This is usually interpreted as a choice of *lex arbitri*.[60] Of course, doing so may give rise to many complex issues and significant legal risks and therefore is not recommended.[61] This is certainly a very rare choice for parties in practice, but it nonetheless remains a possibility, particularly for ad hoc arbitration in China. Given that most national arbitration laws in the world allow for ad hoc arbitration and do provide some gap-filling provisions to help the parties overcome problems in the arbitration proceeding, it is possible that parties may want to take advantage of a national arbitration law's support of ad hoc arbitration and want to voluntarily choose this law to govern their arbitration proceeding in general. In the rare case that parties did choose a *lex arbitri* different from the seat law, however, the SPC's choice-of-law rule may lead to some uncertainties.

If parties have not explicitly chosen a law to govern the validity of their arbitration agreement, but have instead chosen a non-Chinese arbitration law as their *lex arbitri* while they agreed to put the seat of arbitration in China, according to the SPC's choice-of-law rule as it is today, a Chinese court will apply the seat law, i.e. Chinese law, to determine the validity of the ad hoc arbitration agreement.[62] Accordingly, the court will strike down the ad hoc arbitration agreement. Such a result, however, is clearly against the parties' intention to validate the ad hoc arbitration agreement by choosing a *lex arbitri* under which ad hoc arbitration is allowed.

59 *See* Di'erci Quanguo Shewai Shangshi Haishi Shenpan Gongzuo Huiyi Jiyao (第二次全国涉外商事海事审判工作会议纪要) [Minutes of the Second National Working Conference on Adjudication of Foreign-related Commercial and Maritime Cases] (promulgated by the Sup. People's Ct., Dec. 26, 2005, effective Dec. 26, 2005), art. 58 (China).

60 *See* Várady et al., *supra* note 27, at 683.

61 van den Berg, *supra* note 53, at 292.

62 *See, e.g.*, Zuigao Renmin Fayuan Guanyu Shiyong "Zhonghua Renmin Gongheguo Zhongcai Fa" Ruogan Wenti de Jieshi (最高人民法院关于适用《中华人民共和国仲裁法》若干问题的解释) [Interpretation on Certain Issues Concerning the Application of the "Arbitration Law of the People's Republic of China"] (promulgated by the Sup. People's Ct., Aug. 23, 2006, effective Sept. 8, 2006), art. 16 (China) (stating that if the parties do not specify a law governing the arbitration agreement, the court must then look to the law of the seat to determine the agreement's validity).

To the author's knowledge, the SPC has not yet decided a case on similar facts, so this still remains an open question for Chinese courts. Nevertheless, if the SPC adheres to its validity-preferring principle, it should validate the ad hoc arbitration agreement in such a situation because doing so will be consistent with a more reasonable interpretation of the parties' agreement: that their choice of a non-Chinese *lex arbitri* also means a choice of that country's law for determining the validity of the arbitration agreement. As a result, the SPC can complement its choice-of-law rule so that if parties ever choose a law under which ad hoc arbitration agreement is valid, their ad hoc arbitration agreement shall be valid. This will be a clearly validity-preferring rule. In fact, if the SPC did adopt this new rule, it would actually be possible to have an ad hoc arbitration seated in China.

2 Will the SPC allow an ad hoc arbitration seated in China?

Even under the SPC's current rule, ad hoc arbitration seated in China may become possible, at least theoretically. This is because if parties explicitly choose a non-Chinese law under which ad hoc arbitration is allowed as the law governing the validity of their ad hoc arbitration agreement, while placing the seat of arbitration in China, a Chinese court will have to enforce this arbitration agreement given that parties' specific choice takes priority over the seat law under the SPC's rule.[63] In this situation, therefore, a Chinese court should enforce an arbitration agreement calling for ad hoc arbitration within Chinese territory.

It is, however, true that an enforceable ad hoc arbitration agreement alone is far from sufficient for the successful operation of an ad hoc arbitration in China. Because neither the PRC Arbitration Law nor the SPC's judicial interpretations contain any provisions permitting Chinese courts to be involved in an ad hoc arbitration, parties cannot rely on Chinese courts for any guidance or assistance with regards to any procedural matters.[64] The parties need to carefully design a complete mechanism to ensure the arbitration's operation and the enforceability of the ensuing award. In practice, this will surely be very difficult, albeit not entirely impossible.[65] As explained in the previous section, if the SPC allows or supports parties to choose a non-Chinese *lex arbitri* to govern their arbitration procedure, the parties will have a much better chance to have a successful ad hoc arbitration seated in China. In any event, the SPC's rule as it currently stands

63 *See id.*

64 *See generally* Zhongcai Fa (仲裁法) [Arbitration Law] (promulgated by the Standing Comm. Nat'l People's Cong., Aug. 31, 1994, effective Sept. 1, 1995, rev. Sept. 1, 2017) (China); Zuigao Renmin Fayuan Guanyu Shiyong "Zhonghua Renmin Gongheguo Zhongcai Fa" Ruogan Wenti de Jieshi (最高人民法院关于适用《中华人民共和国仲裁法》若干问题的解释) [Interpretation on Certain Issues Concerning the Application of the "Arbitration Law of the People's Republic of China"] (promulgated by the Sup. People's Ct., Aug. 23, 2006, effective Sept. 8, 2006) (China).

65 *See* discussion *infra* Chapter 5.

does open a door for a successful ad hoc arbitration seated in Chinese territory by recognizing the ad hoc arbitration agreement's validity under certain conditions.

V Conclusion

Unlike most, if not all other, jurisdictions in the world, China maintains a legal framework under which an ad hoc arbitration agreement is invalid per se. Given an arbitration agreement's vital status in an arbitration process, this may seemingly suggest that ad hoc arbitration is completely prohibited under Chinese law. It is fortunate for arbitration, however, that the world is connected. Parties do have the freedom to seek arbitration outside China or choose a different law to govern their arbitration agreement. Realizing these ramifications, the SPC has adopted a pro-arbitration choice-of-law rule, under which Chinese courts will enforce many of the ad hoc arbitration agreements that are submitted to them for review. How a country's courts enforce arbitration agreements is a core aspect of that country's arbitration legal framework. While the PRC Arbitration Law's prohibition of ad hoc arbitration agreements undoubtedly manifests its hostility towards ad hoc arbitration in general, the SPC's pro-arbitration stance on enforcing ad hoc arbitration agreements via the choice-of-law rule obviously indicates its willingness to stretch the unfavorable legislation to the largest extent. The chapters to follow will discuss both of these two observations in more depth.

4 Enforceability of ad hoc arbitration awards in China

As discussed in the previous chapter, the parties to an arbitration agreement must designate an arbitration institution in the arbitration agreement under the PRC Arbitration Law; otherwise their arbitration agreement is invalid.[1] Because a valid arbitration agreement is the cornerstone of an enforceable arbitration award, it appears that ad hoc arbitration has lost its legitimacy in China. China, however, cannot unilaterally delegitimize ad hoc arbitration, particularly given that the world is connected. As a contracting party to the New York Convention, China has an obligation to recognize and enforce arbitration awards made in other New York Convention countries, no matter if those awards are ad hoc or institutional. However, will Chinese courts fulfill this international obligation and enforce foreign ad hoc awards in practice? Moreover, what if two parties want to arbitrate their dispute in China on an ad hoc basis? Will an ad hoc award made in China be enforceable under Chinese law? Will the PRC Arbitration Law's institutional arbitration requirement affect the award's enforcement outside China under the New York Convention? These queries are particularly important because enforcement of arbitration awards is perhaps the issue that carries the most weight in the entire arbitration process. After all, if an award is not enforceable, the whole arbitration is obviously of no use. Therefore, this chapter will answer these questions.

For the sake of convenience, in this chapter and other relevant parts of this book, ad hoc arbitrations seated in China will be referred to as "Chinese ad hoc arbitrations," and awards rendered in such arbitrations will be referred to as "Chinese ad hoc arbitration awards" or "Chinese ad hoc awards." Similarly, ad hoc arbitrations seated outside China will be referred to as "foreign ad hoc arbitrations," and awards rendered in such arbitrations will be referred to as "foreign ad hoc arbitration awards" or "foreign ad hoc awards."

I Foreign ad hoc arbitration awards are enforceable in China

Unlike what is normally expected in a country's arbitration legislation, the PRC Arbitration Law does not contain any provisions related to the recognition and

1 *See* Zhongcai Fa (仲裁法) [Arbitration Law] (promulgated by the Standing Comm. Nat'l People's Cong., Aug. 31, 1994, effective Sept. 1, 1995, rev. Sept. 1, 2017), arts. 16–18 (China).

enforcement of foreign arbitration awards in China.[2] The PRC Civil Procedure Law does address this issue, albeit very briefly, by providing that Chinese courts shall deal with the recognition and enforcement of awards rendered by foreign arbitration institutions in accordance with the treaties that China concluded or acceded to or based on the principle of reciprocity.[3] After China's ratification of the New York Convention, the SPC instructed all Chinese courts to apply the New York Convention when hearing cases in which recognition and enforcement of foreign arbitration awards are sought.[4] As a result, Chinese lawmakers have implemented the New York Convention via legislation. In practice, Chinese courts will directly apply the contents of the New York Convention to review foreign awards that parties seek to recognize and enforce in China.

Under Chinese law's assumption and misconception that all arbitrations are institutional, the PRC Civil Procedure Law only mentions enforcement of awards rendered by foreign arbitration institutions, but arguably remains silent on foreign ad hoc awards.[5] In practice, however, Chinese courts recognize and enforce foreign ad hoc awards in the same way as they recognize and enforce foreign institutional awards, as long as the foreign ad hoc awards meet the standards otherwise set forth by the New York Convention. This is largely because Chinese courts directly apply the New York Convention and the New York Convention makes no distinction between ad hoc and institutional awards.

According to Article I(2) of the New York Convention, "[t]he term 'arbitral awards' shall include not only awards made by arbitrators appointed for each case but also those made by permanent arbitral bodies to which the parties have submitted."[6] Because ad hoc arbitration awards are indeed made by arbitrators appointed for each case, they clearly fall within the scope of Article I(2). The New York Convention therefore supports enforcement of foreign ad hoc awards. Moreover, as compared with an institutional award, an ad hoc award will be subject to the same standards of review and therefore will not suffer any disadvantages. The only potential issue for a foreign ad hoc award's enforcement in China probably lies with Article V(1)(a) of the New York Convention, under which a Chinese court may refuse to recognize and enforce an award if the arbitration agreement between the parties is invalid.[7] However, this will likely not

2 *See id.*

3 *See* Minshi Susong Fa (民事诉讼法) [Civil Procedure Law] (promulgated by Nat'l People's Cong., Apr. 9, 1991, effective Apr. 9, 1991, rev. June. 27, 2017), art. 283 (China).

4 *See* Zuigao Renmin Fayuan Guanyu Zhixing Woguo Jiaru de "Chengren ji Zhixing Waiguo Zhongcai Caijue Gongyue" de Tongzhi (最高人民法院关于执行我国加入的《承认及执行外国仲裁裁决公约》的通知) [Notice on the Implementation of the "Convention on the Recognition and Enforcement of Foreign Arbitral Awards" Acceded to by China], (promulgated by the Sup. People's Ct., Apr. 10, 1987, effective Apr. 10, 1987) (China).

5 *See* Minshi Susong Fa (民事诉讼法) [Civil Procedure Law] (promulgated by Nat'l People's Cong., Apr. 9, 1991, effective Apr. 9, 1991, rev. June 27, 2017), art. 283 (China).

6 United Nations Convention on the Recognition and Enforcement of Foreign Arbitral Awards art. I(2), June 10, 1958, 330 U.N.T.S. 38 [hereinafter New York Convention].

7 *See id.* art. V(1)(a).

pose any difficulty for the award, because under Article V(1)(a), the condition for an award's rejection is that the arbitration agreement is invalid according to the law chosen by the parties or, absent any choice, the law at the seat of arbitration. When parties choose to resolve their dispute via ad hoc arbitration outside China, it is very unlikely that they will specifically choose Chinese law, under which ad hoc arbitration is invalid, to govern their arbitration agreement's validity. If the parties did not specifically choose a law to govern their arbitration agreement's validity, the seat law will apply. Because this arbitration is seated outside China, ad hoc arbitration is presumably legal at the seat, which means the ad hoc arbitration agreement is valid under the seat law. As a result, either under the law that the parties chose for their arbitration agreement, or under the seat law absent the parties' specific choice, the ad hoc arbitration agreement will be valid under the applicable law, therefore, Chinese courts should not reject the ad hoc award under the New York Convention Article V(1)(a). In fact, the SPC has confirmed that this is the way that Chinese courts should interpret and apply the New York Convention on this particular issue.[8] Consequently, a Chinese court will not refuse to recognize or enforce a foreign arbitration award under the New York Convention solely on the ground that it is ad hoc. In other words, when a foreign ad hoc arbitration award satisfies the conditions otherwise set forth by the New York Convention, a Chinese court will recognize and enforce it, even though it will not enforce a similar Chinese ad hoc award.

Chinese lawmakers have also indicated their support for ad hoc awards' enforceability in China. In its Commentaries on Arbitration Laws of China, the Legislative Affairs Commission of the Standing Committee of the National People's Congress (NPC) confirmed that foreign ad hoc arbitration awards will be recognized and enforced in China under the New York Convention:

> In the course of drafting the PRC Arbitration Law, the issue of ad hoc arbitration has been studied. The basic opinion was that ad hoc arbitration would be allowed in international economic and trade disputes, but would not be approved of in domestic economic and trade disputes. . . . [T]he PRC Arbitration Law does not provide for ad hoc arbitration . . . [but] the issue of recognition and enforcement of foreign ad hoc arbitration awards has been solved under the New York Convention. China is a party to the New York Convention, so issues relating to ad hoc arbitration awards made in other countries will be resolved according to the Convention.[9]

8 *See* Zuigao Renmin Fayuan Guanyu Shandongsheng Changyi Kunfu Fangzhi Youxian Gongsi Shenqing Chengren yu Zhixing Waiguo Zhongcai Caijue Yi'an de Qingshi de Fuhan (最高人民法院关于对山东省高级人民法院就丰岛株式会社与山东省昌邑琨福纺织有限公司申请承认与执行外国仲裁裁决一案的请示的复函) [Reply Letter to the Request for Instructions by Shandong Province High People's Court Concerning the Recognition and Enforcement of Foreign Arbitration Award Case Between Toyoshima & Co., Ltd. and Shandong Province Changyi Kunfu Textile Co., Ltd.] (promulgated by the Sup. People's Ct., Sept. 24, 2015, effective Sept. 24, 2015) (China).

9 Quanguo Renda Changweihui Fazhi Gongzuo Weiyuanhui (全国人大常委会法制工作委员会) [The Legislative Affairs Comm'n of the Standing Comm. of the Nat'l People's Cong. of

As indicated above, when enacting the PRC Arbitration Law, the NPC was assuming that foreign ad hoc arbitration awards would be recognized and enforced in China according to the New York Convention. The NPC's Commentaries clearly demonstrated that those awards should be recognized and enforced in China as long as they could satisfy the conditions set by the New York Convention.

The SPC has echoed the NPC's view in this regard on several occasions. One of its judicial interpretations provided:

> Where parties apply to a people's court for enforcement of an ad hoc arbitration award . . . made in the Hong Kong Special Administrative Region, the people's court shall review the case according to the Arrangement [on Mutual Enforcement of Arbitration Awards between the Mainland and the Hong Kong Special Administrative Region]. If no situation provided for in Article 7 of the Arrangement exists, such an arbitration award can be enforced in mainland China.[10]

As discussed earlier, Chinese law treats awards made in Hong Kong and Macau as quasi-foreign.[11] Enforcement of these awards by Chinese courts follows similar procedures and standards of foreign awards. Although the New York Convention is not applicable to these awards, the Chinese central government and the governments of Hong Kong and Macau have jointly promulgated special regulations to govern proceedings relating to recognition and enforcement of arbitration awards made in each other's jurisdictions. These special regulations include provisions that are virtually identical to those in the New York Convention.[12] As a result, the SPC's friendly attitude towards ad hoc awards seated in Hong Kong or Macau is indicative of its position on foreign ad hoc awards. The SPC's willingness to recognize and enforce Hong Kong ad hoc awards means that it is willing to recognize and enforce foreign ad hoc arbitration awards in general.

THE PEOPLE'S REPUBLIC OF CHINA], ZHONGHUA RENMIN GONGHEGUO ZHONGCAI FALÜ SHIPING (中华人民共和国仲裁法律释评) [COMMENTARIES ON ARBITRATION LAWS OF CHINA] 38 (1997).

10 Zuigao Renmin Fayuan Guanyu Xianggang Zhongcai Caijue Zai Neidi Zhixing de Youguan Wenti de Tongzhi (最高人民法院关于香港仲裁裁决在内地执行的有关问题的通知) [Notice on Relevant Issues Concerning the Enforcement of Hong Kong Arbitral Awards in Mainland China] (promulgated by the Sup. People's Ct., Dec. 30, 2009, effective Dec. 30, 2009) (China).

11 *See* discussion *supra* Chapter 3 Part II.A.

12 *See* Zuigao Renmin Fayuan Guanyu Neidi yu Xianggang Tebie Xingzhengqu Xianghu Zhixing Zhongcai Caijue de Anpai (最高人民法院关于内地与香港特别行政区相互执行仲裁裁决的安排) [Arrangement on Mutual Enforcement of Arbitration Awards between Mainland and Hong Kong Special Administrative Region] (promulgated by the Sup. People's Ct., Jan. 24, 2000, effective Feb. 1, 2000) (China); Zuigao Renmin Fayuan Guanyu Neidi yu Aomen Tebie Xingzhengqu Xianghu Renke he Zhixing Zhongcai Caijue de Anpai (最高人民法院关于内地与澳门特别行政区相互认可和执行仲裁裁决的安排) [Arrangement on Mutual Recognition and Enforcement of Arbitration Awards between Mainland and Macau Special Administrative Region] (promulgated by the Sup. People's Ct., Dec. 12, 2007, effective Jan. 1, 2008) (China).

During an interview in 2007, a former vice-president of the SPC explicitly confirmed that foreign ad hoc arbitration awards are enforceable in China:

> Question: Does the Arrangement [on Mutual Enforcement of Arbitration Awards in the Mainland and the Macau Special Administrative Region] recognize ad hoc arbitration?
>
> Answer: According to the laws of the Macau Special Administrative Region, Macau has an ad hoc arbitration system. It is known that in Macau SAR, more ad hoc arbitration awards are made than institutional arbitration awards. At present, current laws in Mainland [China] do not provide for ad hoc arbitration, but according to the New York Convention, arbitration awards that are to be mutually recognized and enforced by the contracting states shall include ad hoc arbitration awards. Given that *China*, as a contracting state [to the New York Convention], ***recognizes ad hoc arbitration awards made in other contracting states***, we shall, of course, recognize and enforce ad hoc arbitration awards made in another jurisdiction within [China].[13]

In practice, cases involving recognition and enforcement of foreign ad hoc awards are common before Chinese courts. For example, in 1997, the Guangzhou Maritime Court recognized and enforced a London ad hoc arbitration award.[14] In 2006, the Wuhan Maritime Court recognized and enforced another London ad hoc arbitration award.[15] In fact, the first foreign arbitration award ever recognized and enforced by a Chinese court under the New York Convention is an ad hoc award.[16] Chinese courts have consistently recognized and enforced foreign ad hoc awards, which proves that China will not refuse to recognize or enforce a foreign arbitration award solely because it is ad hoc.

13 Gaofa Fuzeren jiu Qianshu Guanyu "Neidi yu Aomen Tebie Xingzhengqu Xianghu Renke he Zhixing Zhongcai Caijue de Anpai" Dawen (高法负责人就签署《关于内地与澳门特别行政区相互认可和执行仲裁裁决的安排》答问) [Person in Charge Answering Questions Regarding Concluding the "Arrangement on Mutual Recognition and Enforcement of Arbitration Awards between Mainland and Macau Special Administrative Region"] (promulgated by the Sup. People's Ct., Oct. 30, 2007, effective Oct. 30, 2007) (China).

14 *See* Caipulusi Sikangtesida Hangyun Youxian Gongsi Shenqing Chengren he Zhixing Lundun Zhongcai Caijue An (塞浦路斯康特斯达航运有限公司申请承认和执行伦敦仲裁裁决案) [Contestar Shipping Company Limited of Cyprus v. Sinotrans Guandong Zhanjiang Company], (Guangzhou Mar. Ct., July 15, 1998) (pkulaw.cn).

15 *See* Zhibuluotuo Baixiong Youxian Zeren Gongsi yu Zhongguo Jiangdu Yahai Zaochuan Youxian Gongsi Shenqing Chengren Guowai Zhongcai Caijue Xiaoli Jiufen An (直布罗陀白熊有限责任公司与中国江都亚海造船有限公司申请承认国外仲裁裁决效力纠纷案) [White Bear Limited of Gibraltar v. China Jiangdu Yahai Shipbuilding Co., Ltd.], (Wuhan Mar. Ct., June 16, 2006) (pkulaw.cu).

16 *See* Jingzhou Tao, Arbitration Law and Practice in China 224 (3d ed. 2012); Jian Zhou, *Arbitration Agreements in China: Battles on Designation of Arbitral Institution and Ad Hoc Arbitration*, 23 J. Int'l Arb. 145, 163 (2006).

II Seemingly dire prospects for Chinese ad hoc arbitration

Compared with foreign ad hoc awards that enjoy warm hospitality from Chinese lawmakers and courts, a Chinese ad hoc arbitration award is far less favored. As explained in previous chapters, although Chinese law does not impose an outright prohibition on ad hoc arbitration, ad hoc arbitration agreements are invalid under the PRC Arbitration Law. Because a valid arbitration agreement is the only source of an arbitrators' jurisdiction, it is difficult to foresee a successful arbitration proceeding based on an invalid arbitration agreement. Moreover, because the invalidity of an arbitration agreement is a ground for setting aside an award under the PRC Arbitration Law and for refusing recognition and enforcement under the New York Convention, even if two parties were willing to cooperate in a Chinese ad hoc arbitration proceeding, it would seem unlikely that the resulting award would be enforceable. That being said, as later chapters will discuss, this projection may not be entirely correct or accurate.

In practice, the situation is more complex. A closer look at the PRC Arbitration Law reveals that while providing rules and mechanisms for institutional arbitration, the law is silent on essentially all issues related to ad hoc arbitration except for the requirement that parties must appoint an arbitration institution in their arbitration agreement. On this basis, the PRC Arbitration Law and all other related Chinese laws presume that all arbitrations in China are and will be institutional.[17] This suggests that Chinese lawmakers never anticipated that ad hoc arbitration would take place in China. In other words, ad hoc arbitration is not included in the Chinese arbitration legal framework. Under these circumstances, if one ever wants to have a successful ad hoc arbitration in China that results in an enforceable award, it is first necessary to understand fully how ad hoc arbitration is excluded from the Chinese arbitration system and where one may encounter difficulties in the process under Chinese law.

A Successful operation seems impractical under Chinese law

Parties do not always need to rely on courts to enforce an arbitration award. Many parties successfully resolve their dispute via arbitration without any involvement of governments or courts. This typically happens when the losing party voluntarily pays the award. From this perspective, parties can always engage in ad hoc arbitration in China and resolve their dispute successfully if they cooperate fully and in good faith. However, this does not always happen in practice and one party may try to resist arbitration by putting forward challenges in its proceeding.

Successful operation of a Chinese ad hoc arbitration will not be possible or practical when there is a resisting party. This is because it faces two major

17 *See e.g.*, Minshi Susong Fa (民事诉讼法) [Civil Procedure Law] (promulgated by Nat'l People's Cong., Apr. 9, 1991, effective Apr. 9, 1991, rev. June 27, 2017) (China).

obstacles under Chinese law: the invalidity of an ad hoc arbitration agreement and the lack of support mechanisms. This section will analyze exactly where in the course of the arbitration proceeding the parties to a Chinese ad hoc arbitration will run into difficulties, as well as what the consequences of these difficulties are. For purposes of analysis, this section assumes that two parties voluntarily agree to arbitrate in China on an ad hoc basis, failing to specify both the *lex arbitri* and the law governing the validity of their arbitration agreement, and that the tribunal is willing to take jurisdiction and proceed with the arbitration. This section will discuss several questions arising out of this scenario: Can the proceeding go on if one party regrets its decision to arbitrate and decides to obstruct arbitration? How and when can one party obstruct arbitration? What will be the consequences of the obstructions?

1 *Possible internal obstructions*

Despite being a private dispute resolution mechanism, in which parties intentionally avoid involvement of courts, arbitration cannot function completely outside a legal framework. Arbitration may need guidance, support, or assistance from courts on a variety of issues including, e.g. appointment and challenge of arbitrators, interim measures, calling witnesses or experts, and other procedural matters, particularly when parties cannot reach an agreement on such issues.[18] Parties and tribunals in an ad hoc arbitration may require assistance from courts even more often, because there is no arbitration institution administering the arbitration proceeding. Take appointment of a presiding arbitrator for example. There are usually five ways to appoint a presiding arbitrator in an arbitration proceeding: (1) appointment by the parties' agreement; (2) appointment by an arbitration institution; (3) appointment of the third arbitrator by the two party-appointed arbitrators; (4) appointment by courts; and (5) appointment by a special appointing authority created by the parties in their arbitration agreement.[19] In an institutional arbitration, if the parties did not previously agree to a special appointing authority and if they, or their respectively appointed arbitrators, cannot reach an agreement on the appointment of the presiding arbitrator, there are still two options available: appointment by the institution or by courts. In an ad hoc arbitration, however, because there is no arbitration institution involved, the parties will only have one option in this situation, namely they will have to request assistance from courts.

In a Chinese ad hoc arbitration proceeding, the parties unfortunately cannot expect any assistance from Chinese courts with regards to any issues that they may encounter. On the issue of appointment of arbitrators, the PRC Arbitration Law provides that arbitration institutions should make a decision when parties

18 *See* Ilias Bantekas, An Introduction to International Arbitration 131–34 (2015).

19 *See* Tibor Várady et al., International Commercial Arbitration: A Transnational Perspective 504 (6th ed. 2015).

failed to appoint an arbitrator in time.[20] This clearly applies to institutional arbitration only. The Law, together with all other related Chinese laws, is completely silent on this issue in an ad hoc arbitration setting and offers no support whatsoever. Under these circumstances, even if the parties in a Chinese ad hoc arbitration requested a Chinese court for assistance with the matter, the court would likely not offer any help, because it would probably hold that they have no authority to do so. As a result, in a Chinese ad hoc arbitration proceeding, in case the arbitration rules that the parties agreed upon are incomplete or unclear on a certain issue that requires both parties' cooperation for the arbitration to proceed, or if the agreed upon rules point to a Chinese court for assistance, it would be quite easy for either one of the parties to obstruct the arbitration proceeding internally (from within the arbitration proceeding) by simply refusing to cooperate. This refusal to cooperate will lead to a deadlock in the Chinese ad hoc arbitration proceeding.

2 *Possible external obstructions*

Apart from blocking the arbitration proceeding itself, a party who wishes to resist arbitration may also obstruct the arbitration from outside of its proceeding by resorting to judicial authority. If a party no longer wants to participate in an ongoing Chinese ad hoc arbitration proceeding, it has at least two options. First, it can request a Chinese court to hold that the ad hoc arbitration agreement is invalid. Because the arbitration is seated in China, absent any specific choice of law between the parties to govern the validity of their ad hoc arbitration agreement, the court will most likely apply Chinese law and strike down the arbitration agreement.[21] The second option for the party is to file the case in a proper Chinese court to hear the merits of the dispute between the parties. When the court decides whether it should take jurisdiction of the case, it needs to consider the validity of the ad hoc arbitration agreement between the parties. Due to the same reason as mentioned above, the court will likely hold the ad hoc arbitration agreement invalid, and therefore take the case and hear its merits.

No matter which option the obstructing party chooses, it will have a good chance to have the ad hoc arbitration agreement struck down by a Chinese court. Once the arbitration agreement is invalidated officially, the party may walk away from the arbitration proceeding with confidence that any ensuing award will not be enforced by Chinese courts.[22] This is because one of the grounds for not enforcing a Chinese arbitration award under Chinese law is that there is

20 *See* Zhongcai Fa (仲裁法) [Arbitration Law] (promulgated by the Standing Comm. Nat'l People's Cong., Aug. 31, 1994, effective Sept. 1, 1995, rev. Sept. 1, 2017), arts. 32, 36 (China).

21 *See* discussion *supra* Chapter 3, Part III.C.

22 The other party may still want to proceed with the arbitration proceeding, particularly when the resisting party has assets outside China, because the resulting award may still have a chance of being enforced outside China under the New York Convention, especially in a pro-arbitration country such as France. *See* discussion *infra* Part II.C.

no arbitration agreement between the parties.[23] The SPC has interpreted that ground to include the situation where a Chinese court has invalidated an arbitration agreement.[24]

Moreover, Chinese law has not fully adopted the doctrine of Kompetenz-Kompetenz, under which arbitrators have the power to rule on their own jurisdiction.[25] Instead, the PRC Arbitration Law empowers arbitration institutions, rather than arbitrators, to decide arbitrability matters, i.e. arbitrators' jurisdiction.[26] This is obviously another example of Chinese law's misconception that all arbitrations are institutional. In any event, the arbitration rules of Chinese arbitration institutions usually specify that the institutions themselves have the authority to decide jurisdiction issues, although they may choose to delegate such authority to the tribunals when necessary.[27] Moreover, Chinese law stipulates that Chinese courts should decide on the matters related to the validity of an arbitration agreement if the parties cannot agree on whether it should be decided by the courts or the arbitration institution.[28] According to the SPC's judicial interpretation, however, a Chinese court will decide on the validity of an arbitration agreement upon one party's request unless the arbitration institution has already decided on the same issue.[29] In any event, because there is no institution involved in an ad hoc arbitration, a Chinese court does not need to consider any decision on arbitrability or jurisdiction made by an arbitration institution, so this mechanism likely means that a Chinese court can be more comfortable with nullifying an ad hoc arbitration agreement. More importantly, as compared

23 *See* Minshi Susong Fa (民事诉讼法) [Civil Procedure Law] (promulgated by Nat'l People's Cong., Apr. 9, 1991, effective Apr. 9, 1991, rev. June 27, 2017), arts. 237–74 (China); Zhongcai Fa (仲裁法) [Arbitration Law] (promulgated by the Standing Comm. Nat'l People's Cong., Aug. 31, 1994, effective Sept. 1, 1995, rev. Sept. 1, 2017), arts. 63, 71 (China).

24 *See* Zuigao Renmin Fayuan Guanyu Shiyong "Zhonghua Renmin Gongheguo Zhongcai Fa" Ruogan Wenti de Jieshi (最高人民法院关于适用《中华人民共和国仲裁法》若干问题的解释) [Interpretation on Certain Issues Concerning the Application of the "Arbitration Law of the People's Republic of China"] (promulgated by the Sup. People's Ct., Aug. 23, 2006, effective Sept. 8, 2006), art. 18 (China).

25 *See* John J. Barceló III, *Who Decides the Arbitrator's Jurisdiction? Separability and Competence – Competence in Transnational Perspective*, 36 Vand. J. Transnat'l L. 1115, 1124 (2003).

26 *See* Zhongcai Fa (仲裁法) [Arbitration Law] (promulgated by the Standing Comm. Nat'l People's Cong., Aug. 31, 1994, effective Sept. 1, 1995, rev. Sept. 1, 2017), art. 20, para. 1 (China).

27 *See e.g.*, 2015 China International Economic and Trade Arbitration Commission Arbitration Rules, art. 6.1, CIETAC (effective Jan. 1, 2015), *available at* http://cn.cietac.org/index.php?m=Page&a=index&id=42&l=en; 2015 Beijing Arbitration Commission Arbitration Rules, art. 6.4, BAC (effective Apr. 1, 2015), *available at* http://www.bjac.org.cn/page/data_dl/zcgz_en.pdf.

28 *See* Zhongcai Fa (仲裁法) [Arbitration Law] (promulgated by the Standing Comm. Nat'l People's Cong., Aug. 31, 1994, effective Sept. 1, 1995, rev. Sept. 1, 2017), art. 20, para. 1 (China).

29 *See* Zuigao Renmin Fayuan Guanyu Shiyong "Zhonghua Renmin Gongheguo Zhongcai Fa" Ruogan Wenti de Jieshi (最高人民法院关于适用《中华人民共和国仲裁法》若干问题的解释) [Interpretation on Certain Issues Concerning the Application of the "Arbitration Law of the People's Republic of China"] (promulgated by the Sup. People's Ct., Aug. 23, 2006, effective Sept. 8, 2006), art. 13, para. 2 (China).

with a similar request in an institutional arbitration, a Chinese court may be more willing to strike down an ad hoc arbitration agreement whenever one party requests it do so, even when the arbitration proceeding is still ongoing.

3 Timing of obstructions

It is also important to understand at what stages in the arbitration proceeding a resisting party can choose to obstruct arbitration. Successful operation of a Chinese ad hoc arbitration will be impossible if the resisting party is able to obstruct arbitration at virtually any time during the proceeding and no matter how far the arbitration proceeding has progressed.

Although the PRC Arbitration Law, together with many other national laws and the New York Convention, requires that an arbitration agreement be in written form, it nonetheless recognizes a party's intent to accept arbitration by conduct.[30] This intent is usually manifested by a party's substantial participation in an arbitration proceeding. Under the PRC Arbitration Law, a party may be deemed as having waived its right to challenge the validity of the arbitration agreement if that party does not object to the arbitral tribunal's jurisdiction before the first hearing in the arbitration proceeding.[31] The SPC has also promulgated another waiver rule, according to which Chinese courts will hold that a party has accepted the arbitral tribunal's jurisdiction if it has appointed an arbitrator in accordance with the arbitration rules and argued the merits of the case.[32] Therefore, under Chinese law, after substantially participating in an

30 *See* Zhongcai Fa (仲裁法) [Arbitration Law] (promulgated by the Standing Comm. Nat'l People's Cong., Aug. 31, 1994, effective Sept. 1, 1995, rev. Sept. 1, 2017), art. 16 (China); New York Convention, *supra* note 6, art. II(2); *See also* Zhongcai Fa (仲裁法) [Arbitration Law] (promulgated by the Standing Comm. Nat'l People's Cong., Aug. 31, 1994, effective Sept. 1, 1995, rev. Sept. 1, 2017), art. 20, para. 2 (China); Zuigao Renmin Fayuan Guanyu Shiyong "Zhonghua Renmin Gongheguo Zhongcai Fa" Ruogan Wenti de Jieshi (最高人民法院关于适用《中华人民共和国仲裁法》若干问题的解释) [Interpretation on Certain Issues Concerning the Application of the "Arbitration Law of the People's Republic of China"] (promulgated by the Sup. People's Ct., Aug. 23, 2006, effective Sept. 8, 2006), art. 13, para. 1 (China); Di'erci Quanguo Shewai Shangshi Haishi Shenpan Gongzuo Huiyi Jiyao (第二次全国涉外商事海事审判工作会议纪要) [Minutes of the Second National Working Conference on Adjudication of Foreign-related Commercial and Maritime Cases] (promulgated by the Sup. People's Ct., Dec. 26, 2005, effective Dec. 26, 2005), art. 67 (China).

31 *See* Zhongcai Fa (仲裁法) [Arbitration Law] (promulgated by the Standing Comm. Nat'l People's Cong., Aug. 31, 1994, effective Sept. 1, 1995, rev. Sept. 1, 2017), art. 20, para. 2 (China); Zuigao Renmin Fayuan Guanyu Shiyong "Zhonghua Renmin Gongheguo Zhongcai Fa" Ruogan Wenti de Jieshi (最高人民法院关于适用《中华人民共和国仲裁法》若干问题的解释) [Interpretation on Certain Issues Concerning the Application of the "Arbitration Law of the People's Republic of China"] (promulgated by the Sup. People's Ct., Aug. 23, 2006, effective Sept. 8, 2006), art. 13, para. 1 (China).

32 *See* Di'erci Quanguo Shewai Shangshi Haishi Shenpan Gongzuo Huiyi Jiyao (第二次全国涉外商事海事审判工作会议纪要) [Minutes of the Second National Working Conference on Adjudication of Foreign-related Commercial and Maritime Cases] (promulgated by the Sup. People's Ct., Dec. 26, 2005, effective Dec. 26, 2005), art. 67 (China).

arbitration proceeding, a party will be estopped from later arguing that no valid arbitration agreement exists between the parties. If this waiver rule applied to Chinese ad hoc arbitration proceedings, it would seem that a resisting party could not obstruct arbitration after it had already participated in the proceeding substantially.

However, this general waiver rule will not necessarily apply to a Chinese ad hoc arbitration. In other words, substantial participation in a Chinese ad hoc arbitration proceeding will not necessarily endow the ad hoc tribunal with jurisdiction over the case under Chinese law. This is because a reasonable interpretation of the waiver rule indicates that it is only meant to govern an institutional arbitration seated within China and an arbitration seated outside China that is either ad hoc or institutional.

First, the context of the waiver rule in the PRC Arbitration Law indicates that the rule only applies to a Chinese institutional arbitration. The waiver rule in the PRC Arbitration Law is stipulated in Article 20, Paragraph 2 of the Law, preceded in the same article by the paragraph discussing situations where a party intends to challenge the validity of an arbitration agreement.[33] This preceding paragraph clearly contemplates a situation in the setting of a Chinese institutional arbitration by providing that the party can request either the arbitration commission or the people's court to make a decision.[34] This is also another example of the assumption that all arbitrations are institutional under Chinese law.[35] Second, the context of the waiver rule in the SPC's judicial interpretation suggests that it only applies to an arbitration seated outside China. This waiver rule is embedded among rules discussing how Chinese courts should review the validity of a foreign-related arbitration agreement.[36] Having contemplated that arbitration proceedings seated outside China may be on an ad hoc basis, when promulgating this waiver rule, the SPC mentioned arbitration proceedings both under institutions and before tribunals (presumably ad hoc tribunals).[37] Also bearing in mind the Chinese law's overall presumption of institutional arbitration, it is reasonable to interpret the SPC's waiver rule as applicable only to an arbitration, institutional or ad hoc, seated outside China.

The absence of a waiver rule in Chinese ad hoc arbitration may give the respondent in the proceeding an unfair advantage. When the claimant is willing to cooperate in the arbitration proceeding and have the dispute resolved

33 *See* Zhongcai Fa (仲裁法) [Arbitration Law] (promulgated by the Standing Comm. Nat'l People's Cong., Aug. 31, 1994, effective Sept. 1, 1995, rev. Sept. 1, 2017), art. 20 (China).

34 *See id.*

35 *See* discussion *supra* Chapter 2, Part III.

36 *See* Di'erci Quanguo Shewai Shangshi Haishi Shenpan Gongzuo Huiyi Jiyao (第二次全国涉外商事海事审判工作会议纪要) [Minutes of the Second National Working Conference on Adjudication of Foreign-related Commercial and Maritime Cases] (promulgated by the Sup. People's Ct., Dec. 26, 2005, effective Dec. 26, 2005), §6.1 (China).

37 *See id.* art. 67 (China).

by a final decision, the respondent may participate in the arbitration with the knowledge that it can later choose to accept or reject the ensuing award based on whether it finds the award favorable. In a mature legal system, rules or principles like estoppel or good faith are designed to avoid such an outcome. Unfortunately, however, there does not seem to be a clear rule or doctrine under Chinese law that would bring about an estoppel effect in this particular context. Although there is a good faith principle in Chinese Civil Procedure Law,[38] it remains largely theoretical and is seldom applied by Chinese courts in a particular case.[39] Most importantly, Chinese law's hostility towards ad hoc arbitration in general may encourage Chinese judges to decide that domestic, or Chinese, ad hoc arbitrations are illegal per se, no matter what the parties have agreed to or how they have conducted themselves in a proceeding. As a result, under the current Chinese law, the PRC Arbitration Law's requirement of institutional arbitration is mandatory. The Chinese law's preclusion of ad hoc arbitration cannot be overcome by party agreement or conduct. When two parties put the seat of their arbitration in China, even though both of them have manifested their intent to resolve their dispute by ad hoc arbitration, either by concluding an arbitration agreement in writing or by arguing the merits of the dispute before the tribunal, their ad hoc arbitration agreement is still invalid under Chinese law.

In conclusion, a party who intends to resist a Chinese ad hoc arbitration may choose to obstruct the proceeding either by refusing to cooperate or by requesting a Chinese court to invalidate the ad hoc arbitration agreement. Based upon a contextual interpretation of the PRC Arbitration Law and the SPC's judicial interpretations, the resisting party may obstruct at virtually all stages of the arbitration proceeding, even after it has significantly participated in it. As a result, it is not practical for a Chinese ad hoc arbitration to operate under the current Chinese law.

B Awards unenforceable under Chinese law

Even when parties in a Chinese ad hoc arbitration are willing and do manage to cooperate fully with each other, another major obstacle for them is the ensuing award's enforceability. The following two sections will carefully analyze a

38 *See* Minshi Susong Fa (民事诉讼法) [Civil Procedure Law] (promulgated by Nat'l People's Cong., Apr. 9, 1991, effective Apr. 9, 1991, rev. June 27, 2017), art. 13 (China).

39 *See* Wang Qi (王琦), *Minshi Susong Chengshi Xinyong Yuanze de Sifa Shiyong* (民事诉讼诚实信用原则的司法适用) [*Judicial Application of the Bona Fide Doctrine in Civil Litigation*], 4 Zhongguo Faxue (中国法学) [China Legal Sci.] 250, 250–51 (2014); Yang Xiuqing (杨秀清), *Minshi Susong zhong Chengshi Xinyong Yuanze de Kongdonghua ji qi Kefu* (民事诉讼中诚实信用原则的空洞化及其克服) [*The Emptiness of the Bona Fide Doctrine in Civil Litigation and How to Overcome It*], 3 Faxue Pinglun (法学评论) [Law Rev.] 37, 37, 44 (2013); Zhang Weiping (张卫平), *Minshi Susong zhong de Chengshi Xinyong Yuanze* (民事诉讼中的诚实信用原则) [*The Bona Fide Doctrine in Civil Litigation*], 6 Falü Kexue (Xibei Zhengfa Daxue Xuebao) (法律科学(西北政法大学学报)) [Sci. L. (J. Northwest U. Pol. Sci. & L.)] 153, 157–58 (2012).

Chinese ad hoc arbitration award's enforceability respectively under Chinese law and the New York Convention. For purposes of analysis, these sections assume that two parties voluntarily agree to arbitrate in China on an ad hoc basis, failing to specify both the *lex arbitri* and the law governing the validity of the arbitration agreement; that the tribunal is willing to take jurisdiction and proceed with the arbitration; that the parties cooperate through the arbitration proceeding; and that the arbitration tribunal renders an award. These sections will discuss several questions arising out of this scenario: Will a Chinese court enforce the award? Can a Chinese court set aside the award? Can the award be recognized and enforced outside China under the New York Convention?

1 A Chinese court will not enforce the award

A Chinese ad hoc arbitration is not enforceable under Chinese law. First, relevant Chinese laws only authorize a Chinese court to enforce an institutional arbitration award seated in China, but not an ad hoc award. For example, Article 237, Paragraph 1 of the PRC Civil Procedure Law provides that "If a party fails to comply with an award of an arbitral organ established according to the law, the other party may apply for execution to the people's court which has jurisdiction over the case. The people's court applied to shall enforce the award."[40] Because Chinese law assumes that all arbitrations in China are institutional, there is no statutory authority for a Chinese court to enforce a Chinese ad hoc award. Neither has the SPC instructed lower level Chinese courts to do so. Second, a losing party has the option to challenge the award's enforceability when the winning party requests a Chinese court to enforce it. Because an arbitration agreement calling for a Chinese ad hoc arbitration is invalid under Chinese law, the court will not enforce this award.[41]

As a result, a Chinese ad hoc award is not enforceable before Chinese courts. Even if an ad hoc tribunal successfully completed the proceeding and rendered an award, the prevailing party could only hope that the losing party would pay the award voluntarily. If that does not happen, the prevailing party cannot have the award enforced by a Chinese court.

40 Minshi Susong Fa (民事诉讼法) [Civil Procedure Law] (promulgated by Nat'l People's Cong., Apr. 9, 1991, effective Apr. 9, 1991, rev. June. 27, 2017), art. 237, papa. 1 (China) (English translation provided by the Nati'l People's Cong., *available at* http://www.npc.gov.cn/englishnpc/Law/2007-12/12/content_1383880.htm). Here, however, "arbitral institution" may be a better translation than "arbitral organ."

41 *See id.* arts. 237, 274 (China); Zhongcai Fa (仲裁法) [Arbitration Law] (promulgated by the Standing Comm. Nat'l People's Cong., Aug. 31, 1994, effective Sept. 1, 1995, rev. Sept. 1, 2017), arts. 63, 71 (China); Zuigao Renmin Fayuan Guanyu Shiyong "Zhonghua Renmin Gongheguo Zhongcai Fa" Ruogan Wenti de Jieshi (最高人民法院关于适用《中华人民共和国仲裁法》若干问题的解释) [Interpretation on Certain Issues Concerning the Application of the "Arbitration Law of the People's Republic of China"] (promulgated by the Sup. People's Ct., Aug. 23, 2006, effective Sept. 8, 2006), art. 18 (China).

2 *Potential set-aside of the award*

A FORMAL SET-ASIDE PROCEEDING NOT AVAILABLE

Issues related to set-aside are an integral part of any discussions on an award's enforceability at its seat. This is because an arbitration award is usually subject to review in a set-aside proceeding before its seat country's national courts. This gives the parties a chance to challenge the award at its seat country, which has an impact on the award's enforceability both in the seat country and elsewhere in the world due to Article V(1)(e) of the New York Convention.[42] In China, however, because Chinese ad hoc arbitration is not included in the Chinese arbitration legal framework, a formal set-aside proceeding may not be available for a Chinese ad hoc award.

The PRC Arbitration Law classifies arbitration awards made in China as either domestic or foreign-related.[43] "Foreign-related" awards under Chinese law are special domestic awards that usually involve a non-Chinese party, or property located outside Chinese territory.[44] Although foreign-related awards are still Chinese domestic awards, a set of special and more favorable rules under Chinese law applies to foreign-related awards.[45] This also distinguishes foreign-related awards from ordinary domestic awards. Regarding set-aside, there are two different sets of grounds under Chinese law, upon which a domestic or a foreign-related award may be set aside respectively.

Article 58 of the PRC Arbitration Law lays out the grounds upon which a domestic award may be set aside:

> A party may apply for setting aside an arbitration award to *the intermediate people's court in the place where the arbitration commission is located* if he can

42 *See* New York Convention, *supra* note 6, art. V(1)(e).

43 *See* Zhongcai Fa (仲裁法) [Arbitration Law] (promulgated by the Standing Comm. Nat'l People's Cong., Aug. 31, 1994, effective Sept. 1, 1995, rev. Sept. 1, 2017), ch. 7 (China).

44 *See id.*; Minshi Susong Fa (民事诉讼法) [Civil Procedure Law] (promulgated by Nat'l People's Cong., Apr. 9, 1991, effective Apr. 9, 1991, rev. June 27, 2017), ch. 26 (China); Zuigao Renmin Fayuan Guanyu Shenli Zhongcai Sifa Shencha Anjian Ruogan Wenti de Guiding (最高人民法院关于审理仲裁司法审查案件若干问题的规定) [Regulation on Certain Issues Concerning the Adjudication of Cases Involving Judicial Review of Arbitration] (promulgated by the Sup. People's Ct., Dec. 26, 2017, effective Jan. 1, 2018), art. 12 (China); Zuigao Renmin Fayuan Guanyu Shiyong "Zhonghua Renmin Gongheguo Shewai Minshi Guanxi Falü Shiyong Fa" Ruogan Wenti de Jieshi Yi (最高人民法院关于适用《中华人民共和国涉外民事关系法律适用法》若干问题的解释(一)) [Interpretation on Certain Issues Concerning the Application of the "Law on Application of Law in Foreign-related Civil Relations of the People's Republic of China" (I)] (promulgated by the Sup. People's Ct., Dec. 28, 2012, effective Jan. 7, 2013), art. 1 (China).

45 *See* Zhongcai Fa (仲裁法) [Arbitration Law] (promulgated by the Standing Comm. Nat'l People's Cong., Aug. 31, 1994, effective Sept. 1, 1995, rev. Sept. 1, 2017), ch. 7 (China); Minshi Susong Fa (民事诉讼法) [Civil Procedure Law] (promulgated by Nat'l People's Cong., Apr. 9, 1991, effective Apr. 9, 1991, rev. June 27, 2017), ch. 26 (China).

> produce evidence which proves that the arbitration award involves one of the following circumstances:
>
> (1) there is no arbitration agreement . . .[46]

The SPC elaborated on this issue in its judicial interpretation on the PRC Arbitration Law:

> The phrase "there is no arbitration agreement" provided in Article 58, Paragraph 1, Item (1) of the Arbitration Law refers to the situation where the parties did not reach an arbitration agreement. *Where an arbitration agreement is found to be invalid or cancelled, it shall be treated as if there is no arbitration agreement.*[47]

On the other hand, Article 70 of the PRC Arbitration Law sets forth the grounds upon which a foreign-related award may be set aside:

> If a party presents evidence which proves that a foreign-related arbitration award involves one of the circumstances set forth in the first paragraph of Article [274] of the Civil Procedure Law, the people's court shall, after examination and verification by a collegial panel formed by the people's court, rule to set aside the award.[48]

Article 274 of the PRC Civil Procedure Law in turn provides:

> A people's court shall, after examination and verification by a collegial panel of the court, make a written order not to allow the enforcement of *the award rendered by an arbitral organ* of the People's Republic of China handling cases *involving foreign element*, if the party against whom the application for enforcement is made furnishes proof that:
>
> (1) *the parties have not had an arbitration clause in the contract or have not subsequently reached a written arbitration agreement* . . .[49]

46 Zhongcai Fa (仲裁法) [Arbitration Law] (promulgated by the Standing Comm. Nat'l People's Cong., Aug. 31, 1994, effective Sept. 1, 1995, rev. Sept. 1, 2017), art. 58 (China) (English translation provided by the Nat'l People's Cong., *available at* http://www.npc.gov.cn/englishnpc/Law/2007-12/12/content_1383756.htm) (emphasis added).

47 Zuigao Renmin Fayuan Guanyu Shiyong "Zhonghua Renmin Gongheguo Zhongcai Fa" Ruogan Wenti de Jieshi (最高人民法院关于适用《中华人民共和国仲裁法》若干问题的解释) [Interpretation on Certain Issues Concerning the Application of the "Arbitration Law of the People's Republic of China"] (promulgated by the Sup. People's Ct., Aug. 23, 2006, effective Sept. 8, 2006), art. 18 (China) (emphasis added).

48 Zhongcai Fa (仲裁法) [Arbitration Law] (promulgated by the Standing Comm. Nat'l People's Cong., Aug. 31, 1994, effective Sept. 1, 1995, rev. Sept. 1, 2017), art. 70 (China) (English translation provided by the Nat'l People's Cong., *available at* http://www.npc.gov.cn/englishnpc/Law/2007-12/12/content_1383756.htm).

49 Minshi Susong Fa (民事诉讼法) [Civil Procedure Law] (promulgated by Nat'l People's Cong., Apr. 9, 1991, effective Apr. 9, 1991, rev. June 27, 2017), art. 274 (China) (English

The above provisions appear to enable a party to challenge a Chinese ad hoc award via a set-aside proceeding. The challenging party will obviously argue that the ad hoc arbitration agreement is invalid under Chinese law. In case the ad hoc award is a regular domestic award, the challenging party may rely on the SPC's judicial interpretation that an invalid arbitration agreement means that "there is no arbitration agreement" and request its set-aside. If the award is a foreign-related award, although there is no clear judicial interpretation on the same issue, it is still reasonable to expect a Chinese court to reach the same conclusion. However, provisions in both statutes explicitly pointed to institutional arbitration awards. This is once again consistent with Chinese law's assumption that all arbitrations in China are institutional. One can make an argument that Chinese law only endows Chinese courts with the authority to set aside Chinese institutional awards, and that there is no statutory authority for the courts to set aside a Chinese ad hoc award. If the Chinese courts follow this line of logic, there will probably be no formal set-aside proceeding available for Chinese ad hoc awards.

Alternatively, even if Chinese courts were to interpret the above-cited provisions in the relevant Chinese statutes as applicable to ad hoc awards, it would be difficult to ascertain the specific court in which the challenging party should file its request for set-aside. Article 58 of the PRC Arbitration Law provides that a case pertaining to the set-aside of a domestic award should be filed in the intermediate people's court at the place where the arbitration institution resides.[50] Although there is no specific statutory provision setting forth a specific court in which the request to set aside a foreign-related award should be filed, a general provision in the PRC Arbitration Law provides that when there is no specific rule for foreign-related awards, the rules applicable to domestic awards shall apply to foreign-related awards.[51] As a result, the challenging party wishing to set aside a foreign-related award in China should also file its request in the intermediate people's court at the place where the arbitration institution is located. This mechanism will create a practical obstacle for a party wishing to have a Chinese ad hoc arbitration award set aside, simply because there is no arbitration institution involved at all.

The PRC Civil Procedure Law does provide a general venue rule for all civil cases, under which the Chinese court at a defendant's domicile has jurisdiction over cases filed against that defendant.[52] However, it may be difficult for a challenging party to convince this court to take jurisdiction and hear a set-aside petition against a Chinese ad hoc arbitration award. This is because the PRC Civil Procedure Law and other Chinese laws provide various exceptions to the general rule when it comes to choosing the right venue.[53] When these exceptions apply,

translation provided by the Nati'l People's Cong., *available at* http://www.npc.gov.cn/english npc/Law/2007-12/12/content_1383880.htm) (emphasis added).

50 *See* Zhongcai Fa (仲裁法) [Arbitration Law] (promulgated by the Standing Comm. Nat'l People's Cong., Aug. 31, 1994, effective Sept. 1, 1995, rev. Sept. 1, 2017), art. 58 (China).

51 *See id.* art. 65.

52 *See* Minshi Susong Fa (民事诉讼法) [Civil Procedure Law] (promulgated by Nat'l People's Cong., Apr. 9, 1991, effective Apr. 9, 1991, rev. June 27, 2017), art. 21, para. 1 (China).

53 *See, e.g., id.* arts. 22–34; Haishi Susong Tebie Chengxu Fa (海事诉讼特别程序法) [Maritime Special Procedure Law] (promulgated by the Standing Comm. Nat'l People's Cong., Dec. 25, 1999, effective July 1, 2000), arts. 6–9 (China).

specific venue rules will replace the general rule. A set-aside petition against a Chinese arbitration award is an exception provided in the PRC Arbitration Law. As discussed before, in the set-aside proceeding, the specific venue rule is that the intermediate people's court at the place where the arbitration institution resides shall hear the case. This should mean that the general venue rule does not apply in this scenario. However, the practical difficulty is that no court will take the case because there is no arbitration institution involved in the case. There is no clear rule on how this dilemma should be resolved under Chinese law. In practice, however, given that all set-aside proceedings in China are heard by courts at the place where the arbitration institution resides, it is very likely that the court at the defendant's domicile will refuse to hear the set-aside case for a Chinese ad hoc award because it does not consider itself the proper forum.

As a result, setting aside a Chinese ad hoc award formally is difficult in that relevant Chinese laws governing set-aside proceedings of arbitration awards may be reasonably interpreted to encompass institutional awards only, while no such formal proceeding is available for ad hoc awards. Alternatively, even if the laws were interpreted as applicable to ad hoc awards, from a practical perspective, it would be likely that no Chinese court would want to take jurisdiction and hear a set-aside petition against a Chinese ad hoc award.

B DE FACTO SET-ASIDE POSSIBLE

Lack of a formal set-aside proceeding does not necessarily mean an unsatisfied party has no chance to challenge a Chinese ad hoc arbitration award. First, under Chinese law, a losing party has the opportunity to contest an award's enforceability when the winning party requests a Chinese court to enforce the award against the losing party. In this situation, the losing party can request the court not to enforce the award if the arbitration agreement is invalid.[54] Second, as previously analyzed, the party can essentially argue for the ad hoc arbitration agreement's invalidity under Chinese law before a Chinese court at any time, even after it fully participated in the arbitration proceeding.[55] Consequently, although the losing party cannot formally have the award set aside, it has, in effect, successfully challenged it.

Alternatively, the challenging party may choose to file the case with a proper Chinese court to hear the dispute's merits. If this happens, the other party will likely argue that the case should be dismissed on the basis of res judicata, namely it has already been decided by the arbitrators in the ad hoc arbitration. The challenging party can then request the court to disregard the ad hoc arbitration award because the award is based on an invalid arbitration agreement and

54 *See* Minshi Susong Fa (民事诉讼法) [Civil Procedure Law] (promulgated by Nat'l People's Cong., Apr. 9, 1991, effective Apr. 9, 1991, rev. June. 27, 2017), arts. 237, 274 (China); Zhongcai Fa (仲裁法) [Arbitration Law] (promulgated by the Standing Comm. Nat'l People's Cong., Aug. 31, 1994, effective Sept. 1, 1995, rev. Sept. 1, 2017), arts. 63, 71 (China).

55 *See* discussion *supra* Part II.A.3.

is therefore unenforceable. As discussed in the previous sections, the Chinese court will likely agree with the challenging party and proceed to hear the merits of the dispute. Given that the court has ignored the award and relitigated the case, one can potentially argue that the Chinese court has set aside the ad hoc award in a de facto manner.

Because a Chinese ad hoc arbitration award is not legally enforceable under Chinese law, there is essentially no practical need for a formal set-aside proceeding. After all, if the losing party does not want to pay the award, it may simply ignore it and the winning party cannot have the award enforced by Chinese courts. The only concern for the losing party is probably the award's potential enforcement outside China where that party has assets. In this situation, if the losing party can successfully have the award set aside by a Chinese court, that party may have a stronger case against the award's enforcement under the New York Convention, because the losing party can base its arguments on both Article V(1)(a) (invalidity of the arbitration agreement)[56] and Article V(1)(e) (award set aside at the seat)[57] of the New York Convention. In practice, the losing party can perhaps achieve this objective by making the de facto set-aside argument, namely, arguing that a Chinese court has in effect set aside the award. As a result, there is probably no practical need to include a formal set-aside proceeding against a Chinese ad hoc arbitration award under the current Chinese legal framework of arbitration, which may also help explain its non-existence in practice.

C Awards' enforceability doubtful under the New York Convention

Although a Chinese ad hoc arbitration award is not enforceable under Chinese law, if the losing party has assets in another New York Convention country, the prevailing party will certainly want to have the award enforced there. The

56 Article V(1)(a) of the New York Convention reads,

> Recognition and enforcement of the award may be refused, at the request of the party against whom it is invoked, only if that party furnishes to the competent authority where the recognition and enforcement is sought, proof that,
>
> (a) The parties to the agreement referred to in article II were, under the law applicable to them, under some incapacity, or *the said agreement is not valid under the law to which the parties have subjected it or, failing any indication thereon, under the law of the country where the award was made*; (emphasis added)
>
> . . . .

57 Article V(1)(e) of the New York Convention reads,

> Recognition and enforcement of the award may be refused, at the request of the party against whom it is invoked, only if that party furnishes to the competent authority where the recognition and enforcement is sought, proof that,
>
> . . . .
>
> (e) *The award* has *not yet become binding on the parties, or has been set aside or suspended by a competent authority of the country in which*, or under the law of which, *that award was made* (emphasis added).

question then becomes whether a Chinese ad hoc award is enforceable under the New York Convention. As previously mentioned, the mere fact that the award is ad hoc will not affect its enforceability under the New York Convention.[58] However, the losing party will for sure try to rely on other grounds under the Convention to challenge the award's enforceability. Among them, the best options for the challenging party are Article V(1)(a) (invalidity of the arbitration agreement) and Article V(1)(e) (set aside in the award's home jurisdiction).

Before discussing the details of Article V of the New York Convention, it may be helpful to bear in mind a national court's discretion under that article. The first paragraph of Article V(1) of the New York Convention reads, "[r]ecognition and enforcement of the award *may* be refused, at the request of the party against whom it is invoked, only if that party furnishes to the competent authority where the recognition and enforcement is sought, proof. . . ."[59] Accordingly, at least in the English version of the New York Convention, the word "may" indicates that, even though certain grounds for rejecting the recognition and enforcement of an award exist, a national court may nonetheless choose to recognize and enforce it. In practice, courts in different countries, and even within the same country, may well have different views on this particular issue and make inconsistent or even contradictory decisions based on the same or similar facts. As a result, notwithstanding the analysis of whether a Chinese ad hoc arbitration award will be recognized and enforced outside China, it must be readily anticipated that different courts will likely reach different conclusions on this issue.

1 Uncertain prospects under Article V(1)(a)

Under Article V(1)(a) of the New York Convention, recognition and enforcement of an arbitration award may be rejected if the arbitration agreement between the parties is invalid under the applicable law.[60] This seemingly logical and important ground, however, may not be as significant in practice. This is because most of the issues that can affect an arbitration agreement's validity are separately governed by other articles of the New York Convention, such as Article II(2) for formal writing requirement, Article V(2)(a) for non-arbitrable subject matters, and Article V(1)(d) for defects related to the composition of tribunal and other procedural issues.[61] As a result, the only issues potentially governed by Article V(1)(a) are lack of consent (misrepresentation, duress, fraud, or undue influence) in the formation of an arbitration agreement and specific requirements as to the contents of the agreement set by the governing law.[62] That said, the formal

58 *See* discussion *supra* Part I.

59 New York Convention, *supra* note 6, art. V(1) (emphasis added).

60 *See id.* art. V(1)(a).

61 *See* Albert Jan van den Berg, The New York Arbitration Convention of 1958: Towards a Uniform Judicial Interpretation 287-91 (1981); Pieter Sanders, *Consolidated Commentary Volumes III and IV*, 4 Y.B. Com. Arb. 231, 247 (1979).

62 *See* van den Berg, *supra* note 61, at 290–91.

writing requirement set forth in Article II(2) of the New York Convention has significantly reduced the chance that a party can successfully invoke lack of consent to invalidate the agreement. This is because if an arbitration clause in a contract or an arbitration agreement is signed by both parties or is contained in an exchange of letters or telegrams between the parties, as required in Article II(2), it will likely be quite difficult for a party to argue later that such a clause or agreement is concluded without consent.[63] As for the specific requirements of the governing law that invalidate an arbitration agreement, it is understandable that they are rare.[64] Nevertheless, the PRC Arbitration Law's unique requirement of institutional arbitration may provide a perfect example of this, because it is indeed a very specific requirement that invalidates an arbitration agreement.

Moreover, under Article V(1)(a), national courts before which recognition and enforcement of an award is being sought need to identify the law the parties have chosen to apply to their arbitration agreement. Many of these jurisdictions have been pro-arbitration and adopted a validity-preferring rule.[65] Countries like France will apply the "transnational law" to determine the validity of the arbitration agreement and focus on the parties' common intent rather than relying on a national law.[66] Under these circumstances, if a party in a Chinese ad hoc award invokes Article V(1)(a), will the court outside China refuse to recognize and enforce the award just because the PRC Arbitration Law invalidates ad hoc arbitration agreements?

This has to remain an open question. Because of the rarity and complexity of the issues involved, different national courts may reach different conclusions. What may be relevant in a court's decision-making process is that, as discussed, national arbitration laws seldom have specific requirements as to the content of an arbitration agreement. More importantly, non-Chinese courts may have difficulty understanding the logic and reasons behind the PRC Arbitration Law's requirement that arbitration must be institutional and deem this an "idiosyncratic" rule.[67] As a result, courts in pro-arbitration countries could potentially disregard this idiosyncratic requirement and will not reject an otherwise enforceable award solely on the ground that it is ad hoc. For example, when determining the validity and the correct interpretation of an arbitration agreement, French courts rely on "transnational law" instead of the law of any single country and will focus on the "common intent of the parties."[68] Consequently, if a French court is deciding whether it should recognize and enforce a Chinese ad

63 *See id.* at 287.

64 *See id.* at 291.

65 *See* Gary B. Born, International Commercial Arbitration 3465 (2d ed. 2014).

66 *See* Fouchard, Gaillard, Goldman on International Commercial Arbitration 228–30 (Emmanuel Gaillard & John Savage eds., 1999); Julian D. M. Lew, Loukas A. Mistelis & Stefan M. Kröll, Comparative International Commercial Arbitration 123 (2003).

67 *See* discussion *infra* Chapter 6 Part III for reasons behind PRC Arbitration Law's bizarre institutional arbitration requirement.

68 *See* Fouchard, Gaillard, Goldman On International Commercial Arbitration, *supra* note 66, at 228–30; Lew et al., *supra* note 66, at 123.

hoc award, it will likely disregard the PRC Arbitration Law's institutional requirement. This is because from the French court's perspective, this requirement does not exist in the "transnational law" that governs the arbitration agreement's validity and the parties have clearly demonstrated a common intention to arbitrate in China when they concluded their arbitration agreement. Moreover, courts in some other pro-arbitration countries, such as Switzerland, may adopt a validity-preferring choice-of-law rule and choose a non-Chinese law to govern the validity of the arbitration agreement.[69] No matter which route they choose, these courts will probably avoid the PRC Arbitration Law's idiosyncratic requirement and enforce the ad hoc award. At the same time, it is also likely that courts in some other countries that are less pro-arbitration may choose to refuse the recognition and enforcement of a Chinese ad hoc award by reasoning that they will follow the law at the seat of arbitration, namely Chinese law in this case. In any event, Article V(1)(a) provides the challenging party with a highly viable option to fight against a Chinese ad hoc award's enforcement under the New York Convention, absent the parties' explicit choice of a different law to govern the validity of their ad hoc arbitration agreement.

2 *Possible outcomes under Article V(1)(e)*

The New York Convention Article V(1)(e) offers a ground for rejecting an award that has been annulled by a competent authority. As previously discussed, although a formal set-aside proceeding is not available for a Chinese ad hoc award under Chinese law, a challenging party may request a Chinese court to hear the merits of the dispute and then reasonably argue that the award has been annulled by that court in a de facto way. As a result, whether a Chinese ad hoc award will be recognized and enforced by a foreign court depends on the court's attitude towards annulled awards.

Emmanuel Gaillard categorizes three kinds of representations of international arbitration, according to which international arbitration is considered as: (i) a component of a single national legal order (the Monolocal Approach); (ii) anchored in a plurality of national legal orders (the Westphalian Approach); or (iii) an autonomous legal order itself (the Transnational Approach).[70] According to Gaillard, the first representation will treat an international arbitration's legal force as deriving from the law of its seat country, and largely assumes that arbitrators are acting as judges in that legal order.[71] The second representation does not consider an international arbitration's legal force as deriving from any single country in the world, including the seat, but instead as deriving from all the countries that are willing to recognize the force of the award. An award's "international" nature makes it independent of any single

69 *See* Fouchard, Gaillard, Goldman On International Commercial Arbitration, *supra* note 66, at 236–38; Lew et al., *supra* note 66, at 122.

70 *See generally* Emmanuel Gaillard, Legal Theory of International Arbitration (2010).

71 *See id.* at 15.

country.[72] The third representation, while agreeing with the second one that an international arbitration's legal force does not derive from any single country's legal order, takes arbitration itself as a distinct and transnational legal order independent of any country's legal system. Under this representation, arbitrators are not administering justice on behalf of any country, but instead, are doing so for the benefit of the international community.[73]

According to Gaillard's representation theory of international arbitration, if a country adopts the first representation (the Monolocal Approach), it will probably not recognize and enforce an award once it has been set aside or deemed unenforceable in its seat country. This is because under the Monolocal Approach, the award has lost its legal force once set aside or deemed unenforceable at the seat, therefore it cannot be enforced anywhere else. A country adopting the second (the Westphalian Approach) or the third (the Transnational Approach) representation, however, will not be bound by the decision made in the seat country. This country may still recognize and enforce the award even though it has been set aside or deemed unenforceable in its seat country. Under these two approaches, the country should either determine whether an award is valid based on its own conceptions and standards, or be free to recognize and enforce an award according to the international arbitral legal order without feeling the need to obey the legal order of any single jurisdiction at all.[74]

Accordingly, whether a Chinese ad hoc award will be recognized and enforced by a non-Chinese court depends, to a large extent, on that country's conception of international commercial arbitration in general. In a country that adopts the second or third approach, and therefore has a more liberal attitude towards international commercial arbitration (such as France), local courts will likely enforce a Chinese ad hoc arbitration award even though it has been disregarded by a Chinese court or deemed unenforceable under Chinese law. That court will believe that the award's lack of enforceability in China cannot affect its legal force, which originates from the international arbitral legal order; or the court will believe that China, despite being the seat, is no more important than any other country in this multinational framework and that courts in other countries are free to recognize the legal force of the award based on their own standards. Moreover, the foreign court may also find that the PRC Arbitration Law's idiosyncratic requirement that arbitration must be institutional arbitration is not sensible and therefore refuse to follow the Chinese court's "wrongful" decision.

On the other hand, it would not be surprising if a court in a country adopting the first approach refused to recognize and enforce a Chinese ad hoc arbitration award. That court could reason that the award derives its legal force from the legal order of China, the seat of arbitration. By being disregarded in China, the award has lost its legal force and therefore cannot be enforced anywhere else. It could also reason that because a Chinese ad hoc arbitration award is not legally

72 *See id.* at 24.
73 *See id.* at 35.
74 *See id.* at 135–36.

enforceable under Chinese law, the parties, by putting the seat of arbitration in China, accepted the likely consequence that the award would not be enforced by any Chinese court if the losing party refused to pay it; therefore the parties should also accept the possible outcome that a non-Chinese court will not enforce this award by virtue of Article V(1)(e) of the New York Convention. Of course, a strong counter-argument may be that the parties' acceptance that the award is not enforceable in China does not necessarily mean they did not intend for the award to be enforced elsewhere. In any event, a national court adopting the first representation of international arbitration (the Monolocal Approach) may well support the seat court's exclusive judicial power over the award and refuse to enforce the award after it has been set aside at the seat, particularly when the New York Convention allows the court to do so.

As a result, enforceability of a Chinese ad hoc award outside China will remain uncertain, as the outcome may vary from jurisdiction to jurisdiction, both on an international scale and even within one country.[75] The outcome will most likely depend on different national courts' practice and their own interpretation of the New York Convention, as well as their conception of international commercial arbitration as a whole.

III Conclusion

While Chinese courts will not hesitate to fulfill their obligations under the New York Convention and enforce a foreign ad hoc award, the enforcement prospects for a Chinese ad hoc award may be much less encouraging both inside and outside China. Due to the PRC Arbitration Law's strong stance on the invalidity of an ad hoc arbitration agreement, absent any specific agreements between the parties, a Chinese ad hoc arbitration will meet insurmountable barriers in its proceedings. It might be difficult for a party to complete the proceedings successfully in the first place, because the other party may easily obstruct the process if it so wishes. Even when the arbitration proceedings conclude successfully, the ensuing award will likely face fatal challenges if the winning party intends to have it enforced by courts either inside or outside China. As dire as the situation appears, the next chapter will introduce some special drafting strategies which may help improve the enforcement prospects of a Chinese ad hoc award significantly and accordingly salvage a party's wish to conduct ad hoc arbitration proceedings within Chinese territory.

75 E.g., different U.S. courts have made different decisions regarding whether an annulled award can be recognized and enforced in the U.S. *See* Chromalloy Aeroservices v. Arab Republic, 939 F. Supp. 907 (D.D.C 1996); *but cf.* Baker Marine, Ltd. v. Chevron, Ltd., 191 F.3d 194 (2d Cir. 1999), and Termorio S.A. E.S.P. v. Electranta S.P., 487 F.3d 928 (D.C. Cir. 2007).

5 Making ad hoc arbitration work in China under its current law

Given Chinese law's preclusion of ad hoc arbitration, parties in practice obviously need to use extreme caution when it comes to choosing a mechanism to resolve their dispute in China or with a Chinese party. More specifically, the safest strategy would be to choose institutional arbitration in China, or if the parties prefer ad hoc arbitration, they should put the seat of arbitration outside China. However, the choice of dispute resolution method is often made at the bargaining table. Every transaction or dealing has its own characteristics and special circumstances that may require a certain type of dispute resolution mechanism that is most suitable. As a result, it may well be the case that parties in a certain case conclude that the best way for them to resolve their dispute is to have an ad hoc arbitration in China. Then the question is: will that be possible? Of course, the optimal position would be if China could change its law and allow ad hoc arbitration. However, before Chinese lawmakers make that happen, can parties somehow make ad hoc arbitration work in China under the current Chinese law?

I A special drafting strategy

Thankfully, due to arbitration's private and consensual nature, the Chinese legal system and the international arbitration legal framework based upon the New York Convention both recognize and support party autonomy in many aspects when it comes to arbitration related issues. The interaction between these two legal frameworks has created many chances that parties can use to their advantage. For the parties who want to arbitrate their dispute in China on an ad hoc basis, if they adopt a carefully crafted drafting strategy, it may be possible for them to have a successful ad hoc arbitration in China, and later have the ensuing award enforced both inside and outside China.

To achieve these goals, the parties should explicitly agree on a set of issues within their arbitration agreement. First, they should choose a non-Chinese law to govern the validity of their ad hoc arbitration agreement. Second, they should agree to put the seat of arbitration outside China, while at the same time specifying that all hearings will be held in China. Third, the parties should specify that the law at the seat will be the *lex arbitri*. Last but not least, they should choose a set of sophisticated arbitration rules for the arbitration proceedings.

The following sections will discuss relevant issues in depth, but in general, if the parties specifically and explicitly agree on all these four issues, it will likely ensure that they can successfully conduct an ad hoc arbitration in China and have the resulting award enforced. First, because the parties have chosen a non-Chinese law to govern the ad hoc arbitration agreement's validity and put the seat of arbitration outside China, a Chinese court will likely hold the ad hoc arbitration agreement valid under the SPC's choice-of-law rule. This means a party will no longer be able to request a Chinese court to strike down the ad hoc arbitration agreement at any time during the course of the arbitration proceeding. At the same time, the parties can choose to hold hearings in China if doing so will offer them geographical convenience. The explicit choice of a place for hearings different from the seat is well accepted in international arbitration practice and will not cause a change in the seat of arbitration.[1] Second, the choice of a set of sophisticated arbitration rules will help minimize possible loopholes in the arbitration proceeding that may give a resisting party chances to obstruct arbitration. The chosen non-Chinese *lex arbitri*, i.e. the seat law, will also provide a legal framework for the ad hoc arbitration, which means the parties will be able to rely on the assistance and support mechanisms provided under the law when necessary. This will further prevent a resisting party from frustrating the arbitration proceeding by simply refusing to cooperate. Third, putting the seat of arbitration outside China and explicitly choosing the seat law as the *lex arbitri* means Chinese courts will treat the ensuing award as a foreign award, or alternatively a non-domestic award, and review it under the New York Convention instead of Chinese law. Given the explicit party choice on the governing law of the arbitration agreement, this award will not encounter any problem under Article V(1)(a) of the New York Convention. Because this award will become enforceable under the New York Convention, Chinese courts will therefore not set it aside or ignore it; recognition and enforcement of the award outside China under the New York Convention will not run into difficulty under Article V(1)(e) of the Convention.

This mechanism will work to its best particularly when one party is non-Chinese. This is because the SPC have ruled against two Chinese parties submitting their dispute to arbitration outside China.

In a 2012 case, the SPC struck down an arbitration agreement between two Chinese companies.[2] In their contract, the two parties agreed to arbitration un-

1 *See, e.g.*, Model Law on International Commercial Arbitration of the United Nations Commission on International Trade Law, G.A. Res. 61/33, U.N. Doc. A/61/453 (revising G.A. Res. 40/72), art. 20(2) (Dec. 4, 2006); UNCITRAL Arbitration Rules (as revised in 2010, with new article 1, paragraph 4, as adopted in 2013), G.A. Res. 68/109, U.N. Doc. A/68/462, art. 18(2) (Dec. 16, 2013); Gary B. Born, International Commercial Arbitration 1596–97 (2d ed. 2014); Fouchard, Gaillard, Goldman On International Commercial Arbitration 676–77 (Emmanuel Gaillard & John Savage eds., 1999).

2 *See* Zuigao Renmin Fayuan Guanyu Jiangsu Hangtian Wanyuan Fengdian Shebei Zhizao Youxian Gongsi yu Ai'ermu Fengneng Yepian Zhipin Tianjin Youxian Gongsi Shenqing Queren Zhongcai Xieyi Xiaoli Jiufen Yi'an de Qingshi de Fuhan (最高人民法院关于江苏航天万源风电设备制造有限公司与艾尔姆风能叶片制品（天津）有限公司申请确认仲裁协议效力纠纷一案的请示的复函) [Reply Letter to the Request for Instructions Concerning the Confirmation of the Validity of the

der ICC rules in Beijing.[3] Although the two companies were both somewhat related to a foreign country, one being a joint venture between a Chinese company and a Spanish company and the other a wholly owned subsidiary of a Danish company, the SPC held that they were both Chinese companies because both of them had been incorporated and registered in China.[4] The SPC further found that the object of the contract was located in China, and the contract was performed completely in China.[5] Under these circumstances, the SPC held that the contract did not contain a foreign element, so was not a foreign-related contract.[6] The SPC went on to hold that Chinese law did not allow parties to submit a non-foreign-related dispute to a non-Chinese arbitration institution or to an ad hoc tribunal outside China.[7] As a result, the SPC ruled that the arbitration agreement between the parties was invalid.[8]

In another case in 2013, the SPC refused to recognize and enforce a Korean arbitration award based on similar grounds.[9] In this case, both parties were Chinese registered companies, although one party was controlled by a foreign investor.[10] The SPC followed its earlier decision and held that because

---

Arbitration Agreement Dispute in the Case Between Nantong CASC Wanyuan Acciona Wind Turbine Manufacture Co., Ltd. and LM Wind power (Tianjin) Co., Ltd.] (promulgated by the Sup. People's Ct., Aug. 31, 2012, effective Aug. 31, 2012) (China).

3 *See id.*

4 *See id.*; Jiangsusheng Gaoji Fayuan Guanyu Jiangsu Hangtian Wanyuan Fengdian Shebei Zhizao Youxian Gongsi yu Ai'ermu Fengneng Yepian Zhipin Tianjin Youxian Gongsi Shenqing Queren Zhongcai Xieyi Xiaoli Jiufen Yi'an de Qingshi (江苏省高级人民法院关于江苏航天万源风电设备制造有限公司与艾尔姆风能叶片制品（天津）有限公司申请确认仲裁协议效力纠纷一案的请示) [Request for Instructions Concerning the Confirmation of the Validity of the Arbitration Agreement Dispute in the Case Between Nantong CASC Wanyuan Acciona Wind Turbine Manufacture Co., Ltd. and LM Wind power (Tianjin) Co., Ltd.] (promulgated by the Jiangsu Province High People's Ct., Nov. 30, 2011, effective Nov. 30, 2011) (China).

5 *See* Zuigao Renmin Fayuan Guanyu Jiangsu Hangtian Wanyuan Fengdian Shebei Zhizao Youxian Gongsi yu Ai'ermu Fengneng Yepian Zhipin Tianjin Youxian Gongsi Shenqing Queren Zhongcai Xieyi Xiaoli Jiufen Yi'an de Qingshi de Fuhan (最高人民法院关于江苏航天万源风电设备制造有限公司与艾尔姆风能叶片制品（天津）有限公司申请确认仲裁协议效力纠纷一案的请示的复函) [Reply Letter to the Request for Instructions Concerning the Confirmation of the Validity of the Arbitration Agreement Dispute in the Case Between Nantong CASC Wanyuan Acciona Wind Turbine Manufacture Co., Ltd. and LM Wind power (Tianjin) Co., Ltd.] (promulgated by the Sup. People's Ct., Aug. 31, 2012, effective Aug. 31, 2012) (China).

6 *See id.*

7 *See id.*

8 *See id.*

9 *See* Zuigao Renmin Fayuan Guanyu Beijing Chaolai Xinsheng Tiyu Xiuxian Youxian Gongsi Shenqing Chengren Dahan Shangshi Zhongcaiyuan Zuochu de Di 12113-0011 Hao Di 12112-0012 Hao Zhongcai Caijue Anjian Qingshi de Fuhan (最高人民法院关于北京朝来新生体育休闲有限公司申请承认大韩商事仲裁院作出的第12113-0011号、第12112-0012号仲裁裁决案件请示的复函) [Reply Letter to the Request for Instructions Concerning the Application Made by Beijing Chaolai Xinsheng Sports Leisure Co., Ltd. to Recognize and Enforce the No. 12113-0011 and the No. 12112-0012 Arbitration Awards of the Korean Commercial Arbitration Board] (promulgated by the Sup. People's Ct., Dec. 18, 2013, effective Dec. 18, 2013) (China).

10 *See id.*

the case did not contain a foreign-element, Chinese law should apply.[11] Given that Chinese law has not allowed parties in a non-foreign-related dispute to arbitrate outside China by either institutional or ad hoc arbitration, the SPC held the arbitration agreement between the parties invalid and rejected the award based on Article V(1)(a) of the New York Convention.[12] However, the SPC in this case did hold that recognition and enforcement of this award would not run against Chinese public policy as provided in Article V(2)(b) of the New York Convention.[13]

These two SPC decisions are highly problematic and have been heavily criticized.[14] There are at least two obvious flaws in the SPC's reasoning. First, Chinese law does allow parties in a foreign-related contract to submit their dispute for arbitration outside China.[15] However, the SPC interpreted it to mean that Chinese law does not allow parties in a non-foreign-related contract to submit their dispute for arbitration outside China.[16] This line of reasoning is overly strict and at odds with the freedom of contract that parties usually enjoy in the field of arbitration. Second, even if Chinese law did forbid these parties to submit their dispute to arbitration outside China, it still would not have enabled Chinese courts to refuse the recognition and enforcement of the award under Article V(1)(a) of the New York Convention. This is because the condition for rejecting an award under Article V(1)(a) is that the arbitration agreement is invalid under the law chosen by the parties or, if there is no such agreement between

11 *See id.*

12 *See id.*

13 *See id.*

14 *See, e.g.*, Weidong Zhu, *The Recognition and Enforcement of the Foreign Arbitral Awards "with No Foreign Element" in China*, 3 J. Int'l Arb. 351 (2015).

15 *See* Minshi Susong Fa (民事诉讼法) [Civil Procedure Law] (promulgated by Nat'l People's Cong., Apr. 9, 1991, effective Apr. 9, 1991, rev. June. 27, 2017), art. 271 (China); Hetong Fa (合同法) [Contract Law] (promulgated by the Nat'l People's Cong., Mar. 15, 1999, effective Oct. 1, 1999), art. 128, para. 2 (China).

16 *See* Zuigao Renmin Fayuan Guanyu Jiangsu Hangtian Wanyuan Fengdian Shebei Zhizao Youxian Gongsi yu Ai'ermu Fengneng Yepian Zhipin Tianjin Youxian Gongsi Shenqing Queren Zhongcai Xieyi Xiaoli Jiufen Yi'an de Qingshi de Fuhan (最高人民法院关于江苏航天万源风电设备制造有限公司与艾尔姆风能叶片制品（天津）有限公司申请确认仲裁协议效力纠纷一案的请示的复函) [Reply Letter to the Request for Instructions Concerning the Confirmation of the Validity of the Arbitration Agreement Dispute in the Case Between Nantong CASC Wanyuan Acciona Wind Turbine Manufacture Co., Ltd. and LM Wind power (Tianjin) Co., Ltd.] (promulgated by the Sup. People's Ct., Aug. 31, 2012, effective Aug. 31, 2012) (China); Zuigao Renmin Fayuan Guanyu Beijing Chaolai Xinsheng Tiyu Xiuxian Youxian Gongsi Shenqing Chengren Dahan Shangshi Zhongcaiyuan Zuochu de Di 12113-0011 Hao Di 12112-0012 Hao Zhongcai Caijue Anjian Qingshi de Fuhan (最高人民法院关于北京朝来新生体育休闲有限公司申请承认大韩商事仲裁院作出的第12113-0011号、第12112-0012号仲裁裁决案件请示的复函) [Reply Letter to the Request for Instructions Concerning the Application Made by Beijing Chaolai Xinsheng Sports Leisure Co., Ltd. to Recognize and Enforce the No. 12113-0011 and the No. 12112-0012 Arbitration Awards of the Korean Commercial Arbitration Board] (promulgated by the Sup. People's Ct., Dec. 18, 2013, effective Dec. 18, 2013) (China).

the parties, the law at the seat of arbitration.[17] As a result, when reviewing this award, the SPC should not apply Chinese law to invalidate the arbitration agreement and further reject the award on that basis.

There have been some developments in Chinese judicial practice since these two cases that may suggest a different outcome in the future. First, the SPC confirmed in one of its recent judicial interpretations that Chinese courts should look at Article V(1)(a) of the New York Convention in ascertaining the law governing the validity of the arbitration agreement when they decide on recognition and enforcement of an award under the Convention.[18] Second, the SPC was willing to expand the scope of "foreign element" and supported two Chinese companies' choice to arbitrate outside China in some circumstances, particularly related to the free trade zones established all over China in recent years.[19] As a result, before the SPC further elaborates on this issue, there are certain uncertainties and risks under Chinese law regarding whether two Chinese parties can submit their dispute to arbitration seated outside China. Therefore, before the SPC clears up the doubts, the special drafting strategy discussed above shall be reserved for agreements between parties of which at least one is non-Chinese.

II Ad hoc arbitration in China will operate successfully

A External obstructions no longer possible

As previously analyzed in Chapter 3 of this book, an ad hoc arbitration agreement is invalid under the PRC Arbitration Law, and a resisting party in a Chinese ad hoc arbitration may request a Chinese court to strike down the agreement at any time. This can only happen, however, if the Chinese court chooses to apply Chinese law to determine the validity of the ad hoc arbitration agreement. Therefore, the parties may avoid this unwanted result by precluding the Chinese law's application. As per the choice-of-law rule adopted by the SPC, if the parties have explicitly agreed on a law to govern the validity of the arbitration agreement itself, a Chinese court will apply that law.[20] Furthermore, the SPC requires that,

17 *See* United Nations Convention on the Recognition and Enforcement of Foreign Arbitral Awards art. V(1)(a), June 10, 1958, 330 U.N.T.S. 38 [hereinafter New York Convention].

18 *See* Zuigao Renmin Fayuan Guanyu Shenli Zhongcai Sifa Shencha Anjian Ruogan Wenti de Guiding (最高人民法院关于审理仲裁司法审查案件若干问题的规定) [Regulation on Certain Issues Concerning the Adjudication of Cases Involving Judicial Review of Arbitration] (promulgated by the Sup. People's Ct., Dec. 26, 2017, effective Jan. 1, 2018), art. 16 (China).

19 *See* Zuigao Renmin Fayuan Guanyu Ximenzi Guoji Maoyi (Shanghai) Youxian Gongsi Shenqing Chengren yu Zhixing Waiguo Zhongcai Caijue Yian de Qingshi de Fuhan (最高人民法院关于西门子国际贸易(上海)有限公司申请承认与执行外国仲裁裁决一案的请示的复函) [Reply Letter to the Request for Instructions Concerning the Application Made by Siemens International Trading Ltd., Shanghai to Recognize and Enforce a Foreign Arbitration Award] (promulgated by the Sup. People's Ct., Oct. 10, 2015, effective Oct. 10, 2015) (China).

20 *See* Zuigao Renmin Fayuan Guanyu Shiyong "Zhonghua Renmin Gongheguo Zhongcai Fa" Ruogan Wenti de Jieshi (最高人民法院关于适用《中华人民共和国仲裁法》若干问题的解释)

when making this choice, the parties should specify that this law applies to the validity of the arbitration agreement and distinguish it from the substantive law that they have chosen to govern the merits of the larger container contract in which the arbitration agreement is embedded as a clause.[21] If, however, the parties did not specifically choose the law to govern the validity of the arbitration agreement but nonetheless chose the seat of arbitration, the Chinese court will apply the seat law to review the validity of the arbitration agreement.[22]

As a result, when parties explicitly choose a non-Chinese law to govern the validity of their ad hoc arbitration agreement, and put the seat of arbitration outside China, Chinese courts will not apply the PRC Arbitration Law when reviewing its validity. Instead, the court will apply the party chosen law, or alternatively, the seat law. Because they both presumably allow ad hoc arbitration, the Chinese court will not strike down the ad hoc arbitration agreement, but actually enforce it. If Chinese courts will enforce the ad hoc arbitration agreement, neither party will be able to obstruct arbitration from outside its proceeding by requesting a Chinese court to strike down the arbitration agreement.

B Internal obstructions will not happen

Also as previously analyzed in Chapter 3 of this book, a resisting party may obstruct a Chinese ad hoc arbitration from within the arbitration proceeding by refusing to cooperate on issues that are vital for the proceeding to move

---

[Interpretation on Certain Issues Concerning the Application of the "Arbitration Law of the People's Republic of China"] (promulgated by the Sup. People's Ct., Aug. 23, 2006, effective Sept. 8, 2006), art. 16 (China); Di'erci Quanguo Shewai Shangshi Haishi Shenpan Gongzuo Huiyi Jiyao (第二次全国涉外商事海事审判工作会议纪要) [Minutes of the Second National Working Conference on Adjudication of Foreign-related Commercial and Maritime Cases] (promulgated by the Sup. People's Ct., Dec. 26, 2005, effective Dec. 26, 2005), art. 58 (China); Zuigao Renmin fayuan Guanyu Sichuan Huahong Guoji Jingji Jishu Touzi Youxian Gongsi Su Hanguo Hanhua Zhushihuishe Maimai Hetong Jiufen Yian zhong Zhongcai Tiaokuan Xiaoli Wenti de Qingshi de Fuhan (最高人民法院关于四川华宏国际经济技术投资有限公司诉韩国韩华株式会社买卖合同纠纷一案仲裁条款效力问题的请示的复函) [Reply Letter to the Request for Instructions Concerning the Validity of the Arbitration Clause in the Sales Contract Dispute Case Between Sichuan Huahong International Economic and Technical Investment Co., Ltd and Hanwha Corporation (Korea)] (promulgated by the Sup. People's Ct., Aug. 24, 2007, effective Aug. 24, 2007) (China).

21 *See, e.g.*, Zuigao Renmin Fayuan Guanyu Shenli Zhongcai Sifa Shencha Anjian Ruogan Wenti de Guiding (最高人民法院关于审理仲裁司法审查案件若干问题的规定) [Regulation on Certain Issues Concerning the Adjudication of Cases Involving Judicial Review of Arbitration] (promulgated by the Sup. People's Ct., Dec. 26, 2017, effective Jan. 1, 2018), art. 13 (China); Di'erci Quanguo Shewai Shangshi Haishi Shenpan Gongzuo Huiyi Jiyao (第二次全国涉外商事海事审判工作会议纪要) [Minutes of the Second National Working Conference on Adjudication of Foreign-related Commercial and Maritime Cases] (promulgated by the Sup. People's Ct., Dec. 26, 2005, effective Dec. 26, 2005), art. 58 (China) (providing that the substantive law chosen by parties to govern the merits of the container contract cannot be used to determine the validity of the arbitration clause within the container contract).

22 *See* sources cited, *supra* note 20.

forward. This is because neither Chinese law nor Chinese courts will provide any assistance regarding those matters. To prevent this problem, the parties need to ensure that they can avoid loopholes in the proceedings as much as possible, and that they have a set of support mechanisms available in case of a deadlock occurring in the arbitration proceedings.

For those purposes, the parties to a Chinese ad hoc arbitration first need to agree on a set of established, sophisticated, and complete arbitration rules, such as the UNCITRAL Arbitration Rules.[23] Further to that, the parties should make sure that relevant parts of the rules do not point to a Chinese court for assistance. For example, the parties should not choose a Chinese court to be the appointing authority for arbitrators under the rules, but should instead agree on a different person or organization to take on that role. Apart from the arbitration rules, the parties should also specify that the seat law should be the *lex arbitri* that governs their arbitration. Once parties choose the seat of arbitration, the law at the seat will often be interpreted as the *lex arbitri* and govern the arbitration proceeding, however, confusions may possibly occur.[24] Consequently, the parties should make this explicit to avoid any doubts. This non-Chinese *lex arbitri* chosen by the parties will provide an additional support mechanism to the arbitration proceeding in case things go wrong. In case one party tries to obstruct arbitration by refusing to cooperate on vital issues during the arbitration proceedings, such as refusing to appoint an arbitrator, the other party may first rely on the relevant procedures specified in the arbitration rules agreed upon between the parties. Sophisticated and mature arbitration rules like the UNCITRAL Arbitration Rules usually contain detailed provisions that may provide a solution to the situation. In the example of appointment of arbitrators, the UNCITRAL Arbitration Rules provide for an appointing authority who will appoint an arbitrator upon a party's request.[25] If, unfortunately, an issue still cannot be solved by the chosen arbitration rules, the party seeking arbitration may turn to the party-chosen *lex arbitri*. The non-Chinese *lex arbitri* will usually contain gap-filling provisions and support mechanisms that will prevent the arbitration proceeding from reaching an impasse.

As a result, when parties carefully adopt this special drafting strategy, neither of them will be able to obstruct the arbitration proceeding by simply refusing to cooperate.

III The ad hoc arbitration award will be enforceable

Choosing a non-Chinese law to govern the validity of their arbitration agreement, putting the seat of arbitration outside China, as well as specifying the seat

23 *See* UNCITRAL Rules on Arbitration (2010), *available at* http://www.uncitral.org/pdf/english/texts/arbitration/arb-rules-revised/arb-rules-revised-2010-e.pdf.

24 *See* Gary B. Born, International Commercial Arbitration 1620–21 (2d ed. 2014); Fouchard, Gaillard, Goldman On International Commercial Arbitration *supra* note 1, at 635–44 (Emmanuel Gaillard & John Savage eds., 1999).

25 *See* UNCITRAL Rules, *supra* note 23.

law as *lex arbitri* will not only ensure the successful operation of a Chinese ad hoc arbitration, but will also significantly improve the ensuing award's prospects for being enforced, both inside and outside China.

A More chances of being enforced inside China

When an arbitration award is brought before a Chinese court for enforcement purposes, the court first needs to decide what law it should apply to review the award's enforceability. If the award is an institutional award issued by a Chinese arbitration institution, the court will apply Chinese law. If it is a foreign award made outside China, either ad hoc or institutional, the court will apply the New York Convention. As previously discussed, an ad hoc arbitration award is not enforceable under Chinese law, but Chinese courts will enforce an ad hoc award under the New York Convention.[26] If parties adopt the special drafting strategy, a Chinese court will likely apply the New York Convention to the ensuing ad hoc award at the enforcement stage. This is because the New York Convention applies to awards "made in the territory of a State other than the State where the recognition and enforcement of such awards are sought. . . . "[27] If parties explicitly agree that the seat of their arbitration is in a country outside China, the arbitral tribunal will for sure honor that agreement. This result shall not be affected by other procedural aspects in the arbitration proceeding, including e.g. where hearings are held or where arbitrators meet to deliberate the case.[28] In other words, in addition to putting the seat of arbitration outside China, parties can freely agree that all aspects of the arbitration proceeding be held in China for the sake of convenience and cost-saving. This design is separate from and will not change the legal seat of arbitration, or where "the award is made," as used in the wordings of the New York Convention. When the winning party brings the award before a Chinese court for the purpose of recognition and enforcement, the award is a "foreign" award because it was made outside China. Therefore, the Chinese court should apply the New York Convention to review the award's enforceability, which means the ad hoc award is enforceable.

That said, to the best of the author's knowledge, there has not been a case in which the SPC dealt with the situation where parties agree to separate the place of hearings from the seat of arbitration. Therefore, it is unclear how a Chinese court will decide on this matter exactly. In the unlikely situation where the Chinese court finds that the award is seated in China because all hearings are held in China, it is still possible that the court will nonetheless apply the New York Convention. This is because apart from foreign awards, i.e. arbitration awards made outside the country, the New York Convention "shall also apply to arbitral awards not considered as domestic awards in the State where

26 *See* discussion *supra* Chapter 4.

27 New York Convention, *supra* note 17, art. I(1).

28 *See* Born, *supra* note 24, at 1596–97; Fouchard, Gaillard, Goldman On International Commercial Arbitration, *supra* note 1, at 676–77.

their recognition and enforcement are sought."[29] These types of awards are commonly referred to as non-domestic awards. The New York Convention, however, offers no definition of what qualifies as a non-domestic award, but instead leaves this question to the national laws.[30] As a result, Chinese courts need to decide, according to Chinese law, under what circumstances they should hold an award made in China as non-domestic and review its enforceability under the New York Convention.[31]

Unfortunately, the PRC Arbitration Law is silent on what makes a non-domestic award under the New York Convention. The SPC has not articulated any guidelines on this issue, either. Under these circumstances, it can be reasonably expected that different Chinese courts may reach different conclusions on the issue. That being said, if the parties explicitly chose a non-Chinese law to govern their arbitration agreement's validity, tried to put the seat of arbitration outside China, and specified a non-Chinese law as their *lex arbitri*, there are good reasons why a Chinese court should treat the resulting award as non-domestic.

First, treating the award as non-domestic is consistent with a structural interpretation of the PRC Arbitration Law and is supported by Chinese case law. In fact, the PRC Arbitration Law is not explicit on the definitions of domestic arbitration and domestic awards. Because the PRC Arbitration Law assumes that all arbitrations in China are institutional, based upon the context of the Law, its definition of domestic arbitration can be reasonably interpreted as arbitration administered by arbitration commissions established under the PRC Arbitration Law in Chinese territory.[32] If this were the correct definition of domestic awards in China, the award being analyzed should obviously *not* be considered domestic.

In *Züblin International GmbH v. Wuxi Woco General Engineering Rubber Co. Ltd.*, the Intermediate People's Court of Wuxi City held an ICC award made in China as non-domestic.[33] In its decision, the court reasoned that the award does not fall under the definition of a domestic award, even though it was made in Chinese territory, because the arbitration was administered by a foreign arbitration institution. The court thus held that the award did not fit into the Chinese arbitration legal framework, because it was neither a domestic award nor

29 *See* New York Convention, *supra* note 17, art. I(1).

30 *See* Albert Jan van den Berg, The New York Arbitration Convention of 1958: Towards a Uniform Judicial Interpretation 22–27 (1981).

31 *See id.* at 25–27.

32 *See* Zhao Xiuwen (赵秀文), *Feineiguo Caijue de Falü Xingzhi Bianxi* (非内国裁决的法律性质辨析) [*Analysis of the Legal Nature of Non-domestic Awards*], 10 Fa Xue (法学) [Law Sci.] 16, 19 (2007) (China).

33 *See* Deguo Xupulin Guoji Youxian Zeren Gongsi Shenqing Chengren he Zhixing Guowai Zhongcai Caijue An (德国旭普林国际有限责任公司申请承认和执行国外仲裁裁决案) [Application by Züblin International GmbH for Recognition and Enforcement of Foreign Arbitration Award] (Wuxi Interm. People's Ct., July 19, 2006) (pku.cn) (the Court clearly held the award as non-domestic and applied the New York Convention, despite rejecting it on Art. V(1)(a) ground eventually).

a foreign award under Chinese law.[34] It further acknowledged that Chinese law is silent on what would make a non-domestic award under the New York Convention, but reasoned that the award should be held as non-domestic because it was made in accordance with a foreign law.[35] The court's conclusion on this particular issue may be somewhat perplexing, because the court based it on the reason that the award was made according to the ICC Arbitration Rules, which is obviously not a law, domestic or foreign.[36] The court also did not specify what it meant for "foreign law," e.g. a foreign substantive law, a foreign *lex arbitri*, or a foreign law governing the validity of the arbitration agreement. Unfortunately, the court decision did not include all relevant factual information about the case that could suggest an explanation for this conclusion, either. Nevertheless, if the parties adopted the special drafting strategy, particularly by explicitly choosing a non-Chinese law to govern their ad hoc arbitration agreement's validity and a non-Chinese law as *lex arbitri*, there would be little doubt that the ensuing award should be deemed as made in accordance with a foreign law. If a Chinese court follows the line of reasoning in *Züblin*, it should undoubtedly treat this award as non-domestic and apply the New York Convention.

Besides, categorizing the award as non-domestic in *Züblin* is perhaps an inevitable result of the incomplete and problematic structure of the PRC Arbitration Law. Due to Chinese lawmakers' misconception of arbitration, they neglected the possibility of international arbitration institutions operating in China and mistakenly assumed that only Chinese arbitration institutions could administer arbitration within Chinese territory.[37] As a result, the bifurcation of "domestic" and "foreign-related" arbitration under the PRC Arbitration Law was based on the wrongful assumption that they could only be products of Chinese arbitration institutions.[38] Therefore, the Chinese court in *Züblin* found the award impossible to fit into the PRC Arbitration Law framework.[39] The same logic exists in the scenario of a Chinese ad hoc arbitration. Because it equally does not fit into the existing Chinese arbitration legal framework and therefore will pose great difficulties for a Chinese court trying to stretch the PRC Arbitration Law and other relevant Chinese laws to apply them on a Chinese ad hoc award. As a result, it was wise, logical, and practical for the *Züblin* court to hold the award in the case as non-domestic. The SPC, and other Chinese courts, should follow *Züblin* in the comparable situation of a Chinese ad hoc award and hold this award as non-domestic as well.

34 *See id.*
35 *See id.*
36 *See id.*
37 *See* discussion *supra* Chapter 2, Part III.
38 *See* discussion *supra* Chapter 2, Part III.
39 *See* Deguo Xupulin Guoji Youxian Zeren Gongsi Shenqing Chengren he Zhixing Guowai Zhongcai Caijue An (德国旭普林国际有限责任公司申请承认和执行国外仲裁裁决案) [Züblin International GmbH v. Wuxi Woco General Engineering Rubber Co. Ltd], (Wuxi Interm. People's Ct., July 19, 2006) (pku.cn).

Second, practical concerns may make it easier for a Chinese court to treat a Chinese ad hoc award as non-domestic rather than domestic. Treating the award as domestic will lead to an unwanted outcome that creates a difficult dilemma for the court. On the one hand, for domestic awards, only institutional awards are enforceable under Chinese law. If the award is considered domestic, the court will not enforce it. On the other hand, according to the SPC's choice-of-law rule regarding the validity of an arbitration agreement, the ad hoc arbitration agreement in this case is indeed enforceable under the law that the parties explicitly chose to govern its validity.[40] This would have created a paradoxical situation in which an arbitration agreement is enforceable but the ensuing award is not. Obviously, no court should choose to interpret laws to be contradictory. Thus, to make a practically viable and logically sound decision, Chinese courts should treat the award as non-domestic.

As a result, if parties adopt the special drafting strategy by explicitly choosing a non-Chinese law to govern the validity of their ad hoc arbitration agreement, putting the seat of arbitration outside China, and choosing the seat law as *lex arbitri*, a Chinese court will likely treat the ensuing award as a foreign award, or alternatively a non-domestic award, and apply the New York Convention when reviewing for its recognition and enforcement. If so, the award will be enforceable in China.

B *More likely to be enforced outside China*

The special drafting strategy will also significantly increase the award's chances of being enforced outside of China under the New York Convention. Specifically, the risks of rejection that the award faces under Article V(1)(a) (invalidity of the arbitration agreement) and Article V(1)(e) (set aside in the home jurisdiction) of the New York Convention will be significantly reduced at least, if not completely eliminated.

1 *Enforceable under Article V(1)(a) of the New York Convention*

As previously discussed, under Article V(1)(a) of the New York Convention, an award may be rejected for recognition and enforcement if the arbitration agreement between the parties "is not valid under the law to which the parties have subjected it or, failing any indication thereon, under the law of the country where the award was made."[41] This provision identifies two bodies of law against which a court should determine the arbitration agreement's validity, and manifests that party-chosen law takes priority over seat law. Accordingly, if the parties explicitly choose a non-Chinese law, which allows ad hoc arbitration, to govern the validity of their ad hoc arbitration agreement, put the seat of arbitration outside China in a jurisdiction where ad hoc arbitration is allowed, and specify

40 *See* discussion *supra* Chapter 3, Part III.C.
41 *See* New York Convention, *supra* note 17, art. V(1)(a).

that the seat law will be the governing *lex arbitri*, a non-Chinese court that is reviewing the award under the New York Convention will most definitely not consider Chinese law relevant under Article V(1)(a). Accordingly, it should not reject recognition and enforcement of the award under Article V(1)(a) of the New York Convention.

2 Enforceable under Article V(1)(e) of the New York Convention

Article V(1)(e) of the New York Convention authorizes a national court to reject a foreign award's recognition and enforcement if that award has been set aside or suspended by a court in the country where the award is made, or under the law of which the award is made.[42] When parties adopt the special drafting strategy, particularly when they put the seat of arbitration outside China and specify that the seat law will be the *lex arbitri*, it is clear that the award is made in this chosen country and under its law. Therefore, when the award is brought before another country for enforcement purposes, the local court will most definitely not see this award as a Chinese award. If the losing party tries to base any of its arguments on Article V(1)(e) of the New York Convention, the court will need to consider whether the award has been set aside by the court at the seat country, as chosen by the parties. Therefore, it is the seat country's court decision on set aside, not one made by a Chinese court, that will become relevant under Article V(1)(e). Given that this country's law presumably allows ad hoc arbitration, the award will not be set aside solely because it is ad hoc. Therefore, the award will be enforceable under the New York Convention in the place where the winning party is requesting recognition and enforcement.

That said, the losing party may still choose to challenge the award before a Chinese court. Although there is probably no formal set aside proceeding that the losing party may initiate, it can certainly argue against the award's enforcement.[43] As previously discussed, if the winning party requests the award's enforcement before a Chinese court, the Chinese court first needs to decide what law applies to this award. Given the parties specifically chose to put the seat of arbitration outside China and chose that country's law as the *lex arbitri*, the Chinese court will most likely find this award as a foreign award, or alternatively a non-domestic award, and apply the New York Convention. If this happens, the award will be enforceable and therefore will not lead to any Article V(1)(e) problem in another country. If, however, the Chinese court somehow holds this award as a Chinese domestic award and therefore applies Chinese law to it, it will likely not enforce the award because it is based on an ad hoc arbitration agreement. When this happens, it may potentially have an impact on another country's court when that court decides whether it wants to recognize and enforce the award under the New York Convention.

42 *See id.* art. V(1)(e).
43 *See* discussion *supra* Chapter 4, Part II.B.

Thankfully, this country's court will not necessarily be bound by the Chinese decision. It needs to interpret the New York Convention and the agreements between the parties on its own. Given that parties have made explicit choices of the seat of arbitration and the *lex arbitri* in their arbitration agreement, it is difficult to see why this court should not honor the party agreement and deem the award as made in the seat chosen by the parties. If this is the case, this court will very likely hold that the Chinese court's decision not to enforce the award in China is merely a decision not to recognize and enforce the award in China and not a set aside decision under Article V(1)(e). It is completely normal for parties in practice to try to enforce an award in multiple countries under the New York Convention. Consequently, an award's rejection in one country does not bind a court in a different country. The New York Convention arguably only gives more weight to a set-aside decision made by a court at the seat, but if another country's court in our case does not deem China as the seat, it will not feel bound by the Chinese court's decision not to enforce the award in China.

IV Conclusion

In conclusion, although the PRC Arbitration Law's institutional arbitration requirement has created apparently insurmountable barriers to an ad hoc Chinese arbitration, parties can nonetheless resolve their dispute in China via ad hoc arbitration after adopting a special drafting strategy. If the parties explicitly choose a non-Chinese law to govern the validity of their ad hoc arbitration agreement, put the seat of arbitration outside China but agree that all hearings will be held in China, specify that the seat law will the *lex arbitri*, and choose a set of sophisticated arbitration rules, they can have a successful arbitration proceeding in China and have the ensuing award enforced both inside and outside China. This, of course, does not mean parties have to, or are even recommended to adopt this strategy in their contract. This is because they may well choose to have ad hoc arbitration outside China, or institutional arbitration inside China, both of which will result in better legal certainty under Chinese law. However, this design may provide an alternative option for parties who, for whatever reasons, particularly want to resolve their disputes in China using ad hoc arbitration.

6 A system calling for change

The previous chapters illustrated the complex issues related to ad hoc arbitration under Chinese law, including its historical roots and practical intricacies. Parties in practice need to deal with these complexities resulting from the preclusion of ad hoc arbitration under Chinese law very carefully in order to avoid potential pitfalls. At the same time, Chinese law's position of not allowing ad hoc arbitration is indeed puzzling. After all, ad hoc arbitration is the original form of arbitration and countries all around the world see it as completely legitimate. Given all the circumstances, should Chinese law continue this hostility?

I A broken system

Chinese law's attempts to preclude ad hoc arbitration from its legal system have proven to be unsuccessful. As discussed, parties have the freedom to agree to arbitration outside China on an ad hoc basis, and bring the resulting award back into China for enforcement. The Chinese courts are restricting the scope of Chinese law's application when it reviews the validity of an ad hoc arbitration agreement. The parties can also try to get around Chinese law via a set of specific agreements and have ad hoc arbitration in China. These in combination mean that Chinese law's prohibition of ad hoc arbitration is quite ineffective in practice. There are many ways for parties to avoid this unfriendly rule under Chinese law.

This result is inevitable. First, arbitration is private. It is based on party consent and does not always require involvement of a public authority. In practice, if the parties in an arbitration proceeding are willing to cooperate in good faith, their whole dispute resolution process can be completely unnoticed by courts or any other government bodies. From this perspective, any attempt to ban ad hoc arbitration in its entirety must fail.

Second, arbitration is international. The New York Convention has become one of the most successful treaties the world has ever seen. It has established an international arbitration legal framework that connects different legal systems in the world. Under this system, none of the contracting parties can insulate itself from the rest of the world. Instead, the interaction between a national legal system and the international framework provides parties with much room in which to achieve their desired goals. In China's example, the international framework offers parties convenient ways to avoid Chinese law's hostility towards ad hoc arbitration. The easiest way would be for the parties to have ad hoc arbitration outside China and, if necessary, later request Chinese courts to recognize and enforce the ensuing award under the New York Convention.

Most importantly, the ad hoc issue exposes some misconceptions of arbitration under the Chinese legal system. These misconceptions not only caused the hostility towards ad hoc arbitration under Chinese law, but also indicated its serious misunderstandings of the nature of arbitration.

First, Chinese law has yet to recognize, at least recognize fully, arbitration's private nature. As indicated in the history, arbitration did not develop in a bottom-up fashion in China. It did not first become popular among merchants and later achieve recognition by the state as an efficient and legitimate dispute resolution mechanism. Instead, Chinese governments adopted an arbitration system as an alternative to a dysfunctional judicial system particularly incapable of resolving commercial disputes.[1] Therefore, in the Chinese lawmakers' mind, arbitration is not private, but is quasi-public. As a result, party autonomy is not given enough respect and consideration under the Chinese arbitration legal framework.

Second, at least at the very beginning, Chinese law did not realize that arbitration is international, or did not fully understand how the international arbitration legal framework based upon the New York Convention functions. When Chinese lawmakers established their arbitration system, they mostly focused on solving domestic problems and satisfying domestic needs. They did not conceive the legislation in an international setting. This is evidenced by the fact that the PRC Arbitration Law does not even contain any provisions related to the recognition and enforcement of foreign awards or the New York Convention. In other words, Chinese lawmakers designed the Chinese arbitration system in parallel to the international arbitration legal framework but failed to envision that the two systems would inevitably interact and that the Chinese system cannot stay isolated given that China has acceded to the New York Convention. Of course, Chinese lawmakers and courts later complemented the Chinese system in many other ways, but the whole Chinese arbitration legal framework undoubtedly carries this "birth defect."

Apart from the fact that Chinese law's preclusion of ad hoc arbitration is unsuccessful in practice, which is inevitable as shown above, there are also other reasons why the Chinese legal system should end its hostility towards ad hoc arbitration.

1 *See* discussion *supra* Chapter 2 Part III.

II A vague and problematic standard

Chinese law should not have used the distinction between ad hoc and institutional arbitration as a standard to determine an arbitration agreement's validity in the first place, because the dividing line between these two types of arbitration is not always clear in practice. It is true that the common standard used to distinguish ad hoc arbitration from institutional arbitration is whether a professional institution is involved in the process of arbitration.[2] However, perhaps because this distinction does not usually result in any legal significance (except in China), it is not as precise as it appears.

Due to their own characteristics and features, it is understandable that various arbitration institutions in the world have different structures, working styles, and functions in arbitration proceedings. Consequently, their roles in administering arbitration proceedings can be quite different. Some institutions, such as the ICC and CIETAC, adopt relatively "intrusive" approaches and tend to supervise their arbitration proceedings more closely. For example, both the ICC and CIETAC provide frequent advice to tribunals on procedural matters and scrutinize draft awards before a tribunal renders a final decision.[3] Additionally, CIETAC affixes its official seal to the awards to indicate its authority.[4] These features make it quite clear that the arbitrations administered by such organizations are undoubtedly institutional.

Not all institutions, however, administer arbitration proceedings in the same ways that the ICC and CIETAC do. Some other institutions tend to work as organizing bodies that provide services to arbitrators and parties to facilitate arbitrations that in every other respect would be considered ad hoc. They may assist the parties with the appointment of arbitrators and provide them with a venue for holding hearings, but they mostly leave the arbitration proceedings to the tribunals.[5] Usually, awards are not issued under the institutions' names either. The London Maritime Arbitrators Association (LMAA) offers a typical example of such an institution. On its official website, the LMAA describes itself as "not administer[ing] or supervis[ing] the conduct of arbitrations (unlike, for example, the Chambre Arbitrale Maritime in Paris, or the ICC International Court of Arbitration): the arbitrations [the LMAA's] members conduct remain ad hoc

2 *See* discussion *supra* Chapter 1 Part II.B.

3 *See* Int'l Chamber of Commerce, *ICC Rules of Arbitration*, art. 34 (effective Mar. 1, 2017), ***available at*** https://cdn.iccwbo.org/content/uploads/sites/3/2017/01/ICC-2017-Arbitration-and-2014-Mediation-Rules-english-version.pdf.pdf; 2015 China International Economic and Trade Arbitration Commission Arbitration Rules, art. 51, CIETAC (effective Jan. 1, 2015) [hereinafter CIETAC Arbitration Rules], ***available at*** http://cn.cietac.org/index.php?m=Page&a=index&id=42&l=en.

4 *See* CIETAC Arbitration Rules, *supra* note 3, art. 48.4.

5 "Unlike the ICC, the AAA and CPR do not closely supervise their arbitrations." *A Primer on International Arbitration*, Covington & Burling, 6 (May 1998), http://www.cov.com/files/Publication/f394b11c-381d-4838-a6e2-02812ed6b093/Presentation/PublicationAttachment/969db08e-5cc1–4f3f-a72e-034ca2c8e9b2/oid6181.PDF.

and are administered by the tribunals involved."[6] Under these circumstances, it is probably incorrect to classify arbitration under the LMAA as institutional, even though an institution is indeed involved.

There may well be other institutions which operate somewhere between the two extremes represented by the ICC and CIETAC at one end and the LMAA at the other. This would undoubtedly mean that it might be difficult to classify an award as either ad hoc or institutional correctly in practice. For example, before the Hong Kong International Arbitration Centre (HKIAC) changed its arbitration rules in 2005, the arbitrations that it administered were essentially ad hoc.[7] The awards only needed to be signed by the arbitrators when rendered. The HKIAC would not affix its own seal to the awards in general.[8] If the parties so wished, however, the institution might affix its seal to the award as proof that the arbitration award was rendered by arbitrators appointed by the HKIAC.[9] In this scenario, it is likely that an award affixed with the HKIAC's seal would cause some controversy under Chinese law. On one hand, it could be claimed that such an award is still ad hoc, because the mere fact that an arbitration is conducted by arbitrators appointed by an institution does not necessarily make it administered by that institution. On the other hand, it could also be argued that the award should be treated as institutional because HKIAC was involved in the process of arbitration and provided some form of certification function. Particularly, given that all arbitration institutions in China are heavily involved in arbitration proceedings, like CIETAC, it would not be surprising if a Chinese court customarily presumes that an arbitration is institutional as long as an institution's name appears on the award.

This, of course, does not always lead to a problem under the current Chinese law. On one hand, Chinese courts will enforce arbitration awards made outside China according to the New York Convention, regardless of whether they are ad hoc or institutional.[10] On the other hand, Chinese arbitration institutions are all of the intrusive type and no ad hoc arbitration is allowed under the Chinese law, so all arbitrations seated in China and administered by Chinese arbitration institutions are indeed institutional. As analyzed before, however, the Chinese arbitration legal framework was based on Chinese arbitration's "isolation" from

6 *What is the LMAA and What Does it Do?*, London Mar. Arb. Assoc., http://www.lmaa.london/faq.aspx (last visited Jan. 27, 2018).

7 Li Jianqiang (李剑强), *Xianggang Zhongcai Jigou de Linshi Zhongcai ji Qi Qishi* (香港仲裁机构的临时仲裁及其启示) [*Ad Hoc Arbitrations at Hong Kong Arbitration Institutions and Their Indications*], 3 Bejing Zhongcai (北京仲裁) [Arb. Beijing] 82, 85, 93 (2006).

8 This is different today. Article 34.6 of the 2013 *Hong Kong International Arbitration Centre Administered Arbitration Rules* reads, "Subject to any lien, originals of the award signed by the arbitrators and affixed with the seal of HKIAC shall be communicated to the parties and HKIAC by the arbitral tribunal. HKIAC shall be supplied with an original copy of the award." *See* H.K. Int'l Arb. Ctr., *Administered Arbitration Rules*, art. 34.6 (2013), *available at* http://www.hkiac.org/sites/default/files/ck_filebrowser/PDF/arbitration/2013_hkiac_rules.pdf.

9 Li, *supra* note 7, at 85.

10 *See* discussion *supra* Chapter 4, Part I.

the world and did not give enough consideration of arbitration's private and international nature. As a result, this bifurcation will for sure fail to cover many scenarios in practice. For example, in a 2013 case, two parties agreed in their arbitration agreement that the arbitration shall take place at CIETAC but be settled according to UNCITRAL Rules.[11] Clearly, CIETAC is an arbitration institution, but parties did seem to choose a typical set of ad hoc rules. In this situation, is that ad hoc or institutional arbitration? The SPC did not directly address the issue, but did hold the arbitration agreement valid under Chinese law because it mentioned an arbitration institution.[12] As another example, parties may well agree to place the seat of their arbitration in China and choose the rules of a non-Chinese arbitration institution that takes a relatively hands-off approach, such as those of the LMAA. In this situation, it is uncertain whether Chinese courts will find this arbitration to be ad hoc or institutional. Although a Chinese court may hold that the arbitration is non-domestic so that the New York Convention applies to the award while the PRC Arbitration Law does not, which means the award will be enforceable no matter if it is ad hoc or institutional, it is not clear whether the SPC will support this position.[13]

In any event, the distinction between ad hoc and institutional arbitration is not always clear. Considering the vast number of arbitral institutions in the world, and the different features of their organization and work styles, this vagueness may be inevitable. As a result, it is problematic to use the distinction between ad hoc and institutional arbitration as the basis for determining an arbitration agreement's validity in the first place. From this perspective, Chinese law should not adopt the dichotomy of ad hoc and institutional arbitration and require that arbitration be institutional.

III Rationale behind the hostility no longer exists

Apart from the impracticality, or even impossibility, of banning ad hoc arbitration, as well as the inherent imprecision of the dichotomy between ad hoc and institutional arbitration, another reason for China to abandon its hostility

11 *See* Zuigao Renmin Fayuan Guanyu Zhejiang Yisheng Shihua Youxian Gongsi Shenqing Queren Zhongcai Tiaokuan Xiaoli Yi'an de Qingshi de Fuhan (最高人民法院关于浙江逸盛石化有限公司申请确认仲裁条款效力一案请示的复函) [Reply Letter to the Request for Instructions Concerning the Confirmation of the Validity of the Arbitration Agreement Case Filed by Zhejiang Yisheng Petrochemical Co., Ltd.] (promulgated by the Sup. People's Ct., Dec. 18, 2013, effective Dec. 18, 2013) (China).

12 *See id.*

13 *See* Deguo Xupulin Guoji Youxian Zeren Gongsi Shenqing Chengren he Zhixing Guowai Zhongcai Caijue An (德国旭普林国际有限责任公司申请承认和执行国外仲裁裁决案) [Application by Züblin International GmbH for Recognition and Enforcement of Foreign Arbitration Award] (Wuxi Interm. People's Ct., July 19, 2006) (pku.cn) (holding the ICC award in this case is a non-domestic award under Chinese law); Zhao Xiuwen (赵秀文), *Feineiguo Caijue de Falü Xingzhi Bianxi* (非内国裁决的法律性质辨析) [*Analysis on the Legal Nature of Non-domestic Awards*], 10 Fa Xue (法学) [Law Sci.] 16, 19 (2007) (China).

towards ad hoc arbitration is that the historical reasons for China to adopt this policy no longer exist today. In fact, it is quite difficult to understand Chinese law's hostility towards ad hoc arbitration to start with. After all, ad hoc is the original form of arbitration and, to a large extent, represents what arbitration really is. Due to its many advantages, ad hoc arbitration is popular among parties on many occasions. Nowadays, ad hoc arbitration is legitimate in essentially all of the world apart from China. This makes it difficult to understand why China is so hostile toward it.

A Reasons given by the Chinese lawmakers

The Chinese lawmakers offered two reasons as an explanation for why the PRC Arbitration Law did not include ad hoc arbitration into its legal framework:

> In the course of drafting the PRC Arbitration Law, we investigated whether ad hoc arbitration should be included. The basic opinion was that ad hoc arbitration would be allowed in international economic and trade disputes, but not in domestic economic and trade disputes. There are two main reasons why the PRC Arbitration Law did not provide for ad hoc arbitration. First, in the development history of arbitration as a legal institution, ad hoc arbitration appeared before institutional arbitration. Ad hoc arbitration is on the decline from the perspective of future development. Second, China only has a short history of arbitration, during which there has only been institutional arbitration, but no ad hoc arbitration. . . .[14]

The explanation offered by the Chinese lawmakers is very puzzling and far from persuasive. First, it is true that ad hoc arbitration precedes institutional arbitration in time. However, it is difficult to see how this should serve as a justification to abandon ad hoc arbitration. After all, things that are older are not necessarily worse than things that are newer.

Second, the claim that ad hoc arbitration is declining in use is baseless. Due to their distinctive characteristics, ad hoc and institutional arbitration complement each other and coexist in the international commercial world.[15] Because parties have distinct practical needs in different disputes, each of the two types of arbitration has certain advantages over the other that make it a better choice for resolving a particular dispute. In fact, in some fields such as admiralty and maritime law, ad hoc arbitration's flexibility and efficiency make it the preferred

14 Quanguo Renda Changweihui Fazhi Gongzuo Weiyuanhui (全国人大常委会法制工作委员会) [The Legislative Affairs Comm'n of the Standing Comm. of the Nat'l People's Cong. of the People's Republic of China], Zhonghua Renmin Gongheguo Zhongcai Falü Shiping (中华人民共和国仲裁法律释评) [Commentaries on Arbitration Laws of China] 38 (1997).

15 *See* discussion *supra* Chapter 1 Part II.

method of dispute resolution.[16] Therefore, ad hoc arbitration and institutional arbitration are both essential to a complete arbitration system in the sense that each provides parties with a dispute resolution mechanism that fits their distinct practical needs.

Third, it does not make sense to preclude ad hoc arbitration because China only has a short history of arbitration and has never had ad hoc arbitration before. Ad hoc arbitration's flexible and largely self-sufficient nature will only make it easier to be established or incorporated into a legal institution. This means that ad hoc arbitration is a good candidate when lawmakers are designing a new arbitration system, and does not explain its exclusion from the PRC Arbitration Law. Also, logically speaking, never having something in the past should not justify refusing to have it in the future. As a result, China's intentional choice to have institutional arbitration but not ad hoc arbitration cannot be reasonably explained by a short history or lack of experience.

B A more convincing explanation

As previously discussed in Chapter 2 of this book, arbitration followed a very different path in its historical development in China compared to the one in the Western world. In the West, arbitration as a legal institution developed in a bottom-up pattern. It originated in the form of ad hoc arbitration, which best suited merchants' needs for an impartial and efficient dispute resolution mechanism. Institutional arbitration appeared only relatively recently when commercial disputes became much more frequent, with the aim to provide professional services to parties and arbitrators. In China, however, arbitration developed in a top-down pattern. Largely due to the prolonged underdevelopment of commercial activities, in China there never existed a practical need for arbitration until drastic social and economic reforms arose at the beginning of the twentieth century as well as in the late 1970s. During both of these times, the Chinese government tried to promote commerce in order to develop the Chinese economy. Then, because the judicial systems at the time were unable to meet the fast growing needs for dispute resolution, the Chinese government established arbitration institutions so that business entities might have their commercial disputes successfully resolved. When Chinese lawmakers finally established arbitration as a legal institution in both of these periods, they only chose institutional arbitration and never adopted ad hoc arbitration in the system.

In other words, unlike the "natural" growth pattern in the West, the Chinese arbitration system was largely "government-made." When Chinese lawmakers decided to take on reforms and set up an arbitration system, they probably did not feel obliged to fully adopt arbitration's classic model, which indisputably

16 *See* Soc'y of Mar. Arbitrators, Inc., Guide to Maritime Arbitration in New York: Answers to Frequently-Asked Questions about Arbitration under the rules of the Society of Maritime Arbitrators, Inc., Question 9 (1997), ***available at*** http://www.smany.org/new-york-maritime-arbitration-guide.html.

includes ad hoc arbitration. Given the pressing needs that they were facing at the time, they were perhaps only interested in what they found most useful: an alternative dispute resolution system that could resolve commercial disputes outside courts in an environment of rapidly increasing business activities. For this purpose, a curtailed arbitration system containing only institutional arbitration was able to satisfy their needs and probably would work the best. Instead of slowly cultivating a culture of private dispute resolution embodied in ad hoc arbitration, it would be much easier and faster to organize and establish a number of arbitration institutions in different parts of the country. Furthermore, through these institutions, it would be easy to promote simple, standard, and uniform practices, which would be helpful for parties and legal practitioners who likely had never had any experience or knowledge of arbitration before. From this perspective, institutional arbitration was the most efficient and suitable option for the Chinese government at the relevant moments in time. Ad hoc arbitration, on the other hand, was not as useful. In addition, given that at that time in China there was essentially no one who would want to use ad hoc arbitration by themselves, the Chinese lawmakers likely found no need to include ad hoc arbitration in the newly designed Chinese arbitration legal framework.

More importantly, the economic and political contexts in Chinese society at the time when the PRC Arbitration Law was enacted had significant impacts on its preclusion of ad hoc arbitration. As discussed earlier, the PRC instituted a planned economy system until 1978, when a shift towards a market economy began.[17] This transition, which was by no means an easy task and arguably is still in progress even today, has had such a profound influence on Chinese society that it cannot be neglected in any study of the Chinese legal system, including its arbitration legal framework.

In a planned economy, the government strictly controls all economic activities.[18] Everything is publicly owned and run, including all dispute resolution processes.[19] In contrast, this is exactly what arbitration, especially ad hoc arbitration, tries to avoid. One of the main reasons why business entities choose ad hoc arbitration is to avoid government control as much as possible and resolve their disputes in private.[20] Moreover, the nature of ad hoc arbitration, namely its flexibility and efficiency, makes it extremely difficult for the public power to govern or control it closely.[21] Particularly when both parties are willing to cooperate in good faith, an ad hoc arbitration can take place while being completely unnoticed by any outsiders, including the government or courts. Therefore, planned

17 *See* The Legislative Affairs Comm'n of the Standing Comm. of the Nat'l People's Cong. of the People's Republic of China, *supra* note 14, at 1–2.

18 *See* Donald C. Clarke, *What's Law Got to Do with It? Legal Institutions and Economic Reform in China*, 10 *UCLA Pac. Basin L.J.* 1, 5 (1991).

19 *See* Donald C. Clarke, *Dispute Resolution in China*, 5 J. Chinese L. 245, 250–51 (1991).

20 *See* Gary B. Born, International Commercial Arbitration 70 (2d ed. 2014).

21 Wei-Jen Chen, *Separate but Equal in Arbitration? – An Analysis on* Ad Hoc *Arbitration of Taiwan and East Asia*, 5 Contemp. Asia Arb. J. 107, 120–21 (2012).

economy and ad hoc arbitration are "natural enemies" from the perspective of government control.

The transition from a planned economy to a market economy is a journey from one extreme to another and therefore not easy or risk-free. From the very beginning, the Chinese government was highly cautious about what reform measures to adopt and always preferred small and steady progress to massive and drastic changes.[22] Due to arbitration's private nature, which is directly contrary to the public nature of a planned economy and a socialist regime, it was politically very sensitive to design and establish an arbitration system in China at the time. In fact, when the PRC Arbitration Law was enacted, the law itself represented the "spirit of reform."[23] For example, the PRC Arbitration Law's provision that arbitration commissions would be independent of and not subordinate to any administrative authorities was seen as an extremely decentralized move at that time.[24] Under these circumstances, it is understandable that the Chinese lawmakers wanted to implement the reform slowly and carefully. A slower transition could allow the Chinese government more time to gradually loosen its control over private business entities, and private business entities would in the interim develop experience and expertise with the new arbitration system. As compared with ad hoc arbitration, institutional arbitration undoubtedly serves this purpose better. It is much easier for the government to exercise some measure of control over the institutions, which, in turn, may exercise some measure of control over the arbitration cases. Ad hoc arbitration, on the other hand, was probably too progressive for the lawmakers at the time. The government would lose control over dispute resolution almost completely, and business entities probably were not ready for such a huge change either. In other words, ad hoc arbitration might pose too big a threat to the success of a steady reform process. As a result, from the government's standpoint, it was much more acceptable to start the reform with institutional arbitration first, as a trial, before deciding whether to incorporate ad hoc arbitration in the future.

Hence, when enacting the PRC Arbitration Law in 1994, the Chinese government's intended goal was not necessarily to implement a flawless arbitration system. Instead, the lawmakers were only trying to establish a transitional, albeit imperfect, arbitration framework that best fit the then-existing political and economic background of Chinese society.

C Changes in nowadays China

Chinese society has gone through radical changes since the adoption of the reform and open up policies in the late 1970s. The policies have successfully

22 *See* Osman Suliman, *Reform and Macroeconomic Stability in China: An Overview*, *in* China's Transition to a Socialist Market Economy 23, 24 (Osman Suliman ed., 1998).

23 *See* Hu Kangsheng (胡康生), *Zhongcai de Benzhi Shi Minjian Xing* (仲裁的本质是民间性) [*The Nature of Arbitration is Private*], Fazhi Ribao (法制日报) [Legal Daily], Sept. 8, 2004 (China)

24 *See id.*

transformed the country in many ways. Given that the more convincing reasons why China refused to allow ad hoc arbitration in the PRC Arbitration Law were essentially all related to China's historical, social, economic, and political contexts at the time of the law's promulgation in 1994, there is obviously a need to rethink this preclusion today.

First, the planned economy has basically been dismantled.[25] Today, the Chinese government no longer plans all of the country's economic affairs. Nor do Chinese business entities receive governmental directions on how to run their business operations. Chinese economy is no longer predominantly based on public ownership, and the private sector has become an essential and powerful component of an economy that is market-based. Although China's market economy still has many problems and is by no means perfect, there is no doubt that it has become the backbone of Chinese society. The era of planned economy is long gone and China is not going back.

Second, government centralization is declining.[26] The Chinese government no longer controls every aspect of Chinese society as it used to. Particularly in the context of commercial activities, Chinese government is retreating from full control and is giving more freedom to business entities. For example, Chinese laws now respect party autonomy as a principle.[27] For dispute resolution processes, parties are free to choose negotiation, mediation, (institutional) arbitration, or litigation as they wish.[28] The government or courts will not become directly involved unless the parties want them to.

Third, Chinese business entities and legal practitioners have gained much experience with arbitration since 1994. Arbitration is no longer a novel dispute resolution mechanism; it is a relatively mature and popular solution for businesses. CIETAC has become a leading arbitral institution in the world. In recent years, CIETAC's caseload ranks the highest among all the arbitration institutions globally. At the same time, Chinese businesses are also assisted by a large number of professional lawyers. China now has many lawyers and arbitrators with extensive experience in arbitration.[29]

25 *See* Xianfa art. 15 (1982) (China) (stating that China practices a socialist market economy); Albert H.Y. Chen, *The Developing Theory of Law and Market Economy in Contemporary China*, *in* Legal Developments in China: Market Economy & Law 3, 3–5 (Wang Guiguo & Wei Zhenying eds., 1996).

26 *See* Bin Liang, The Changing Chinese Legal System, 1978-Present: Centralization of Power and Rationalization of the Legal System 70 (2008).

27 *See, e.g.*, Bing Ling, Contract Law in China 40–41 (2002) (stating that the PRC Contract Law adopts freedom of contract as a basic principle).

28 *See* Vai Io Lo, *Arbitration of Commercial Disputes in China*, Md. Series in Contemp. Asian Stud., no. 5, 2001 at 1 *available at* http://digitalcommons.law.umaryland.edu/cgi/viewcontent.cgi?article=1165&context=mscas.

29 *See generally China Lawyer's Role in Domestic Arbitration and International Arbitration*, China Law. Blog (Jan. 27, 2018, 17:16 PM), http://www.chinalawblog.org/law-topics/legal-counsel/148-china-lawyers-role-in-domestic-arbitration-and-international-arbitration.

Fourth, the Chinese legal system and judicial system have greatly improved. For the purposes of resolving commercial disputes, China now has a complete commercial law system that includes both substantive and procedural laws. Chinese judges are now predominately well educated and many have rich experience and expertise. Courts all over China hear a very large number of commercial disputes every year. They are very effective in resolving commercial disputes.

As a result, most, if not all, of the reasons for excluding ad hoc arbitration under Chinese law are no longer relevant. The goal of the Chinese arbitration system is no longer to provide an alternative for a dysfunctional judicial system. Instead, it should be to enable parties to choose the dispute resolution mechanism that they find most efficient or that best fits their needs. At the same time, arbitration, particularly ad hoc arbitration, is no longer a politically sensitive legal institution. The private nature of arbitration is gradually accepted by Chinese society. Most importantly, it will not pose any threat to any of the government's political agenda. Moreover, Chinese government no longer needs to worry about parties not knowing what to do with ad hoc arbitration, because they may well already have much experience themselves, and if not, they can very easily obtain legal assistance. Therefore, the reasons for the preclusion of ad hoc arbitration under Chinese law are no longer existent.

IV Conclusion

In summation, there are multiple reasons why China should change its law to remove its prohibition of ad hoc arbitration. First, the current attempts under Chinese law to ban ad hoc arbitration are not, and cannot be, successful due to the private and international nature of arbitration as a dispute resolution mechanism. There are always ways that parties can avoid the institutional arbitration requirement under Chinese law. Second, the distinction between ad hoc and institutional arbitration is never crystal clear and should not become the deciding factor for an arbitration agreement's validity in the first place. Third, Chinese law's hostility towards ad hoc arbitration was clearly historically shaped and politically motivated. The current prohibition of ad hoc arbitration was closely tied to the political, economic, and social contexts of Chinese society at the time when the PRC Arbitration Law was promulgated in 1994. Chinese society, however, has gone through significant changes since then. Those contexts that found ad hoc arbitration intolerable no longer exist in China today. Instead, and as will be explained in the next chapter, China is ready for ad hoc arbitration. Moreover, legitimizing ad hoc arbitration will only benefit China. As a result, China should change its law to legitimize ad hoc arbitration fully.

7 Re-thinking China's ad hoc arbitration legal framework

I China should have ad hoc arbitration

As discussed in the previous chapters, there are multiple reasons why Chinese law should abandon its requirement that all arbitrations must be institutional. First, Chinese law's preclusion of ad hoc arbitration is, and is destined to be, unsuccessful in practice. Due to arbitration's private and international nature, parties can avoid the Chinese law's requirement by resorting to the New York Convention and by specific party agreements. Second, the distinction between ad hoc and institutional arbitration is never clear-cut. Arbitration institutions' different organizational structures and work styles dictate that it is not practical to accurately distinguish ad hoc arbitration from institutional arbitration in practice. More importantly, ad hoc and institutional arbitration have so much in common that they are not easily separable from each other. Therefore, recognizing the legitimacy of only one and not the other is not a good strategy to begin with. Third, Chinese law's hostility against ad hoc arbitration was historically shaped and politically motivated. The development history of arbitration in China indicated that the preclusion of ad hoc arbitration under Chinese law resulted from the social, political, and economic contexts of the Chinese society at the time when the legal transplant of arbitration in China took place. However, after the radical economic and social changes that China has gone through in recent decades, the reasons or concerns for not legitimizing ad hoc arbitration in China have disappeared. Moreover, history indicates that the current PRC Arbitration Law represents a tentative or interim legal framework that came into existence during the transition period from a planned economy to a market economy. Given that there are no compelling arguments against the full recognition of ad hoc arbitration in China's legal system, China will only benefit from legitimizing ad hoc arbitration.[1]

Moreover, having a good arbitration system may contribute to a country's economic development.[2] When foreign investors and merchants make

1 *See* discussion *infra* Part II.A for an analysis and critique of arguments against legitimizing ad hoc arbitration in China.

2 *See generally,* Eric A. Schwartz, *The Role of International Arbitration in Economic Development*, 12 Int'l Trade & Bus. L. Rev. 127 (2009).

international investments or conduct international transactions, they usually care about how future disputes will be resolved.[3] Therefore, an efficient and just dispute resolution mechanism is essential for foreign parties to be assured that their rights and interests will be adequately protected.[4] Because arbitration serves as the dominant dispute resolution mechanism for international commercial disputes,[5] having a complete, efficient, and effective arbitration system may help China attract foreign business as much as possible, continue the move towards a market economy, remain active in the globalization process, and become more involved in the world's international commercial arbitration system.[6]

It is difficult to see why and how a good arbitration system can possibly preclude ad hoc arbitration. Flexibility is a very important reason why parties choose arbitration to resolve their disputes. The consensual nature of arbitration usually allows the parties to decide what kinds of arbitration procedure they want. Because of its obvious advantages, there will always be parties who want to choose ad hoc arbitration. Therefore, a complete and efficient arbitration system should allow parties to choose ad hoc arbitration if the parties find that it best suits their needs, particularly when there is no valid policy reason to forbid the parties to

3 *See id.* at 127–28.

4 *See id.* at 128.

5 *See* Christian Bühring-Uhle, Lars Kirchhoff & Gabriele Scherer, Arbitration and Mediation in International Business 27 (2d ed. 2006); Gerald Aksen, *Arbitration and Other Means of Dispute Settlement*, *in* International Joint Ventures: A Practical Approach to Working with Foreign Investors in the U.S. and Abroad 287, 287–88 (David N. Goldsweig & Roger H. Cummings eds., 1990).

6 Many Chinese scholars have discussed and supported complete legitimization of ad hoc arbitration in China, although some different opinions do exist. *See, e.g.*, Wang Yan (王岩) & Song Lianbin (宋连斌), *Shilun Linshi Zhongcai ji Qi Zai Woguo de Xianzhuang* (试论临时仲裁及其在我国的现状) [*Ad Hoc Arbitration and Its Current Status in China*], 1 Beijing Zhongcai (北京仲裁) [Arb. Beijing] 1 (2005) (China); Chen Fang (陈芳), *Woguo Chengren Linshi Zhongcai de Yingran Xing Fenxi* (我国承认临时仲裁的应然性分析) [*Analysis on Why China Should Recognize Ad Hoc Arbitration*], 4 Lilun Guancha (理论观察) [Theoretic Observation] 128 (2006) (China); Huang Shan (黄珊), *Woguo Jianli Linshi Zhongcai Zhidu de Sikao* (我国建立临时仲裁制度的思考) [*On the Establishment of China's Adhockery [sic] Arbitration System*], 12 Ha'erbin Xueyuan Xuebao (哈尔滨学院学报) [J. Harbin U.] 52 (2006) (China); Hao Haiqing (郝海青), *Zai Woguo Jianli Linshi Zhongcai Zhidu de Falü Sikao* (在我国建立临时仲裁制度的法律思考) [*Legal Thinking on Establishing Ad Hoc Arbitration System in China*], 2 Zhongguo Haiyang Daxue Xuebao (Shehui Kexue Ban) (中国海洋大学学报(社会科学版)) [J. Ocean Univ. China (Soc. Sci.)] 95 (2003) (China) (for opinions supporting such legitimization). *But see, e.g.*, Liu Maoliang (刘茂亮), *Linshi Zhongcai Yingdang Huanxing* (临时仲裁应当缓行) [*Ad Hoc Arbitration Should be on Hold*], 1 (北京仲裁) Beijing Zhongcai [Arb. Beijing] 8 (2005) (China); Ye Xiaochun (叶晓春), *Lun Zhongguo Dui Linshi Zhongcai Zhidu Yingyou de Lixing yu Taidu* (论中国对临时仲裁制度应有的理性与态度) [*China's Proper Rationality and Attitude Towards Ad Hoc Arbitration System*], 5 Yunnan Caimao Xueyuan Xuebao (Shehui Kexue Ban) (云南财贸学院学报(社会科学版)) [J. Yunnan Fin. & Econ. U.] 116 (2006) (China); Gong Xiaoning (宫晓凝), *Qianxi Linshi Zhongcai Zhidu Zai Woguo de Goujian* (浅析临时仲裁制度在我国的构建) [*Analysis on the Construction of Ad Hoc Arbitration System in China*], 30 Fazhi yu Shehui (法制与社会) [Legal Sys. & Soc'y] 53 (2008) (China) (for opinions against such legitimization).

do so. Moreover, in the field of international commercial arbitration, the world is closely connected. A national law's special or bizarre provisions and practices, like the preclusion of ad hoc arbitration under Chinese law, may create complex scenarios and produce unexpected outcomes through its dissonance with the international system. As a result, the current Chinese law's hostility towards ad hoc arbitration may become a considerable uncertainty and possibly a deterring factor for foreign business entities.[7] Therefore, in order to construct a complete, stable, flexible, and efficient arbitration system that will help China further develop its economy, China should bring its law into line with international practice and fully legitimize ad hoc arbitration.

Last but not least, apart from providing service to businesses and industries, arbitration is an industry itself. Many countries and regions in the world are actively developing and implementing strategies towards becoming leaders in the arbitration industry with the hope that this will generate income for the country as a whole.[8] If China fully endorses ad hoc arbitration, one can naturally assume this will bring more business for its arbitration practitioners, the entire legal service industry, and potentially many related services including hotel and entertainment industries. Business opportunities like these will certainly benefit China's economy. In fact, the Chinese arbitration industry has already made attempts to incorporate ad hoc arbitration. In 2017, China Online Arbitration Alliance, initiated and spearheaded by Guangzhou Arbitration Commission, issued the China Internet Arbitration Alliance Rule for Bridging Ad Hoc Arbitration and Institutional Arbitration.[9] In this set of rules, parties in an ad hoc arbitration can choose to convert their ad hoc arbitration procedure into an institutional arbitration procedure.[10] The arbitration institution chosen by the parties will confirm the award rendered by the ad hoc tribunal and convert it into an institutional award.[11] This clearly indicates a significant amount of interest among the Chinese arbitration industry to expand into the ad hoc arbitration territory.

7 At the very least, the PRC Arbitration Law has prompted numerous international law firms to write guides to advise their clients on the potential pitfalls of arbitration in China. While it is undoubtedly impossible to calculate the added cost of these undertakings, one can reasonably assume that such efforts have consumed significant energy and resources solely because of China's unusual position against ad hoc arbitration. *See generally, e.g.*, CHINESE ARBITRATION: A SELECTION OF PITFALLS (Ass'n for Int'l Arbitration ed. 2009); JINGZHOU TAO, ARBITRATION LAW AND PRACTICE IN CHINA 1 (2d ed. 2008).

8 *See, e.g.*, Michael Hwang et al., *National Report for Singapore (2015)*, *in* ICCA INTERNATIONAL HANDBOOK ON COMMERCIAL ARBITRATION 1, 2 (Jan Paulsson and Lise Bosman eds., 1984, Supp. No. 86, Oct. 2015).

9 *See* China Internet Arbitration Alliance Rule for Bridging Ad Hoc Arbitration and Institutional Arbitration, China Internet Arbitration Alliance (effective as of Sept. 19, 2017), http://www.gzac.org/WEB_CN/AboutInfo.aspx?AboutType=4&KeyID=081cc689-cb45-4c1a-8ac9-62caa8e5a600.

10 *See id.* art. 22.

11 *See id.* art. 23.

II China can have ad hoc arbitration

A Doubts are unnecessary

Many scholars have advocated incorporating ad hoc arbitration into the Chinese arbitration system. They find China's arbitration system incomplete and support legitimizing ad hoc arbitration because of its various advantages.[12] Some others, however, have expressed concerns or cautions and were particularly unsure about whether Chinese society is ready for ad hoc arbitration. They argued, among other things, that ad hoc arbitration is not practical in China because it will be difficult for Chinese parties to find good arbitrators without assistance provided by arbitration institutions; that institutional arbitration can be very flexible and therefore there is no need for ad hoc arbitration; that the lack of a mature credit system in China means some parties may engage in bad faith practices which will result in the failure of the ad hoc arbitration proceeding; and that some parties may form a conspiracy and participate in a fake ad hoc arbitration for purposes of money laundering and embezzlement of state assets.[13]

These arguments and concerns against legitimizing ad hoc arbitration under Chinese law are unpersuasive or unnecessary. First, no one cares more about the quality of the arbitrators and having a just and fair proceeding than the parties themselves. They will never give up until they find the right person to hear and decide their dispute. Given the current large body of lawyers and arbitration practitioners in China, as well as the professional advice that parties can receive from their counsel, there is no need to worry about parties being unable to find an appropriate arbitrator.

Second, it is correct that institutional arbitration can also be very flexible, particularly given that many institutions in the world have adopted rules that

12 *See, e.g.*, Wang & Song, *supra* note 6; Chen, *supra* note 6; Huang, *supra* note 6; Hao, *supra* note 6; ZhangXinquan (张心泉) & Zhang Shengcui (张圣翠), *Lun Woguo Linshi Zhongcai Zhidu de Goujian* (论我国临时仲裁制度的构建) [*On the Establishment of Ad Hoc Arbitration System in China*], 4 HUADONG ZHENGFA DAXUE XUEBAO (华东政法大学学报) [J. EAST CHINA UNIV. POL. SCI. & L.] 149 (2010); Li Changchao (李昌超) & Chen Lei (陈磊), *Lun Woguo Linshi Zhongcai Zhidu zhi Goujian* (论我国临时仲裁制度之构建) [*Establishment of Ad Hoc Arbitration System in China*], 1 HUBEI JINGJI XUEYUAN XUEBAO (湖北经济学院学报) [J. HUBEI UNIV. ECON.] 116 (2014); Yang ling (杨玲), *Wanjin Zhongguo Zhongcai Zhidu de Biange yu Fazhan Qushi* (晚近中国仲裁制度的变革与发展趋势) [*Reform and Trend of Development of Arbitration System of Modern and Contemporary China*], 2 NANTONG DAXUE XUEBAO (SHEHUI KEXUE BAN) (南通大学学报(社会科学版)) [J. NANTONG UNIV. (SOC. SCI.)] 37 (2016).

13 *See, e.g.*, Liu, *supra* note 6; Ye, *supra* note 6; Gong, *supra* note 6; Liu Xiaohong (刘晓红) & Zhou Qi (周祺), *Woguo Jianli Linshi Zhongcai Libi Fenxi he Shiji Xuanze* (我国建立临时仲裁利弊分析和时机选择) [*The Pros and Cons and Timing for Introduction of Ad hoc Arbitration in the P.R.C.*], 9 NANJING SHEHUI KEXUE (南京社会科学) [NANJING J. SOC. SCI.] 95 (2012); Zhang Zitan (张紫檀), *Dui zai Woguo Goujian Linshi Zhongcai Zhidu de Zaisikao* (对在我国构建临时仲裁制度的再思考) [*System of Ad Hoc Arbitration in China*], 3 XI'AN WENLI XUEYUAN XUEBAO (SHEHUI KEXUE BAN) (西安文理学院学报(社会科学版)) [J. XI'AN UNIV. (SOC. SCI.)] 56 (2013).

allow a very high level of flexibility to attract parties.[14] However, the issue does not lie in whether ad hoc is more flexible than institutional arbitration but in whether parties are free to choose the dispute resolution mechanism that they find best suits their needs. Parties may have various reasons to choose ad hoc arbitration. No matter what the reason is, in a complete and effective arbitration system, they should be allowed to use ad hoc arbitration if that is what they want.

Third, while it is true that ad hoc arbitration will run more smoothly when parties cooperate with each other in good faith and may encounter a certain level of difficulty if one party tries to resist and obstruct arbitration, as discussed in previous chapters, if parties use caution when drafting their arbitration agreement, they can avoid future problems in the proceeding and have a successful ad hoc arbitration. Also, a party trying to resist arbitration will do so in both ad hoc and institutional arbitration. It will likely engage in delaying tactics in other dispute resolution mechanisms, such as litigation, as well. This problem is not specific to ad hoc arbitration and therefore should not be the reason for its continuing preclusion.

Finally and similarly, it is possible that ad hoc arbitration can be abused, and so can other dispute resolution mechanisms. The lawmakers could establish a better supervision system over state interest, which will hopefully prevent conspiracies to embezzle state assets via all channels. Ad hoc arbitration should not become the scapegoat.

B Mediation offers a good example

There is yet another reason why Chinese society could very easily accept ad hoc arbitration. Despite never having ad hoc arbitration in the history of its legal system, China is very familiar with its "sibling," i.e. mediation.

Mediation has long been a part of Chinese society.[15] In ancient times Chinese people were already practicing mediation in the Zhou dynasty (1046–256 B.C).[16]

14 *Soo* Gary B. Born, International Commercial Arbitration 85–86 (2d ed. 2014).

15 *See* Hou Yuanzhen (侯元贞) & Liao Yong'an (廖永安), *Lun Woguo Renmin Tiaojie Zhidu de Bianqian — Jiufen Jiejueguan, Tiaojie Zuzhe he Tiaojie Gongneng* (论我国人民调解制度的变迁——纠纷解决观、调解组织和调解功能) [*Concept of Dispute Resolution, Organization of Mediation and Function of Mediation: On the Vicissitudes of People's Mediation System in China*], 2 Shihezi Daxue Xuebao (Zhexue Shehui Kexue Ban) (石河子大学学报(哲学社会科学版)) [J. Shihezi Univ. (Phil. & Soc. Sci.)] 44, 44–45 (2016); Huang E (黄娥), *Lishi de Chuancheng: Zhongguo Gudai Tiaochu Zhidu — Jianyu Xiandai Tiaojie Zhidu Bijiao* (历史的传承: 中国古代调处制度——兼与现代调解制度比较) [*The Historical Preservation: Mediation System in Ancient China — Comparing with Modern Mediation System*], 4 Zhongnan Caijing Zhengfa Daxue Yanjiusheng Xuebao (中南财经政法大学研究生学报) [J. Postgraduate Zhongnan Univ. Econ. & L.] 128, 128–29 (2007); John S. Mo, *Understanding the Role of People's Mediation in the Age of Globalization*, 17 Asia Pac. L. Rev. 75, 82 (2009); Zeng Xianyi, *Mediation in China — Past and Present*, 17 Asia Pac. L. Rev. 1, 2–7 (2009).

16 *See* Hou & Liao, *supra* note 15, at 44–45; Huang, *supra* note 15, at 128.

Since then, mediation has always played an important role in traditional Chinese culture and community. One of the main reasons for mediation's popularity in traditional China is its compatibility with many classic Chinese schools of thoughts including, most importantly, Confucianism.[17] Confucianism was the mainstream ideology throughout most parts of Imperial China.[18] It has fundamentally shaped Chinese culture in many important ways, and arguably still has a major impact on today's Chinese society.[19] At the center of Confucianism lies the concept of harmony. According to this concept, in an ideal society, people should live in harmony with one another and there is no need for litigation.[20] Therefore, when disputes do arise in a real world, the best practice would be to resolve them in a non-confrontational way that still preserves a litigation-free world.[21] Mediation obviously makes a perfect tool for this theory. In addition, mediation also has an educational function, in the sense that disputed parties can learn about relevant morality in the process, which will again help achieve a litigation-free society in the long run.[22] Apart from the ideological reasons, there might also be economic or social reasons for mediation's popularity in traditional China.[23] For instance, China is a very large country, and has been built on agriculture throughout its history. Most people live in small communities formed by kinships and closed social ties and they seldom leave. As a result, mediation offers a conveniently accessible and economically low-cost solution to disputes among people in the small communities and is perhaps best at preserving their important relationships with a focus on putting the dispute behind them and moving forward. All these reasons made mediation a very important dispute resolution mechanism in traditional China that lasted until the beginning of the twentieth century.

Mediation in traditional China came in various forms. The government officials, or judges,[24] mediated in their official capacity when they heard disputes in litigation. Senior family members and local chiefs mediated disputes within

17 *See* Hou & Liao, *supra* note 15, at 45, 47; Huang, *supra* note 15, at 129–31; Stanley Lubman, *Mao and Mediation: Politics and Dispute Resolution in Communist China*, 55 CAL. L. REV. 1284, 1290–91 (1967); Zeng, *supra* note 15, at 7–8.

18 *See* GEOFFREY MACCORMACK, THE SPIRIT OF TRADITIONAL CHINESE LAW 3–4 (1996); John H. Matheson, *Convergence, Culture, and Contract Law in China,* 15 MINN. J. INT'L L. 329, 372 (2006); Patricia Pattison & Daniel Herron, *The Mountains Are High and the Emperor is Far Away: Sanctity of Contract Law in China,* 40 AM. BUS. L.J. 459, 478 (2003).

19 *See* Anne M. Burr, *Law and Harmony: An In-Depth Look at China's First American-Style Law School,* 28 UCLA PAC. BASIN L.J. 25, 34 (2010); Matheson, *supra* note 18, at 372; Pattison & Herron, *supra* note 18, at 478.

20 *See* JOHN KING FAIRBANK, THE UNITED STATES AND CHINA 118–20 (4th ed. 1979); Hou & Liao, *supra* note 15, at 45; Huang, *supra* note 15, at 128.

21 *See* Burr, *supra* note 19, at 34; Hou & Liao, *supra* note 15, at 45; Huang, *supra* note 15, at 128.

22 *See* Hou & Liao, *supra* note 15, at 47–48; Huang, *supra* note 15, at 131.

23 *See* Hou & Liao, *supra* note 15, at 48; Huang, *supra* note 15, at 130.

24 In imperial China, there was no separation of powers. As a result, there were no separate courts. The functions of courts were carried out by executive officials. *See* ESTHER LAM, CHINA AND THE WTO: A LONG MARCH TOWARDS THE RULE OF LAW 13 (2009); Hayden Windrow, *A Short*

their own communities. There was also cooperation between these official and unofficial processes. When a judge heard a dispute and felt it could be resolved via mediation by the parties' family or community, he could refer the case to their family or community leader and recommend mediation.

Mediation has also played an active role in contemporary China. The Republic of China adopted mediation in its laws.[25] Perhaps more important and relevant for the discussions on the current Chinese legal system, mediation always takes on a central role in the political and legal processes adopted by the Communist Party of China (CPC). Starting from the 1920s, the CPC began using mediation as the predominant dispute resolution mechanism in the area that it controlled.[26] After the founding of the PRC, the CPC further reinforced mediation's position. Mediation was frequently used by all branches of the government, including by courts in the litigation process. The Chinese government also created a new, free-standing mediation system called "People's Mediation."[27] Under this system, many People's Mediation Commissions were created at the local level across the country. These commissions could mediate disputes among parties. In the planned economy era, however, this mediation system was gradually converted to a political tool to spread communist ideology, with its dispute resolution function marginalized.[28] With the reform and open-up policy in place in the late 1970s, mediation was reinstated with its original function of dispute resolution.[29]

Nowadays, mediation is still a centerpiece of the PRC legal system. First, there is the free-standing People's Mediation system, in which parties may submit their disputes to a People's Mediation Commission and seek amicable resolution.[30] Furthermore, administrative bodies of the government frequently mediate between parties when they deal with certain kinds of disputes, such as labor disputes, patent disputes, consumer disputes, traffic accident disputes, and so

---

History of Law, Norms, and Social Control in Imperial China, 7 ASIAN-PAC. L. & POL'Y J. 244, 246 (2006)

25 *See* Wen Bingcun (温丙存) & Xing Hongfei (邢鸿飞), *Tiaojie de Bainian Shanbian: Benyuan, Yihua, Xinsheng yu Chonggou—Jiyu Minshi Jiufen Tiaochu Shijian de Lishi Kaocha (1912—2012)* (调解的百年嬗变：本原、异化、新生与重构——基于民事纠纷调处实践的历史考察(1912—2012)) [*The Century Evolution of Mediation: Principle, Heterization, Rebirth, Reconfiguration*], 2 ZHONGGUO NONGYE DAXUE XUEBAO (SHEHUI KEXUE BAN) (中国农业大学学报(社会科学版)) [CHINA AGRIC. UNIV. J. SOC. SCI.] 68, 68–70 (2014).

26 *See* Hou & Liao, *supra* note 15, at 45–46; Wang Dandan (王丹丹), *Falü Zhidu de Gongneng ji Qi Yihua — Renmin Tiaojie Zhidu Yanbian Shi* (法律制度的功能及其异化——人民调解制度演变史) [*The Function of the Legal System and Its Alienation — Evolution of the People's Mediation Syestem* [sic]], 6 ZHENGFA LUNTAN (政法论坛) [TRIB. POL. SCI. & L.] 126, 127–29 (2016).

27 *See* Hou & Liao, *supra* note 15, at 46–47; Wang, *supra* note 26, at 129–30.

28 *See* Hou & Liao, *supra* note 15, at 47; Lubman, *supra* note 17, at 1339–49; Wang, *supra* note 26, at 131–34; Wen & Xing, *supra* note 25, at 70–71.

29 *See* Hou & Liao, *supra* note 15, at 47; Wen & Xing, *supra* note 25, at 71–74.

30 *See* Renmin Tiaojie Fa (人民调解法) [People's Mediation Law] (promulgated by the Standing Comm. Nat'l People's Cong., Aug. 28, 2010, effective Jan. 1, 2011) (China); Mo, *supra* note 15, at 78.

on.[31] Perhaps most importantly, Chinese courts and judges also heavily rely on mediation in the litigation process.

The current PRC Civil Procedure Law contains sophisticated provisions on mediation.[32] Judges can mediate at all stages of the litigation process, and are often encouraged to do so whenever it is feasible.[33] In the last decade, there has been a political campaign to promote mediation in the adjudication process.[34] Some Chinese courts even encourage judges to achieve the goal of "zero judgment" and evaluate judges on the basis of how many of the cases they hear were successfully resolved by mediation.[35] Many scholars have voiced their strong concerns about and opposition to this mediation-supremacy system, because they find it contrary to the rule of law principles and see it as damaging to the Chinese judiciary.[36]

31 *See* Fan Yu (范愉), *Dangdai Zhongguo Feisusong Jiufen Jiejue Jizhi de Wanshan yu Fazhan* (当代中国非诉讼纠纷解决机制的完善与发展) [*Perfection and Development of Alternative Dispute Resolution Mechanisms in Modern China*], 1 Xuehai (学海) [Academia Bimestrie] 77, 83 (2003); Peng Zhen (彭震), *Lun Woguo Xingzheng Tiaojie Xieyi de Falü Xiaoli* (论我国行政调解协议的法律效力) [Research on the Force of Law to Administrative Mediation Agreements in China], 6 Zhongnan Caijing Zhengfa Daxue Yanjiusheng Xuebao (中南财经政法大学研究生学报) [J. Postgraduate Zhongnan Univ. Econ. & L.] 155, 155 (2009); Wang Dongwei (王东伟), Lun Woguo Xingzheng Zhengyi de Xingzheng Tiaojie Jiejue Jizhi (论我国行政争议的行政调解解决机制) [On Our Country's Administrative Mediation Mechanisms in Administrative Dispute Resolution], 3 Huanan Ligong Daxue Xuebao (Shehui Kexue Ban) (华南理工大学学报(社会科学版)) [J. South China Univ. Tech. (Sco. Sci.)] 92, 92 (2016).

32 *See* Minshi Susong Fa (民事诉讼法) [Civil Procedure Law] (promulgated by Nat'l People's Cong., Apr. 9, 1991, effective Apr. 9, 1991, rev. June. 27, 2017), chap. 8 (China).

33 *See id.* arts. 122, 133, 142, 172; Zuigao Renmin Fayuan Guanyu Jinyibu Guanche "Tiaojie Youxian, Tiaopan Jiehe" Gongzuo Yuanze de Ruogan Yijian (最高人民法院关于进一步贯彻"调解优先、调判结合"工作原则的若干意见) [Opinions on Certain Issues Concerning the Further Implementation of the "Priority of Mediation, Combination of Mediation and Adjudication" Principle] (promulgated by the Sup. People's Ct., June 7, 2010, effective June 7, 2010), art. II(4) (China); Zuigao Renmin Fayuan Guanyu Renmin Fayuan Minshi Tiaojie Gongzuo Ruogan Wenti de Guiding (最高人民法院关于人民法院民事调解工作若干问题的规定) [Regulation on Certain Issues Concerning Mediation in the People's Courts] (promulgated by the Sup. People's Ct., Sept. 16, 2004, effective Nov. 1, 2004, amended Dec. 16, 2008), arts. 1, 6 (China); Wang Liming, *Characteristics of China's Judicial Mediation System*, 17 Asia Pac. L. Rev. 67, 72 (2009).

34 *See* Wang Fuhua (王福华), *Da Tiaojie Shiye zhong de Shenpan* (大调解视野中的审判) [*Adjudication from the Perspective of Grand Mediation*], 4 Huadong Zhengfa Daxue Xuebao (华东政法大学学报) [ECUPL J.] 102, 102–06 (2012); Zhang Xianchu, *Rethinking the Mediation Campaign*, 2 J. Comp. L. 44, 44–51 (2015).

35 *See* Li Bingshuo (李炳烁), *Lun Sifa Tiaojie Guifanhua de Shijian Wenti yu Lujing Xuanze* (论司法调解规范化的实践问题与路径选择) [*On the Practical Problems of Judicial Mediation Standardization and the Path Chosen*], 12 Faxue Zazhi (法学杂志) [L. Sci. Mag.] 52, 53 (2016); Suli (苏力), *Guanyu Nengdong Sifa yu Da Tiaojie* (关于能动司法与大调解) [*Judicial Activism and Extensive Mediation*], 1 Zhongguo Faxue (中国法学) [China Legal Sci.] 5, 9 (2010); Tian Ping'an (田平安) & Lü Hui (吕辉), *"Tiaojie Youxian" Zhiyi Lun* ("调解优先"质疑论) [*Questions About "Mediation Priority"*], Henan Daxue Xuebao (Shehui Kexue Ban) (河南大学学报(社会科学版)) [J. Henan Univ. (Sco. Sci.)] 54, 56 (2013).

36 *See e.g.*, Li Hao (李浩), *Tiaojie Gui Tiaojie, Shenpan Gui Shenpan: Minshi Shenpan zhong de Tiaoshen Fenli* (调解规调解, 审判归审判: 民事审判中的调审分立) [*Mediation Is Mediation,*

The above discussions indicate that mediation is nothing novel to Chinese legal culture and the legal system. Chinese people and legal elites are very familiar with mediation as a traditional, common, and efficient dispute resolution mechanism. At the same time, arbitration, particularly ad hoc arbitration, is in fact similar to mediation in many aspects.

They first share a common origin. In the early time of human society, when two parties had a dispute that they did not want to resolve by force, they would likely find a third person who they both considered neutral, just, and knowledgeable and let that person hear and decide their dispute. Because this was a time when concepts like law, government, or court did not exist, the third person's decision would not become "legal binding" on the parties in the sense that we understand it nowadays. However, the disputed parties would likely still be willing to accept the result and perform accordingly, due to many concerns such as moral obligations or the prestigious and authoritative status of the decision maker. This dispute resolution mechanism can be seen as the origin of both arbitration and mediation.

It is hard to distinguish the two from each other at this stage because the biggest difference between arbitration and mediation, at least according to these concepts as understood in the Western world today, is that an arbitration award is legally binding upon the parties while the mediation result is not.[37] Although mediation carries with it the effect and legal force of a contract, it will only be enforceable by a court after a substantive litigation process. Arbitration, on the other hand, is a quasi-judicial process. Therefore, an arbitration award is "directly" enforceable by a court and is subject to only procedural challenges but not those on its merits. In case of a court-conducted mediation, for example, the mediation result can be formalized by a judgment or order, which will become legally binding on the parties.[38] But in this context, it is the judicial act of issuing a judgment and not the mediation itself that makes the final result binding.

That being said, mediation in China is perhaps slightly different from the Western concept of mediation. It always has a semi-official status, which means that it is binding on the parties to some extent.[39] As discussed above, in both traditional and communist China, mediation would take place under an official ideology, either Confucianism or communism, that dictated all the norms of Chinese society at the time. In addition, government or courts would frequently

Adjudication Is Adjudication: Separation of Mediation and Adjudication in Civil Cases], 3 Zhongguo Faxue (中国法学) [China Legal Sci.] 5 (2013); Li, *supra* note 35; Long Zongzhi (龙宗智), *Guanyu "Da Tiaojie" he "Nengdong Sifa" de Sikao* (关于"大调解"和"能动司法"的思考) [*Thinking About "Grand Mediation" and "Judicial Activism"*], 4 Zhengfa Luntan (政法论坛) [Trib. Pol. Sci. & L.] 98 (2010); Suli, *supra* note 35; Tian & Lü, *supra* note 35; Wang, *supra* note 34; Zhang, *supra* note 34.

37 *See* Born, *supra* note 14, at 272.

38 *See, e.g.*, Carolina Secondo Magila, *Why Not Mediation*, 7 Disp. Resol. Int'l 159, 167 (2013).

39 *See* Hou & Liao, *supra* note 15, at 45; Huang, *supra* note 15, at 131.

use mediation in their official capacity, or direct an unofficial body to conduct the mediation. From this perspective, they could be seen as binding upon the parties in a de facto manner. Therefore, mediation in China is very similar to arbitration, which may make ad hoc arbitration easily acceptable to the Chinese people.

Moreover, mediation and ad hoc arbitration are both extra-judicial, so both their proceedings are usually informal and flexible. A very important reason why parties choose to mediate or arbitrate their dispute can be that they want to shy away from the formal and rigid litigation procedures. Therefore, it is reasonable to expect that Chinese parties will find ad hoc arbitration comfortable and easy to work with because of its informality and flexibility.

As a result, because of the shared origin and the many similar features between ad hoc arbitration and mediation, although ad hoc arbitration has never been part of the Chinese legal system or legal culture, it may not be completely alien to Chinese people and legal elites. Given mediation's popularity in Chinese society, it is reasonable to expect that Chinese parties will find ad hoc arbitration familiar and easily acceptable.

III Towards a complete ad hoc arbitration system

A The SPC's role

As the highest court in China, the SPC interprets Chinese law, including its preclusion of ad hoc arbitration. Its stance on this issue, however, is not always coherent. On the one hand, it has tried to be more tolerant towards ad hoc arbitration in many aspects. On the other hand, it sometimes interprets Chinese law's institutional requirement in an unnecessarily strict way.

1 Pro-arbitration stances

The SPC has taken some steps that can be seen as pro-arbitration when it comes to the ad hoc issue. As discussed in earlier chapters, when determining the validity of an ad hoc arbitration agreement, the SPC has adopted a choice-of-law rule under which it does not always apply Chinese law. This choice-of-law rule has maximized the chances for a Chinese court to enforce an ad hoc arbitration agreement. In its new judicial interpretation, the SPC also explicitly added a validity preferring approach into this choice-of-law rule. It specified that when deciding on the law to govern the validity of an arbitration agreement, Chinese courts should choose the law that will validate the agreement.[40] In any event, as a result of the SPC's pro-arbitration choice-of-law

40 *See* Zuigao Renmin Fayuan Guanyu Shenli Zhongcai Sifa Shencha Anjian Ruogan Wenti de Guiding (最高人民法院关于审理仲裁司法审查案件若干问题的规定) [Regulation on Certain Issues Concerning the Adjudication of Cases Involving Judicial Review of Arbitration] (promulgated by the Sup. People's Ct., Dec. 26, 2017, effective Jan. 1, 2018), art. 14 (China).

rule, many ad hoc arbitration agreements are indeed enforced by Chinese courts in practice.

Since 2013, the Chinese central government has established a number of Free Trade Zones in many cities across China, including, e.g., Shanghai and Tianjin.[41] Businesses that operate in these Free Trade Zones enjoy many special, flexible, and usually preferential governmental policies regarding foreign investment and trade. This government strategy aims at deepening China's reforms and opening-up policies, promoting China's economic development, and furthering China's participation in the globalization process.[42] In 2016, the SPC formulated a judicial interpretation, which provides that Chinese courts should validate an arbitration agreement that calls for ad hoc arbitration in mainland China as long as the agreement is concluded between businesses that are both registered inside Free Trade Zones.[43] Although the SPC did not specify many related issues, such as how the resulting award should be enforced or challenged, this is clearly a welcoming sign that the SPC is open to legitimizing ad hoc arbitration seated in China to the largest possible extent.

2 Overly Strict Interpretation

More often than not, however, the SPC does not support ad hoc arbitration seated in China. This is perhaps understandable because the SPC probably feels bound by the clear provision under Chinese law and thus cannot support ad hoc arbitration seated in China. To make matters worse, the SPC sometimes interprets and applies Chinese law's institutional arbitration requirement in an overly strict manner, which could cause many undesirable and unnecessary results.

In international arbitration practice, it is very common for an arbitration agreement to refer to an arbitration institution's rules instead of the institution

41 *See, e.g.*, Guowuyuan Guanyu Yinfa Zhongguo (Shanghai) Ziyou Maoyi Shiyanqu Zongti Fang'an de Tongzhi (国务院关于印发中国(上海)自由贸易试验区总体方案的通知) [Notice on Issuing the Framework Plan for China (Shanghai) Pilot Free Trade Zone] (promulgated by the St. Council, Sept. 18, 2013, effective Sept. 18, 2013) (China); Guowuyuan Guanyu Yinfa Zhongguo (Tianjin) Ziyou Maoyi Shiyanqu Zongti Fang'an de Tongzhi (国务院关于印发中国(天津)自由贸易试验区总体方案的通知) [Notice on Issuing the Framework Plan for China (Tianjin) Pilot Free Trade Zone] (promulgated by the St. Council, Apr. 8, 2015, effective Apr. 8, 2015) (China).

42 *See, e.g.*, Guowuyuan Guanyu Yinfa Zhongguo (Shanghai) Ziyou Maoyi Shiyanqu Zongti Fang'an de Tongzhi (国务院关于印发中国(上海)自由贸易试验区总体方案的通知) [Notice on Issuing the Framework Plan for China (Shanghai) Pilot Free Trade Zone] (promulgated by the St. Council, Sept. 18, 2013, effective Sept. 18, 2013) (China).

43 *See* Zuigao Renimn Fayuan Guanyu wei Ziyou Maoyi Shiyanqu Jianshe Tigong Sifa Baozhang de Yijian (最高人民法院关于为自由贸易试验区建设提供司法保障的意见) [Opinions on Providing Judicial Safeguard for Building Pilot Free Trade Zones] (promulgated by the Sup. People's Ct., Dec. 30, 2016, effective Dec. 30, 2016), art. IV(9) (China).

itself.[44] This is apparent from the standard arbitration clauses drafted by various arbitration institutions. For example, the standard arbitration clause recommended by the International Chamber of Commerce International Court of Arbitration (ICC), one of the most prestigious arbitration institutions in the world, reads as follows: "All disputes arising out of or in connection with the present contract shall be finally settled under the Rules of Arbitration of the International Chamber of Commerce by one or more arbitrators appointed in accordance with the said Rules."[45]

This standard arbitration clause is accepted by most of the world's jurisdictions as a valid arbitration agreement.[46] However, the SPC used to take a different position. In 2004, it struck down an arbitration agreement that said "ICC Rules, Shanghai shall apply" reasoning that Chinese law requires that parties appoint an arbitration institution in their arbitration agreement, and that a mere choice of arbitration rules is not equivalent to a designation of arbitration institution.[47] It is true that parties can ask a different arbitration institution to administer their arbitration under the ICC Rules or even conduct an ad hoc arbitration and ask the tribunal to apply ICC Rules to the largest extent possible. Such an arrangement, however, should be an exception which requires explicit wording in the arbitration agreement rather than the presumed meaning of the wording as quoted above. Therefore, this decision was clearly overly strict. Two years later in 2006, the SPC promulgated the Interpretation on Certain Issues Concerning the Application of the "Arbitration Law of the People's Republic of China" (SPC Arbitration Law Interpretation), which provided that when parties only agree on applicable arbitration rules but do not specify the arbitration institution, the arbitration agreement shall be valid if an arbitration institution can be ascertained from the agreed arbitration rules.[48] While this

44 *See* Born, *supra* note 14, at 1388; Fouchard, Gaillard, Goldman on International Commercial Arbitration 179–80 (Emmanuel Gaillard & John Savage eds., 1999); Julian D. M. Lew, Loukas A. Mistelis & Stefan M. Kröll, Comparative International Commercial Arbitration 171–72 (2003).

45 *Arbitration Clause—Standard ICC Arbitration Clause*, Int'l Chamber Com., https://iccwbo.org/dispute-resolution-services/arbitration/arbitration-clause/ (last visited Jan. 29, 2018).

46 *See* Yves Derains & Eric A. Schwartz, A Guide to the ICC Rules of Arbitration 388 (2d ed. 2005) (in discussing the use of the ICC's standard arbitration clause, the authors identify China as a notable exception to the general practice that an arbitration agreement will be valid even though the standard clause refers only to the institution's rules.).

47 *See* Deguo Xupulin Guoji Youxian Zeren Gongsi yu Wuxi Woke Tongyong Gongcheng Xiangjiao Youxian Gongsi Shenqing Queren Zhongcai Xieyi Xiaoli An (德国旭普林国际有限责任公司与无锡沃可通用工程橡胶有限公司申请确认仲裁协议效力案) [Züblin Int'l GmbH v. Wuxi Woco Gen. Rubber Eng'g Co. Ltd.] (People's Ct. of Wuxi High-tech Indus. Dev. Dist., Sept. 2, 2004) (China).

48 *See* Zuigao Renmin Fayuan Guanyu Shiyong "Zhonghua Renmin Gongheguo Zhongcai Fa" Ruogan Wenti de Jieshi (最高人民法院关于适用《中华人民共和国仲裁法》若干问题的解释) [Interpretation on Certain Issues Concerning the Application of the "Arbitration Law of the People's Republic of China"] (promulgated by the Sup. People's Ct., Aug. 23, 2006, effective Sept. 8, 2006), art. 5 (China).

appeared encouraging for the case just discussed, the SPC in 2009 once again struck down another arbitration agreement calling for arbitration under ICC Rules, reasoning that no arbitration institution could be ascertained from the ICC Rules.[49] Given that the ICC is responsible for many administrative and supervisory duties under the then applying ICC Rules, this holding by the SPC was again overly strict.[50] The problem was not finally resolved until the 2012 ICC Rules came into effect. The 2012 Rules states that "[t]he [ICC] is the only body authorized to administer arbitrations under the Rules . . ." and that "[b]y agreeing to arbitration under the Rules, the parties have accepted that the arbitration shall be administered by the [ICC]."[51] In 2013, the SPC confirmed that when parties agreed on the ICC Rules but did not choose any other arbitration institution to administer their arbitration, the ICC could be ascertained as the arbitration institution from the choice of the ICC Rules.[52] Therefore, the SPC validated such an arbitration agreement.

Realizing Chinese courts' overly strict position on this issue, the ICC recommends a special standard arbitration clause for parties who intend to arbitrate under ICC Rules in mainland China, which reads:

> All disputes arising out of or in connection with the present contract *shall be submitted to the International Court of Arbitration of the International Chamber of Commerce* and shall be finally settled under the Rules

49 *See* Zuigao Renmin Fayuan Guanyu Xiaxin Dianzi Gufen Youxian Gongsi yu Bilishi Chanpin Youxian Gongsi Queren Jingxiao Xieyi Zhongcai Tiaokuan Xiaoli de Qingshi de Fuhan (最高人民法院关于夏新电子股份有限公司与比利时产品有限公司确认经销协议仲裁条款效力的请示的复函) [Reply Letter to the Request for Instructions Concerning Determination of the Validity of the Distribution Agreement's Arbitration Clause in the Case Between Amoi Tech. Co., Ltd and Société de Production Belge AG] (promulgated by the Sup. People's Ct., Mar. 20, 2009, effective Mar. 20, 2009) (China).

50 *See generally* Int'l Chamber of Commerce, *Rules of Arbitration of the International Chamber of Commerce* (effective Jan. 1, 1998), *reprinted in* Tibor Várady et al., Documents Supplements to International Commercial Arbitration: A Transnational Perspective 238 (4th ed. 2009).

51 Int'l Chamber of Commerce, *Rules of Arbitration of the International Chamber of Commerce* (effective Jan. 1, 2012), *reprinted in* Tibor Várady et al., Documents Supplements to International Commercial Arbitration: A Transnational Perspective 273 (5th ed. 2012). The same provisions were kept in the new 2017 ICC Rules. *See* Int'l Chamber of Commerce, *ICC Rules of Arbitration*, arts. 1(2) & 6(2) (effective Mar. 1, 2017), *available at* https://cdn.iccwbo.org/content/uploads/sites/3/2017/01/ICC-2017-Arbitration-and-2014-Mediation-Rules-english-version.pdf.pdf.

52 *See* Zuigao Renmin Fayuan Guanyu Ningboshi Beilun Licheng Runhuayou Youxian Gongsi yu Famowanchi Gongsi Maimai Hetong Jiufen Yi'an Zhongcai Tiaokuan Xiaoli Wenti Qingshi de Fuhan (最高人民法院关于宁波市北仑利成润滑油有限公司与法莫万驰公司买卖合同纠纷一案仲裁条款效力问题请示的复函) [Reply Letter to the Request for Instructions Concerning the Validity of the Arbitration Clause in the Sales Contract Dispute Case Between Ningbo Beilun Li Cheng Lubricating oil Co., Ltd. and Formal Venture Corp.] (promulgated by the Sup. People's Ct., Dec. 5, 2013, effective Dec. 5, 2013) (China).

of Arbitration of the International Chamber of Commerce by one or more arbitrators appointed in accordance with the said Rules.[53]

As a related issue, parties sometimes choose two arbitration institutions in their arbitration agreement and agree that any future dispute may be submitted to either one of them. Courts around the world usually allow such an arrangement and will generally give whoever is the claimant the chance to choose from the two previously agreed institutions.[54] Chinese courts, however, do not allow such a mechanism. According to the SPC Arbitration Law Interpretation, "[w]here two or more arbitration institutions are agreed in an arbitration agreement, the parties may agree to choose one of the arbitration institutions and apply for arbitration; where the parties cannot reach an agreement on the choice of arbitration institution, the arbitration agreement is invalid."[55] As a result, a party wishing to resist arbitration in such a situation may easily do so by refusing to reach a supplementary agreement to eliminate one of the two agreed institutions.

Despite the fact that a choice between two institutions may cause some minor practical difficulty, the arbitration agreement concluded between the parties does not logically conflict with the PRC Arbitration Law's requirement that arbitration must be institutional. By agreeing on two possible institutions, parties have clearly demonstrated their intent to arbitrate and their willingness to have their arbitration administered by an institution. This certainly satisfies Chinese law's institutional arbitration requirement. Additionally, there are ways to solve problems caused by naming two institutions in one arbitration agreement, such as giving whoever is the claimant the right to choose from the two agreed institutions. Therefore, there is no need to invalidate such an arbitration agreement. By requiring that parties must agree to eliminate one of the two appointed institutions after a dispute arises, the SPC has essentially redefined and expanded Chinese law's requirement on the appointment of "an institution" in an arbitration agreement to "only one institution."[56]

53 *Arbitration Clause—Other Recommendations*, INT'L CHAMBER COM., https://iccwbo.org/dispute-resolution-services/arbitration/arbitration-clause/ (last visited Jan. 29, 2018) (emphasis added).

54 *See* Weixia Gu, *The Changing Landscape of Arbitration Agreements in China: Has the SPC-Led Pro-Arbitration Move Gone Far Enough?*, 22 N.Y. INT'L L. REV. 1, 38 (2009); Norbert Horn, *The Arbitration Agreement in Light of Case Law of the UNCITRAL Model Law (Arts 7 and 8)*, 5 INT'L ARB. L. REV. 146, 149 (2005).

55 Zuigao Renmin Fayuan Guanyu Shiyong "Zhonghua Renmin Gongheguo Zhongcai Fa" Ruogan Wenti de Jieshi (最高人民法院关于适用《中华人民共和国仲裁法》若干问题的解释) [Interpretation on Certain Issues Concerning the Application of the "Arbitration Law of the People's Republic of China"] (promulgated by the Sup. People's Ct., Aug. 23, 2006, effective Sept. 8, 2006), art. 5 (China).

56 Nothing in the PRC Arbitration Law provides that parties must select only one particular institution in their arbitration agreement. *See generally* Zhongcai Fa (仲裁法) [Arbitration Law] (promulgated by the Standing Comm. Nat'l People's Cong., Aug. 31, 1994, effective Sept. 1, 1995, rev. Sept. 1, 2017) (China).

As a summary, the SPC has played a vital role in clarifying Chinese law's position on ad hoc arbitration. It has exercised its discretion in certain situations and enforced many ad hoc arbitration agreements and awards, either directly itself or by instructing lower level Chinese courts to do so. However, constrained by Chinese legislation, the SPC stopped short of fully supporting ad hoc arbitration and sometimes interpreted relevant laws in an overly strict manner. This indicates that the SPC cannot solve the ad hoc problem under Chinese law by itself. Any meaningful and complete solution has to happen via legislative action.

B Legislative action is the only choice

There are certainly prospects for revising the PRC Arbitration Law as well as other Chinese legislation related to arbitration and full legitimizing ad hoc arbitration. After all, the current arbitration legal framework built around the PRC Arbitration Law was only meant to be transitional. An NPC official once stated that issues relating to ad hoc arbitration could be further studied in practice, and the PRC Arbitration Law could be perfected "after common ground has been reached."[57] But how exactly can China do that?

Unsurprisingly, the first step should be to eliminate the requirement that parties must appoint an arbitration institution in their arbitration agreement. An arbitration agreement should be valid as long as the parties indicate a clear intention to arbitrate, irrespective of whether they agree to submit their dispute to an arbitration institution or an ad hoc tribunal. This is, however, only the beginning. The complete legitimization of ad hoc arbitration under Chinese law demands much more than simply getting rid of this requirement. The ad hoc issue relates to multiple sections of the PRC Arbitration Law, because Chinese lawmakers assumed that arbitration in China could only be institutional and designed many of the rules under that statute on that basis. For example, under the PRC Arbitration Law, the jurisdiction of a court in a set aside procedure is decided by the residence of the arbitration commission;[58] the jurisdiction, or arbitrability, issue is decided by the arbitration commission rather than the tribunal;[59] and the official seal of the arbitration commission must be affixed to the award.[60] Because of these interconnected rules within the statute, incorporation of ad hoc arbitration requires a complete and systematic revision of all relevant parts of the PRC Arbitration Law. Apart from this special arbitration statute, many other related Chinese laws, such as the PRC Civil Procedure Law, are also based on this same assumption that arbitration in China is only

57 *See* Hu Kangsheng (胡康生), *Zhongcai de Benzhi Shi Minjian Xing* (仲裁的本质是民间性) [*The Nature of Arbitration is Private*], Fazhi Ribao (法制日报) [Legal Daily], Sept. 8, 2004 (China).

58 *See* Zhongcai Fa (仲裁法) [Arbitration Law] (promulgated by the Standing Comm. Nat'l People's Cong., Aug. 31, 1994, effective Sept. 1, 1995, rev. Sept. 1, 2017), art. 58 (China).

59 *See id.* art. 20.

60 *See id.* art. 54.

institutional.[61] Therefore, a complete review and revision of all the Chinese laws that relate to arbitration is needed.

Moreover, the new law needs to provide support mechanisms for ad hoc arbitration. These are a range of issues that are necessary for the smooth operation of ad hoc proceedings but they may not be needed in institutional arbitration. Possible examples include who should act as the default appointing authority when parties fail to reach an agreement on the appointment of arbitrators; who will exercise the authority to decide on challenges of arbitrators; and whether and how an ad hoc tribunal can grant provisional measures, call experts and witnesses, and so on.

Perhaps most importantly, Chinese law should correct its misconceptions of ad hoc arbitration and arbitration in general. All lawmakers and judges should be conscious of arbitration's private nature. It is not part of the state apparatus, so it should not be subject to excessive state control. The focus should instead stay on the parties' rights and freedom of choice. From this perspective, ad hoc arbitration is absolutely the same as institutional arbitration. They are both arbitration, a private and informal dispute resolution mechanism that is built on party autonomy. As a result, laws and judges should treat ad hoc and institutional arbitration equally. For example, the law should explicitly adopt the Kompetenz-Kompetenz doctrine, under which arbitrators, not the institutions, have the authority to decide on their own jurisdiction; courts should support an ad hoc tribunal's decision to take provisional measures in the same way as they support those made by an arbitration institution; judges should apply the same standards when reviewing an ad hoc award as they do when reviewing an institutional award and should not be overly aggressive towards the ad hoc award. The list goes on.

As suggested, full recognition of ad hoc arbitration under Chinese law means a full scale rewriting of the PRC Arbitration Law and amending of all the related Chinese legislation. Chinese lawmakers may look to the UNCITRAL Model Law on International Commercial Arbitration for reference. They can of course choose to adopt this very well crafted document as many other countries that wanted to build a pro-arbitration legal system did, or draft a new piece of arbitration legislation, using it as a model.

61 Minshi Susong Fa (民事诉讼法) [Civil Procedure Law] (promulgated by Nat'l People's Cong., Apr. 9, 1991, effective Apr. 9, 1991, rev. June. 27, 2017), art. 257 (China).

8 Conclusion

Arbitration plays a very important role in today's world. It is the preferred method for resolving disputes arising from cross-border business transactions and investments. As China becomes more integrated into the global economy, it has grown to be an increasingly important player in the field of international arbitration. With Chinese economic influence rising worldwide, more arbitration will involve Chinese parties or even take place in China, and more arbitral awards will need enforcement in Chinese courts. As a result, the world needs to have a good understanding of the Chinese arbitration legal framework, particularly how it interacts with the international arbitration system based on the New York Convention.

Ad hoc arbitration is a classic type of arbitration dating back to the dawn of civilization. With many benefits such as flexibility, low cost, and efficiency, ad hoc arbitration is recognized in almost all of the jurisdictions in the world. It is also highly favored in some industries. Despite its efficacy and popularity, the Chinese legal system remains extremely hostile towards ad hoc arbitration. The PRC Arbitration Law precludes ad hoc arbitration by requiring that parties must appoint an arbitration institution in their arbitration agreement. An ad hoc arbitration agreement is therefore invalid per se under Chinese law. Apart from directly impacting the determination of an arbitration agreement's validity, the preclusion of ad hoc arbitration infiltrates the entire Chinese arbitration legal framework. It forms a fundamental basis and premise of Chinese law when it relates to arbitration, including e.g. enforcing an arbitral award or setting it aside. As a result, the ad hoc issue is the "hidden" central issue of Chinese arbitration law.

As important as it is, there is not enough discussion in the current literature on the topic of ad hoc arbitration in China. Although many books and articles have touched upon this issue, they fall short of analyzing it comprehensively. This book has, for the first time, systematically examined the complex issues surrounding ad hoc arbitration in China, including concerns arising in legal practice, its historical background, and the rationale behind Chinese law's hostility towards it. This book has also offered suggestions to parties regarding how they can, as far as possible, avoid Chinese law's preclusion of ad hoc arbitration and made strong arguments as to why Chinese lawmakers should change the law to legitimize ad hoc arbitration fully. Through its discussion of this central topic, this book has also provided new and – hopefully – stimulating insights into Chinese arbitration law and more generally into Chinese law as a whole.

This book has carried out a comprehensive doctrinal analysis of the intricate legal issues surrounding ad hoc arbitration in China. Despite Chinese law's hostility towards ad hoc arbitration, which most importantly includes its extreme stance on invalidating ad hoc arbitration agreements, China cannot single-handedly ban ad hoc arbitration. The international arbitration legal framework based upon the New York Convention unquestionably allows and supports ad hoc arbitration. Due to arbitration's private and international nature, parties still have channels to avoid the unwelcoming institutional arbitration requirement under Chinese law. That said, the interaction between the Chinese and international legal frameworks on arbitration is by no means simple or straightforward. Parties and practitioners need to use extreme caution when dealing with this evidently complex legal issue. This book has suggested a special drafting strategy for parties to adopt in practice. Under this strategy, parties may be able to engage in ad hoc arbitration in China if they decide doing so best fits their needs due to concerns such as time, costs, and so on. Accordingly, the book has provided business entities and legal practitioners with clear guidance on how to avoid possible pitfalls and resolve their disputes in the way that they desire. Such clear guidance is missing in the existing literature, and this book has filled that gap.

Moreover, Chinese law's hostility towards ad hoc arbitration appears truly puzzling when taken at face value. Its ill feeling against this universally popular and evidently useful dispute resolution mechanism is indeed perplexing. The existing literature failed to provide a satisfactory explanation, or indeed any explanation at all, for this apparently bizarre position. This book has offered an answer to this puzzle by analyzing arbitration's history in China from a comparative perspective and proclaiming that Chinese law's hostility towards ad hoc arbitration is historically shaped and politically motivated. The book has placed particular emphasis on the misconception of arbitration's nature among Chinese lawmakers and legal elites. The true nature of arbitration is that it is a private dispute resolution mechanism that caters to party autonomy to the largest extent permitted by law. However, Chinese lawmakers have always conceptualized arbitration as a quasi-public apparatus complementary to the country's judicial system. This is a fundamental misconception that has grave consequences. It not only directly resulted in Chinese law's preclusion of ad hoc arbitration but has also formed the foundation of the Chinese arbitration legal framework in many other aspects. This book is the first to identify this misconception of arbitration in China, which must be corrected before any attempt to improve the Chinese arbitration legal framework can bear fruit.

To explain the puzzle, this book has assessed arbitration's historical development in China using legal transplant theories. Arbitration, as a modern legal institution, was legally transplanted to China from the West. Chinese lawmakers, at different times in the past hundred years, made multiple attempts to transplant arbitration to China. The sophisticated arbitration legal framework, as well as the vibrant arbitration community of present day China, undoubtedly offers an example of a successful legal transplant. However, the legal transplant of arbitration in China provides interesting insights into the relevant theories. It first confirms that a legal transplant is very closely connected with the receiving country's political, economic, and social contexts. It was precisely because of these factors that Chinese lawmakers decided to transplant only institutional arbitration but not ad hoc arbitration. However, the history of arbitration in China suggests that a legal transplant is not wholly determined by existing social and cultural factors. It may take place even though those factors are not completely "ready," but as long as sufficient political will is present. In the present day world, forces of globalization, including needs for economic development, international trade patterns, and international legal instruments, may contribute to that political will significantly.

In addition, the legal transplant of arbitration in China suggests that a legal transplant can take place in different phases as a result of the receiving country's conscious choice. Although China chose not to borrow ad hoc arbitration in the past, it may be ready and willing to do so in the near future. Some Chinese lawmakers have expressed interest in ad hoc arbitration. The SPC has also supported ad hoc arbitration in the Free Trade Zones recently established all over the country. That being said, it is of course subject to future debate as to whether this phased strategy is good or bad for the transplanted law or system, and thus whether it is the best way to conduct a legal transplant.

This book's main argument and proposal is that China should change its law to legitimize and legalize ad hoc arbitration fully. The book has given multiple reasons to support this conclusion. First, the sophisticated doctrinal analysis in the book suggested that parties may adopt a carefully designed drafting strategy to avoid Chinese law's mandatory institutional arbitration requirement. This essentially means that the intended preclusion of ad hoc arbitration under Chinese law has not been successful in practice. More importantly, this prohibition is destined to fail due to arbitration's private and international nature as well as ad hoc arbitration's legitimacy at the international level. In other words, Chinese law can never ban ad hoc arbitration successfully, as long as China wishes to interact globally.

Second, this book has shown that Chinese law's hostility towards ad hoc arbitration is historically shaped and politically motivated. It is the direct result of a conscious cherry-picking process during the legal transplant of arbitration in China. The political and ideological environment in China at the time when the PRC Arbitration Law was promulgated in 1994 meant that ad hoc arbitration could not possibly be tolerated: it was considered incompatible with the socialist system that China had adopted and was deemed too drastic as a reform measure. However, as time has passed, the political contexts that were once hostile towards ad hoc arbitration and responsible for its preclusion from the Chinese legal system no longer exist in China today. Instead, the social and economic context of today's China is clearly favorable towards ad hoc arbitration. One example is the SPC's support in legitimizing ad hoc arbitration in various Free Trade Zones established all over China in recent years. Therefore, it is time to complete the final stage of the legal transplant by fully incorporating ad hoc arbitration into the current Chinese law.

Third, the distinction between ad hoc and institutional arbitration is not always clear cut. Due to the different processes and practices of the various arbitration institutions in the world, it can sometimes be difficult to differentiate clearly between the two types of arbitration. Moreover, because both forms of arbitration are legitimate all over the world, the dichotomy largely remains a theoretical distinction without legal significance. As a result, there is perhaps no need on the international level to reach a consensus on the exact definitions of the two types of arbitration. In practice, there are no exact definitions. Given this lack of clarity, the distinction between ad hoc and institutional arbitration should never have become a deciding factor for the legitimacy of an arbitration process in the first place.

Finally, legitimizing ad hoc arbitration will not cause any damage for China, but can only benefit the country on the whole. Parties in practice need ad hoc arbitration because of its advantages compared with other dispute resolution mechanisms, including litigation and institutional arbitration. Among the advantages, flexibility, efficiency, and low cost are perhaps most appealing, particularly for those cases involving smaller claims. Legitimizing ad hoc arbitration in China will give business entities more options to resolve their disputes effectively, which will make the Chinese economy more efficient. Besides, legitimizing ad hoc arbitration in China will necessarily create more opportunities for the Chinese and international arbitration community. Particularly, opening up the possibility of ad hoc arbitration in China will bring business to the Chinese legal service industry as well as other related industries such as consultancy and hotels. Moreover, China's long and strong tradition of mediation, with which ad hoc arbitration shares the same origin and many similarities, means that it would be very easy for Chinese society to accept ad hoc arbitration. Therefore, incorporating ad hoc arbitration into the current Chinese legal framework is unlikely to cause any disruption in practice.

Looking ahead, legislative action nevertheless remains the only way to resolve completely the ad hoc arbitration problem under Chinese law. Based on the comprehensive analyses from multiple perspectives conducted earlier in the book, this book calls on Chinese lawmakers to recognize and correct the previous misconception of arbitration and incorporate ad hoc arbitration fully into the Chinese legal system.

Apart from addressing the issues related to arbitration law in China, this book has also shed light on the Chinese legal system overall. First, the legal transplant of arbitration in China was by no means a rare incident, but instead is highly representative of the development path of the entire Chinese legal system. China has experienced multiple waves of legal borrowing from the West ever since its legal modernization process began at the turn of the twentieth century. Even today, Chinese lawmakers and legal elites are still paying close attention to different legal systems and legal institutions around the world, particularly those in the West. At the same time, they are clearly conscious of the particular political, economic, and social context of Chinese society and always attempt to adjust the borrowed laws to take account of this. This is the case not only for arbitration law in China, but also for contract, corporate, banking, and many other areas of law. As a result, by analyzing the historical development of Chinese arbitration laws, this book has provided useful insights that can form a starting point for Western readers who want to understand the Chinese legal system and how it is developing as a whole.

Second, the ad hoc arbitration issue offers a typical example of how closely the Chinese legal system is connected with the rest of the world. This book has explained why China cannot unilaterally ban ad hoc arbitration as long as it wishes to interact globally. Just as in the case of arbitration, China cannot insulate its legal system from the world, or the "Western" approaches to law and legality, insomuch as China continues its interaction with the world. Provided that China intends to participate in the globalization process, it will inevitably need to rethink and possibly reform its legal system constantly.

Third, the Chinese legal system has gone through drastic changes in recent decades. It is still rapidly and continually evolving. Ad hoc arbitration offers a very good example in this respect. Although the PRC Arbitration Law prohibits ad hoc arbitration outright, the SPC's attitude has been gradually softening. Chinese lawmakers are also potentially open to changing the law. This should remind those who want to assess the Chinese legal system that one should probably avoid rushing to conclusions based on observations and analyses of Chinese laws at a certain point in time. Instead, it is always important to be aware of the long term development of the Chinese legal system.

Last but not least, the book portrayed a proactive and liberal Chinese court system that is not often observed in the literature. Despite a clear legislative prohibition of ad hoc arbitration, the Chinese judiciary, represented by the SPC, has taken a pro-arbitration stance and has endeavored to support ad hoc arbitration. For example, when reviewing the validity of an ad hoc arbitration agreement, the SPC has gone as far as adopting a choice-of-law rule to avoid applying Chinese law as much as possible, with the effect that Chinese courts are able to enforce many ad hoc arbitration agreements submitted before them. The SPC also never shies away from enforcing foreign ad hoc arbitration awards. Although its vigorous efforts understandably have to fall short in some scenarios and give way to explicit legislation, it is undeniable that the SPC is doing its best to ensure that China complies with its obligations under international norms based on the New York Convention. This depiction of the Chinese judiciary is perhaps different from its usual image. The world often sees courts in China as a weak party in the Chinese constitutional or political structure, and mostly subordinate to other stronger institutions or arms of the government. The SPC's stance on ad hoc arbitration, however, indicates that Chinese courts are in fact trying very hard to be proactive. This book thus contributes to painting a more objective and complete picture of the Chinese legal system as a whole.

APPENDICES

Appendix A

Arbitration Law of the People's Republic of China[1]

(Adopted at the Ninth Meeting of the Standing Committee of the Eighth National People's Congress on August 31, 1994, revised for the first time at the Tenth Meeting of the Standing Committee of the Eleventh National People's Congress on August 27, 2009, and revised for the second time at the Twenty-Ninth Meeting of the Standing Committee of the Twelfth National People's Congress on September 1, 2017.)

Chapter I: General provisions

Article 1

This Law is formulated in order to ensure the impartial and prompt arbitration of economic disputes, to protect the legitimate rights and interests of the parties and to safeguard the sound development of the socialist market economy.

Article 2

Contractual disputes and other disputes over rights and interests in property between citizens, legal persons and other organizations that are equal subjects may be arbitrated.

Article 3

The following disputes may not be arbitrated:

1. marital, adoption, guardianship, support and succession disputes;
2. administrative disputes that shall be handled by administrative organs as prescribed by law.

1 Official translation by the National People's Congress of the People's Republic of China, available at http://www.npc.gov.cn/englishnpc/Law/2007-12/12/content_1383756.htm. The author has provided comments to facilitate understanding.

Article 4

The parties' submission to arbitration to resolve their dispute shall be on the basis of both parties' free will and an arbitration agreement reached between them. If a party applies for arbitration in the absence of an arbitration agreement, the arbitration commission shall not accept the case.

Article 5

If the parties have concluded an arbitration agreement and one party institutes an action in a people's court, the people's court shall not accept the case, unless the arbitration agreement is null and void.[2]

Article 6

The arbitration commission shall be selected by the parties through agreement. In arbitration, there shall be no jurisdiction by level and no territorial jurisdiction.[3]

Article 7

In arbitration, disputes shall be resolved on the basis of facts, in compliance with the law and in an equitable and reasonable manner.

Article 8

Arbitration shall be carried out independently according to law and shall be free from interference of administrative organs, social organizations or individuals.

Article 9

A system of a single and final award shall be practised for arbitration. If a party applies for arbitration to an arbitration commission or institutes an action in a people's court regarding the same dispute after an arbitration award has been made, the arbitration commission or the people's court shall not accept the case.

If an arbitration award is set aside or its enforcement is disallowed by the people's court in accordance with the law, a party may apply for arbitration on the basis of a new arbitration agreement reached between the parties, or institute an action in the people's court, regarding the same dispute.

2 Here, "invalid" may be a better translation than "null and void."

3 The second sentence of this article means that arbitration commissions are not subject to the venue provisions in the PRC Civil Procedure Law.

Chapter II: Arbitration commissions and the arbitration association

Article 10

Arbitration commissions may be established in municipalities directly under the Central Government and in cities that are the seats of the people's governments of provinces or autonomous regions. They may also be established in other cities divided into districts, according to need.[4] Arbitration commissions shall not be established at each level of the administrative divisions.

People's governments of the cities referred to in the preceding paragraph shall arrange for the relevant departments and chambers of commerce to organize arbitration commissions in a unified manner.

The establishment of an arbitration commission shall be registered with the administrative department of justice of the relevant province, autonomous region or municipality directly under the Central Government.

Article 11

An arbitration commission shall meet the conditions set forth below:

1 to have its own name, domicile and charter;
2 to have the necessary property;
3 to have the personnel that are to form the commission; and
4 to have appointed[5] arbitrators.

The charter of an arbitration commission shall be formulated in accordance with this Law.

Article 12

An arbitration commission shall be composed of one chairman, two to four vice chairmen and seven to eleven members.

The offices of chairman, vice chairman and members of an arbitration commission shall be held by experts in the field of law, economy and trade and persons with practical working experience. Experts in the field of law, economy and trade shall account for at least two thirds of the people forming an arbitration commission.

Article 13

An arbitration commission shall appoint[6] its arbitrators from among righteous and upright persons.

4 A better translation for this sentence may be, "They may also be established in other cities, which have districts thereunder, according to need."
5 Here, "engaged" may be a better translation than "appointed."
6 Here, "engage" may be a better translation than "appoint."

An arbitrator shall meet one of the conditions set forth below:

1 to have passed the national legal profession qualification exam and obtained such qualification, and have been engaged in arbitration work for at least eight years;
2 to have worked as a lawyer for at least eight years;
3 to have served as a judge for at least eight years;
4 to have been engaged in legal research or legal education, possessing a senior professional title; or
5 to have acquired the knowledge of law, engaged in the professional work in the field of economy and trade, etc., possessing a senior professional title or having an equivalent professional level.

An arbitration commission shall have a register of arbitrators in different specializations.

Article 14

Arbitration commissions shall be independent from administrative organs and there shall be no subordinate relationships between arbitration commissions and administrative organs. There shall also be no subordinate relationships between arbitration commissions.

Article 15

China Arbitration Association is a social organization with the status of a legal person. Arbitration commissions are members of China Arbitration Association. The charter of China Arbitration Association shall be formulated by its national congress of members.

China Arbitration Association is a self-disciplined organization of arbitration commissions. It shall, in accordance with its charter, supervise arbitration commissions and their members and arbitrators as to whether or not they breach discipline.

China Arbitration Association shall formulate rules of arbitration in accordance with this Law and the relevant provisions of the Civil Procedure Law.

Chapter III: Arbitration agreement

Article 16

An arbitration agreement shall include arbitration clauses stipulated in the contract and agreements of submission to arbitration that are concluded in other written forms before or after disputes arise.

An arbitration agreement shall contain the following particulars:

1 an expression of intention to apply for arbitration;
2 matters for arbitration; and
3 a designated arbitration commission.

Article 17

An arbitration agreement shall be null and void[7] under one of the following circumstances:

1 the agreed matters for arbitration exceed the range of arbitrable matters as specified by law;
2 one party that concluded the arbitration agreement has no capacity for civil conducts or has limited capacity for civil conducts; or
3 one party coerced the other party into concluding the arbitration agreement.

Article 18

If an arbitration agreement contains no or unclear provisions concerning the matters for arbitration or the arbitration commission, the parties may reach a supplementary agreement. If no such supplementary agreement can be reached, the arbitration agreement shall be null and void.[8]

Article 19

An arbitration agreement shall exist independently. The amendment, rescission, termination or invalidity of a contract shall not affect the validity of the arbitration agreement.

The arbitration tribunal shall have the power to affirm[9] the validity of a contract.

Article 20

If a party challenges the validity of the arbitration agreement, he[10] may request the arbitration commission to make a decision or apply to the people's court for a ruling. If one party requests the arbitration commission to make a decision

7 Here, "invalid" may be a better translation than "null and void."
8 Here, "invalid" may be a better translation than "null and void."
9 Here, "determine" may be a better translation than "affirm."
10 The gender specific language used here and elsewhere in this Appendix reflects the original text in the official translation.

and the other party applies to the people's court for a ruling, the people's court shall give a ruling.

A party's challenge of the validity of the arbitration agreement shall be raised prior to the arbitration tribunal's first hearing.

Chapter IV: Arbitration proceedings

Section 1: Application and acceptance

Article 21

A party's application for arbitration shall meet the following requirements:

1 there is an arbitration agreement;
2 there is a specific arbitration claim and there are facts and reasons therefore; and
3 the application is within the scope of the arbitration commission's acceptability.[11]

Article 22

To apply for arbitration, a party shall submit to the arbitration commission the written arbitration agreement and a written application for arbitration together with copies thereof.

Article 23

A written application for arbitration shall specify the following particulars:

1 the name, sex, age, occupation, work unit and domicile of each party, or the name and domicile of legal persons or other organizations and the names and positions of their legal representatives or chief responsible persons;
2 the arbitration claim and the facts and reasons on which it is based; and
3 the evidence, the source of the evidence and the names and domiciles of witnesses.

Article 24

When an arbitration commission receives a written application for arbitration and considers that the application complies with the conditions for acceptance, it shall accept the application and notify the party within five days from the date of receipt. If the arbitration commission considers that the application does not comply with the conditions for acceptance, it shall inform the party in writing of its rejection of the application and explain the reasons for rejection within five days from the date of receipt.

11 Here, "remit" may be a better translation than "acceptability."

Article 25

After an arbitration commission accepts an application for arbitration, it shall, within the time limit specified in the rules of arbitration, deliver a copy of the rules of arbitration and the register of arbitrators to the claimant, and serve one copy of the application for arbitration together with the rules of arbitration and the register of arbitrators on the respondent.

After receiving the copy of the application for arbitration, the respondent shall submit a written defense to the arbitration commission within the time limit specified in the rules of arbitration. After receiving the written defense, the arbitration commission shall serve a copy thereof on the claimant within the time limit specified in the rules of arbitration. Failure on the part of the respondent to submit a written defense shall not affect the progress of the arbitration proceedings.

Article 26

If the parties have concluded an arbitration agreement and one party has instituted an action in a people's court without declaring the existence of the arbitration agreement and, after the people's court has accepted the case, the other party submits the arbitration agreement prior to the first hearing, the people's court shall dismiss the case unless the arbitration agreement is null and void.[12] If, prior to the first hearing, the other party has not raised an objection to the people's court's acceptance of the case, he shall be deemed to have renounced the arbitration agreement and the people's court shall continue to try the case.

Article 27

The claimant may renounce or amend its arbitration claim. The respondent may accept or refuse an arbitration claim and shall have the right to make a counter-claim.

Article 28

A party may apply for property preservation if it may become impossible or difficult for the party to implement the award due to an act of the other party or other causes.

If a party applies for property preservation, the arbitration commission shall submit the party's application to the people's court in accordance with the relevant provisions of the Civil Procedure Law.

If an application for property preservation has been wrongfully made, the applicant shall compensate the person against whom the application has been made for any loss incurred from property preservation.

12 Here, "invalid" may be a better translation than "null and void."

Article 29

A party or statutory agent may appoint a lawyer or other agent to carry out arbitration activities. To appoint a lawyer or other agent to carry out arbitration activities, a power of attorney shall be submitted to the arbitration commission.

Section 2: Formation of arbitration tribunal

Article 30

An arbitration tribunal may be composed of either three arbitrators or one arbitrator. An arbitration tribunal composed of three arbitrators shall have a presiding arbitrator.

Article 31

If the parties agree that the arbitration tribunal shall be composed of three arbitrators, they shall each appoint or entrust the chairman of the arbitration commission to appoint one arbitrator. The parties shall jointly select or jointly entrust the chairman of the arbitration commission to appoint the third arbitrator who shall be the presiding arbitrator.

If the parties agree that the arbitration tribunal shall be composed of one arbitrator, they shall jointly appoint or jointly entrust the chairman of the arbitration commission to appoint the arbitrator.

Article 32

If the parties fail to agree on the method of formation of the arbitration tribunal or to select the arbitrators within the time limit specified in the rules of arbitration, the arbitrators shall be appointed by the chairman of the arbitration commission.

Article 33

After the arbitration tribunal has been formed, the arbitration commission shall notify the parties in writing of the tribunal's formation.

Article 34

In one of the following circumstances, the arbitrator must withdraw, and the parties shall also have the right to challenge the arbitrator for a withdrawal:

1 the arbitrator is a party in the case or a close relative of a party or of an agent in the case;
2 the arbitrator has a personal interest in the case;

3 the arbitrator has other relationship with a party or his agent in the case which may affect the impartiality of arbitration; or
4 the arbitrator has privately met with a party or agent or accepted an invitation to entertainment or gift from a party or agent.

Article 35

If a party challenges an arbitrator, he shall submit his challenge, with a statement of the reasons therefore, prior to the first hearing. If the matter giving rise to the challenge became known after the first hearing, the challenge may be made before the conclusion of the final hearing of the case.

Article 36

The decision as to whether or not the arbitrator should withdraw shall be made by the chairman of the arbitration commission. If the chairman of the arbitration commission serves as an arbitrator, the decision shall be made collectively by the arbitration commission.

Article 37

If an arbitrator cannot perform his duties due to his withdrawal or for other reasons, a substitute arbitrator shall be selected or appointed in accordance with this Law.

After a substitute arbitrator has been selected or appointed on account of an arbitrator's withdrawal, a party may request that the arbitration proceedings already carried out should be carried out anew. The decision as to whether to approve it or not shall be made by the arbitration tribunal. The arbitration tribunal may also make a decision of its own motion as to whether or not the arbitration proceedings already carried out should be carried out anew.

Article 38

If an arbitrator is involved in the circumstances described in item (4) of Article 34 of this Law and the circumstances are serious or involved in the circumstances described in item (6) of Article 58 of this Law, he shall assume legal liability according to law and the arbitration commission shall remove his name from the register of arbitrators.

Section 3: Hearing and award

Article 39

Arbitration shall be conducted by means of oral hearings. If the parties agree to arbitration without oral hearings, the arbitration tribunal may render an arbitration award on the basis of the written application for arbitration, the written defense and other material.

Article 40

Arbitration shall be conducted in camera. If the parties agree to public arbitration, the arbitration may be public unless State secrets are involved.

Article 41

The arbitration commission shall notify the parties of the date of the hearing within the time limit specified in the rules of arbitration. A party may, within the time limit specified in the rules of arbitration, request a postponement of the hearing if he has justified reasons therefore. The arbitration tribunal shall decide whether or not to postpone the hearing.

Article 42

If the claimant fails to appear before the arbitration tribunal without justified reasons after having been notified in writing or leaves the hearing prior to its conclusion without the permission of the arbitration tribunal, he may be deemed to have withdrawn his application for arbitration.

If the respondent fails to appear before the arbitration tribunal without justified reasons after having been notified in writing or leaves the hearing prior to its conclusion without the permission of the arbitration tribunal, a default award may be made.

Article 43

Parties shall provide evidences in support of their own arguments.

The arbitration tribunal may, as it considers necessary, collect evidences on its own.

Article 44

If the arbitration tribunal considers that a special issue requires appraisal, it may refer the issue for appraisal to an appraisal department agreed on by the parties or to an appraisal department designated by the arbitration tribunal.

If requested by a party or required by the arbitration tribunal, the appraisal department shall send its appraiser to attend the hearing. Subject to the permission of the arbitration tribunal, the parties may question the appraiser.

Article 45

The evidence shall be presented during the hearings and may be examined by the parties.

Article 46

Under circumstances where the evidence may be destroyed or lost or difficult to obtain at a later time, a party may apply for preservation of the evidence. If a party applies for preservation of the evidence, the arbitration commission shall submit his application to the basic people's court[13] in the place where the evidence is located.

Article 47

The parties shall have the right to carry on debate in the course of arbitration. At the end of the debate, the presiding arbitrator or the sole arbitrator shall solicit final opinions from the parties.

Article 48

The arbitration tribunal shall make records of the hearings in writing. The parties and other participants in the arbitration shall have the right to apply for supplementation or correction of the record of their own statements if they consider that such record contains omissions or errors. If no supplementation or corrections are to be made, their application therefore shall be recorded.

The record shall be signed or sealed by the arbitrators, the recordist, the parties and other participants in the arbitration.

Article 49

After an application for arbitration has been made, the parties may settle their dispute on their own. If the parties have reached a settlement agreement, they may request the arbitration tribunal to make an arbitration award in accordance with the settlement agreement; alternatively, they may withdraw their application for arbitration.

Article 50

If a party repudiates the settlement agreement after the application for arbitration has been withdrawn, he may apply for arbitration again in accordance with the arbitration agreement.

Article 51

The arbitration tribunal may carry out conciliation prior to giving an arbitration award. The arbitration tribunal shall conduct conciliation if both parties voluntarily seek conciliation. If conciliation is unsuccessful, an arbitration award shall be made promptly.

If conciliation leads to a settlement agreement, the arbitration tribunal shall make a written conciliation statement or make an arbitration award in accordance

13 Here, "people's court at the basic level" may be a better translation than "basic people's court."

with the result of the settlement agreement. A written conciliation statement and an arbitration award shall have equal legal effect.

Article 52

A written conciliation statement shall specify the arbitration claim and the results of the settlement agreed upon between the parties. The written conciliation statement shall be signed by the arbitrators, sealed by the arbitration commission, and then served on both parties.

The written conciliation statement shall become legally effective immediately after both parties have signed for receipt thereof.

If the written conciliation statement is repudiated by a party before he signs for receipt thereof, the arbitration tribunal shall promptly make an arbitration award.

Article 53

The arbitration award shall be made in accordance with the opinion of the majority of the arbitrators. The opinion of the minority of the arbitrators may be entered in the record. If the arbitration tribunal is unable to form a majority opinion, the arbitration award shall be made in accordance with the opinion of the presiding arbitrator.

Article 54

An arbitration award shall specify the arbitration claim, the facts of the dispute, the reasons for the decision, the results of the award, the allocation of arbitration fees and the date of the award. If the parties agree that they do not wish the facts of the dispute and the reasons for the decision to be specified in the arbitration award, the same may be omitted. The arbitration award shall be signed by the arbitrators and sealed by the arbitration commission. An arbitrator with dissenting opinions as to the arbitration award may sign the award or choose not to sign it.

Article 55

In arbitration proceedings, if a part of the facts involved has already become clear, the arbitration tribunal may first make an award in respect of such part of the facts.

Article 56

If there are literal or calculation errors in the arbitration award, or if the matters which have been decided by the arbitration tribunal are omitted in the arbitration award, the arbitration tribunal shall make due corrections or supplementation. The parties may, within thirty days from the date of receipt of the award, request the arbitration tribunal to make such corrections or supplementation.

Article 57

The arbitration award shall be legally effective as of the date on which it is made.

Chapter V: Application for setting aside arbitration award

Article 58

A party may apply for setting aside an arbitration award to the intermediate people's court in the place where the arbitration commission is located if he can produce evidence which proves that the arbitration award involves one of the following circumstances:

1 there is no arbitration agreement;
2 the matters decided in the award exceed the scope of the arbitration agreement or are beyond the arbitral authority of the arbitration commission;
3 the formation of the arbitration tribunal or the arbitration procedure was not in conformity with the statutory procedure;[14]
4 the evidence on which the award is based was forged;
5 the other party has withheld the evidence which is sufficient to affect the impartiality of the arbitration;[15] or
6 the arbitrators have committed embezzlement, accepted bribes or done malpractices for personal benefits or perverted the law in the arbitration of the case.

The people's court shall rule to set aside the arbitration award if a collegial panel formed by the people's court verifies upon examination that the award involves one of the circumstances set forth in the preceding paragraph.

If the people's court determines that the arbitration award violates the public interest, it shall rule to set aside the award.

Article 59

A party that wishes to apply for setting aside the arbitration award shall submit such application within six months from the date of receipt of the award.

Article 60

The people's court shall, within two months from the date of accepting an application for setting aside an arbitration award, rule to set aside the award or to reject the application.

14 Here, "procedure provided by law" may be a better translation than "statutory procedure."
15 A better translation for this sentence may be "The opposing party has concealed evidence that may sufficiently affect the just finding of the case."

Article 61

If, after accepting an application for setting aside an arbitration award, the people's court considers that the case may be re-arbitrated by the arbitration tribunal, it shall notify the tribunal that it shall re-arbitrate the case within a certain time limit and shall rule to stay the setting-aside procedure. If the arbitration tribunal refuses to re-arbitrate the case, the people's court shall rule to resume the setting-aside procedure.

Chapter VI: Enforcement

Article 62

The parties shall perform the arbitration award. If a party fails to perform the arbitration award, the other party may apply to the people's court for enforcement in accordance with the relevant provisions of the Civil Procedure Law. The people's court to which the application has been made shall enforce the award.

Article 63

If the party against whom the enforcement is sought presents evidence which proves that the arbitration award involves one of the circumstances set forth in the second paragraph of Article 217 [renumbered as Article 237] of the Civil Procedure Law, the people's court shall, after examination and verification by a collegial panel formed by the people's court, rule to disallow the award.

Article 64

If one party applies for enforcement of the arbitration award and the other party applies for setting aside the arbitration award, the people's court shall rule to suspend the procedure of enforcement.

If the people's court rules to set aside the arbitration award, it shall rule to terminate the enforcement procedure. If the people's court rules to reject the application for setting aside the arbitration award, it shall rule to resume the enforcement procedure.

Chapter VII: Special provisions for arbitration involving foreign elements

Article 65

The provisions of this Chapter shall apply to the arbitration of disputes arising from economic, trade, transportation and maritime activities involving a foreign element. For matters not covered in this Chapter, the other relevant provisions of this Law shall apply.

Article 66

Foreign-related arbitration commissions may be organized and established by the China Chamber of International Commerce.

A foreign-related arbitration commission shall be composed of one chairman, a certain number of vice chairmen and members.

The chairman, vice chairmen and members of a foreign-related arbitration commission may be appointed by the China Chamber of International Commerce.

Article 67

A foreign-related arbitration commission may appoint[16] arbitrators from among foreigners with special knowledge in the fields of law, economy and trade, science and technology, etc.

Article 68

If a party to a foreign-related arbitration applies for preservation of the evidence, the foreign-related arbitration commission shall submit his application to the intermediate people's court in the place where the evidence is located.

Article 69

A foreign-related arbitration tribunal may enter the details of the hearings in written records or make written minutes thereof. The written minutes may be signed or sealed by the parties and other participants in the arbitration.

Article 70

If a party presents evidence which proves that a foreign-related arbitration award involves one of the circumstances set forth in the first paragraph of Article 260 [renumbered as Article 274] of the Civil Procedure Law, the people's court shall, after examination and verification by a collegial panel formed by the people's court, rule to set aside the award.

Article 71

If the party against whom the enforcement is sought presents evidence which proves that the foreign-related arbitration award involves one of the circumstances set forth in the first paragraph of Article 260 [renumbered as Article 274] of the Civil Procedure Law, the people's court shall, after examination and verification by a collegial panel formed by the people's court, rule to disallow the enforcement.

16 Here, "engaged" may be a better translation than "appointed."

Article 72

If a party applies for enforcement of a legally effective arbitration award made by a foreign-related arbitration commission and if the party against whom the enforcement is sought or such party's property is not within the territory of the People's Republic of China, he shall directly apply to a competent foreign court for recognition and enforcement of the award.

Article 73

Foreign-related arbitration rules may be formulated by the China Chamber of International Commerce in accordance with this Law and the relevant provisions of the Civil Procedure Law.

Chapter VIII: Supplementary provisions

Article 74

If prescription for arbitration is provided by law, such provisions shall apply. In the absence of such provisions, the prescription for litigation shall apply to arbitration.[17]

Article 75

Prior to the formulation of rules of arbitration by China Arbitration Association, arbitration commissions may formulate provisional rules of arbitration in accordance with this Law and the relevant provisions of the Civil Procedure Law.

Article 76

Parties shall pay arbitration fees according to regulations.[18]

Measures[19] for charging arbitration fees shall be submitted to the price control authorities for examination and approval.

Article 77

Regulations concerning arbitration of labor disputes and agricultural contractor's contract disputes arising within the agricultural collective economic organizations shall be formulated separately.[20]

17 A better translation for this article may be, "Where the law provides a statute of limitation for arbitration, such provisions shall apply. Where the law does not provide any statute of limitation for arbitration, the statute of limitation for litigation shall apply."

18 A better translation for this article may be, "Parties shall pay arbitration fees according to relevant provisions."

19 Here, "Schedules" may be a better translation than "Measures."

20 A better translation for this article may be, "Arbitration of labor disputes and disputes arising from agricultural contracting contracts within agricultural collective economic organizations shall be subject to other regulations."

Article 78

If regulations governing arbitration promulgated prior to the implementation of this Law contravene the provisions of this Law, the provisions of this Law shall prevail.

Article 79

Arbitration institutions established prior to the implementation of this Law in the municipalities directly under the Central Government, in the cities that are the seats of the people's governments of provinces or autonomous regions and in other cities divided into districts[21] shall be reorganized in accordance with this Law. Those of such arbitration institutions that have not been reorganized shall terminate upon the end of one year from the date of the implementation of this Law.

Other arbitration institutions established prior to the implementation of this Law that do not comply with the provisions of this Law shall terminate on the date of the implementation of this Law.

Article 80

This Law shall go into effect as of September 1, 1995.

21 Here, "cities, which have districts thereunder" may be a better translation than "cities divided into districts."

Appendix B

Civil Procedure Law of the People's Republic of China[22] (selected provisions)

(Adopted at the Fourth Meeting of the Seventh National People's Congress on April 9, 1991, revised for the first time at the Thirtieth Meeting of the Standing Committee of the Tenth National People's Congress on October 28, 2007, revised for the second time at the Twenty-eighth Meeting of the Standing Committee of the Eleventh National People's Congress on August 31, 2012, and revised for the third time at the Twenty-Eighth Meeting of the Standing Committee of the Twelfth National People's Congress on June 27, 2017.)

Chapter XX: Application for execution[23] and referral

. . . .

Article 237

If a party fails to comply with an award of an arbitral organ[24] established according to the law, the other party may apply for execution[25] to the people's court which has jurisdiction over the case. The people's court applied to shall enforce the award.

If the party against whom the application is made furnishes proof that the arbitral award involves any of the following circumstances, the people's court shall, after examination and verification by a collegial panel, make a written order not to allow the enforcement:

1 the parties have had no arbitration clause in their contract, nor have subsequently reached a written agreement on arbitration;[26]
2 the matters dealt with by the award fall outside the scope of the arbitration agreement or are matters which the arbitral organ[27] has no power to arbitrate;

22 Official translation by the National People's Congress of the People's Republic of China, available at http://www.npc.gov.cn/englishnpc/Law/2009-02/20/content_1471601.htm. The author has provided comments to facilitate understanding and adjusted certain numerics to reflect the law's recent amendments.

23 Here, "enforcement" may be a better translation than "execution."

24 Here, "arbitration institution" may be a better translation than "arbitral organ."

25 Here, "enforcement" may be a better translation than "execution."

26 Here, "nor have they subsequently reached a written agreement on arbitration" may be a better translation than "nor have subsequently reached a written agreement on arbitration."

27 Here, "arbitration institution" may be a better translation than "arbitral organ."

3 the composition of the arbitration tribunal or the procedure for arbitration contradicts the procedure prescribed by the law.
4 the evidence, which the arbitral award is based on, is falsified;
5 the opposing party conceals from the arbitral institution evidence that is sufficient to affect the impartiality of the arbitration; or
6 the arbitrators have committed embezzlement, accepted bribes or done malpractice for personal benefits or perverted the law in the arbitration of the case.

If the people's court determines that the execution[28] of the arbitral award is against the social and public interest, it shall make an order not to allow the execution.[29]

The above-mentioned written order shall be served on both parties and the arbitral organ.[30]

If the execution[31] of an arbitral award is disallowed by a written order of the people's court, the parties may, in accordance with a written agreement on arbitration reached between them, apply for arbitration again; they may also bring an action in a people's court.

Chapter XXVI: Arbitration

. . . .

Article 271

In the case of a dispute arising from the foreign economic, trade, transport or maritime activities of China, if the parties have had an arbitration clause in the contract concerned or have subsequently reached a written arbitration agreement stipulating the submission of the dispute for arbitration to an arbitral organ[32] in the People's Republic of China handling cases involving foreign element,[33] or to any other arbitral body, they may not bring an action in a people's court.

If the parties have not had an arbitration clause in the contract concerned or have not subsequently reached a written arbitration agreement, they may bring an action in a people's court.

Article 272

If a party has applied for preservation measures, the arbitral organ[34] of the People's Republic of China handling cases involving foreign element[35] shall refer the party's application for a decision to the intermediate people's court of the place where the party against whom the application is made has his domicile or where his property is located.

28 Here, "enforcement" may be a better translation than "execution."
29 Id.
30 Here, "arbitration institution" may be a better translation than "arbitral organ."
31 Here, "enforcement" may be a better translation than "execution."
32 Here, "arbitration institution" may be a better translation than "arbitral organ."
33 Here, "involving a foreign element" may be a better translation than "involving foreign element."
34 Here, "arbitration institution" may be a better translation than "arbitral organ."
35 Here, "involving a foreign element" may be a better translation than "involving foreign element."

Article 273

In a case in which an award has been made by an arbitral organ[36] of the People's Republic of China handling cases involving foreign element, the parties may not bring an action in a people's court. If one party fails to comply with the arbitral award, the other party may apply for its enforcement to the intermediate people's court of the place where the party against whom the application for enforcement is made has his domicile or where his property is located.

Article 274

A people's court shall, after examination and verification by a collegial panel of the court, make a written order not to allow the enforcement of the award rendered by an arbitral organ[37] of the People's Republic of China handling cases involving foreign element,[38] if the party against whom the application for enforcement is made furnishes proof that:

1 the parties have not had an arbitration clause in the contract or have not subsequently reached a written arbitration agreement;
2 the party against whom the application for enforcement is made was not given notice for the appointment of an arbitrator or for the inception of the arbitration proceedings or was unable to present his case due to causes for which he is not responsible;
3 the composition of the arbitration tribunal or the procedure for arbitration was not in conformity with the rules of arbitration; or
4 the matters dealt with by the award fall outside the scope of the arbitration agreement or which the arbitral organ was not empowered to arbitrate.[39]

If the people's court determines that the enforcement of the award goes against the social and public interest of the country, the people's court shall make a written order not to allow the enforcement of the arbitral award.

Article 275

If the enforcement of an arbitral award is disallowed by a written order of a people's court, the parties may, in accordance with a written arbitration agreement reached between them, apply for arbitration again; they may also bring an action in a people's court.

36 Here, "arbitration institution" may be a better translation than "arbitral organ."
37 Id.
38 Here, "involving a foreign element" may be a better translation than "involving foreign element."
39 Here, "or are of a type which the arbitral institution was not empowered to arbitrate" may be a better translation than "or which the arbitral organ was not empowered to arbitrate."

Chapter XXVII: Judicial assistance

. . . .

Article 282

In the case of an application or request for recognition and enforcement of a legally effective judgment or written order of a foreign court, the people's court shall, after examining it in accordance with the international treaties concluded or acceded to by the People's Republic of China or with the principle of reciprocity and arriving at the conclusion that it does not contradict the basic principles of the law of the People's Republic of China nor violates[40] State sovereignty, security and social and public interest of the country, recognize the validity of the judgment or written order, and, if required, issue a writ of execution to enforce it in accordance with the relevant provisions of this Law; if the application or request contradicts the basic principles of the law of the People's Republic of China or violates State sovereignty, security and social and public interest of the country, the people's court shall not recognize and enforce it.

Article 283

If an award made by a foreign arbitral organ[41] requires the recognition and enforcement by a people's court of the People's Republic of China, the party concerned shall directly apply to the intermediate people's court of the place where the party subjected to enforcement has his domicile or where his property is located. The people's court shall deal with the matter in accordance with the international treaties concluded or acceded to by the People's Republic of China or with the principle of reciprocity.

. . . .

40 Here, "violate" may be a better translation than "violates."

41 Here, "arbitration institution" may be a better translation than "arbitral organ."

Appendix C

The Supreme People's Court's interpretation on certain issues concerning the application of the "Arbitration Law of the People's Republic of China"[42]

(Adopted at No. 1375 Meeting of the Adjudication Committee of the Supreme People's Court on December 26, 2005, effective as of September 8, 2006.)

In accordance with the "Arbitration Law of the People's Republic of China," the "Civil Procedure Law of the People's Republic of China" and other laws, the following interpretation is made concerning certain issues relating to the application of law in arbitration cases heard by the people's courts:

Article 1

Arbitration agreements in "other written forms" as provided in Article 16 of the Arbitration Law include agreements calling for arbitration reached in forms of contract, letter, data message (including telegraph, telex, facsimile, electronic data interchange, and e-mail) and other forms.

Article 2

Where parties agree in general that subject matters for arbitration are contract disputes, disputes arising from the formation, validity, amendment, transfer, performance, liability for breach, interpretation and rescission of a contract may all be found as subject matters for arbitration.

Article 3

Where the name of the arbitration institution agreed in an arbitration agreement is inaccurate, but a specific arbitration institution could be ascertained, it should be found that an arbitration institution has been chosen.

Article 4

Where the arbitration agreement only agrees on the applicable arbitration rules for the dispute, it shall be deemed that no arbitration institution has

42 English translation prepared by the author.

been agreed, except that the parties reach a supplementary agreement or the arbitration institution could be ascertained according to the agreed arbitration rules.

Article 5

Where two or more arbitration institutions are agreed in an arbitration agreement, the parties may agree to choose one of the arbitration institutions and apply for arbitration; where the parties cannot reach an agreement on the choice of arbitration institution, the arbitration agreement is invalid.

Article 6

Where it is agreed in an arbitration agreement to arbitrate under an arbitration institution at a certain place, if there is only one arbitration institution at such place, then this arbitration institution is deemed as the agreed arbitration institution. If there are two or more arbitration institutions at such place, the parties may agree to choose one of the arbitration institutions and apply for arbitration; if the parties cannot reach an agreement on the choice of arbitration institution, the arbitration agreement is invalid.

Article 7

Where the parties agree that they may either apply for arbitration to an arbitration institution or file a lawsuit to a people's court to resolve their dispute, the arbitration agreement is invalid, except that one party applies for arbitration to an arbitration institution and the other party does not raise any objection within the time limit provided in Article 20, Paragraph 2 of the Arbitration law.

Article 8

Where a party merges with others or separates itself after concluding an arbitration agreement, the arbitration agreement is binding upon the successor to its rights and obligations.

Where a party deceases after concluding an arbitration agreement, the arbitration agreement is binding upon the heir inheriting the party's rights and obligations of the subject matters for arbitration.

Situations provided in the two preceding paragraphs shall not apply if the parties agree otherwise when concluding the arbitration agreement.

Article 9

Where rights and obligations are transferred in parts or in whole, the arbitration agreement is binding upon the transferee, except that parties agree otherwise, or that the transferee opposes it when accepting the rights and obligations, or that the transferee does not know of the existence of a separate arbitration agreement.

Article 10

Where the contract does not take effect after being formed, or is cancelled, Article 19, Paragraph 1 of the Arbitration Law shall apply when determining the validity of the arbitration agreement.

Where the parties reach an arbitration agreement when concluding a contract, the non-formation of the contract does not affect the validity of the arbitration agreement.

Article 11

Where it is agreed in a contract that a valid arbitration clause contained in another contract or document shall apply to the resolution of disputes, when contractual disputes arise, the parties shall call for arbitration according to such arbitration clause.

Where there are arbitration provisions in a relevant international treaty which shall apply to a foreign-related contract, when contractual disputes arise, the parties shall call for arbitration according to the arbitration provisions in the international treaty.

Article 12

Cases in which a party applies to the people's court to determine the validity of an arbitration agreement shall fall into the jurisdiction of the intermediate people's court at the place where the arbitration institution agreed in the arbitration agreement resides; if the arbitration institution agreed in the arbitration agreement is not clear, the case shall fall into the jurisdiction of the intermediate people's court at the place where the arbitration agreement is concluded, or where the respondent domiciles.

Cases in which a party applies to determine the validity of a foreign-related arbitration agreement shall fall into the jurisdiction of the intermediate people's court at the place where the arbitration institution agreed in the arbitration agreement resides, where the arbitration agreement is concluded, or where the applicant or the respondent domiciles.

Cases relating to the validity of an arbitration agreement in admiralty or maritime disputes shall fall into the jurisdiction of the maritime court at the place where the arbitration institution agreed in the arbitration agreement resides, where the arbitration agreement is concluded, or where the applicant or the respondent domiciles; if there is no maritime court at the above places, the case shall fall into the jurisdiction of the nearest maritime court.

Article 13

According to Article 20, Paragraph 2 of the Arbitration Law, where a party does not raise any dispute concerning the validity of the arbitration agreement before the first hearing is held by the arbitration tribunal, but subsequently applies to the people's court to invalidate the arbitration agreement, the people's court shall not accept the case.

After an arbitration institution has made a decision on the validity of an arbitration agreement, if a party applies to the people's court to determine the validity of the arbitration agreement or to set aside the arbitration institution's decision, the people's court shall not accept the case.

Article 14

The "first hearing" provided in Article 26 of the Arbitration Law refers to the first trial hearing organized by the people's court after the defense period expires, excluding all kinds of activities in the pre-trial proceedings.

Article 15

When hearing cases concerning determination of the validity of an arbitration agreement, the people's court shall form a collegial panel to conduct examination, and to question the parties.

Article 16

When reviewing the validity of a foreign-related arbitration agreement, the law chosen by the parties shall apply; where the parties failed to agree on the applicable law, but did agree on the place of arbitration, the law at the place of arbitration shall apply; where the parties agreed on neither the applicable law nor the place of arbitration, or otherwise the place of arbitration agreed on is not clear, the law at the place of the court shall apply.

Article 17

Where a party applies to set aside an arbitration award relying upon reasons other than those provided in Article 58 of the Arbitration Law or Article 260 [renumbered as Article 274] of the Civil Procedure Law, the people's court shall not sustain such application.

Article 18

The phrase "there is no arbitration agreement" provided in Article 58, Paragraph 1, Item (1) of the Arbitration Law refers to the situation where the parties did not reach an arbitration agreement. Where an arbitration agreement is found to be invalid or cancelled, it shall be treated as if there is no arbitration agreement.

Article 19

Where a party applies to set aside an arbitration award relying on the reason that matters decided in the award fall outside the scope of the arbitration agreement, if it has been found true after review, the people's court shall set aside the part of the arbitration award that is outside the scope. However, if the part outside the scope is not severable from other matters in the award, the people's court shall set aside the arbitration award.

Article 20

The "not in conformity with the statutory procedure"[43] provision in Article 58 of the Arbitration Law refers to situations in violation of the arbitration proceeding provided in the Arbitration Law and the arbitration rules chosen by the parties, that may affect the correct decision on the case.

Article 21

Where the case in which a party applies for setting aside a domestic award falls into one of the situations mentioned below, the people's court may, according to Article 61 of the Arbitration Law, notify the arbitration tribunal to re-arbitrate within a certain period:

1 the evidence on which the award is based was forged;
2 the other party has withheld evidence which is sufficient to affect the impartiality of the arbitration.[44]

The people's court shall specify its detailed reason for requiring re-arbitration within the notification.

Article 22

Where an arbitration tribunal starts to re-arbitrate within the time limit specified by the people's court, the people's court shall rule to terminate the procedure for setting aside; where the re-arbitration is not started, the people's court shall rule to resume the procedure for setting aside.

43 Translated as in the official translation of the *PRC Arbitration Law* prepared by the National People's Congress. A better translation for this sentence may be, "not in conformity with procedure provided by law."

44 Translated as in the official translation of the *PRC Arbitration Law* prepared by the National People's Congress. A better translation for this sentence may be, "The opposing party has concealed evidence that may sufficiently affect the just finding of the case."

Article 23

Where a party does not agree with the re-arbitration award, it may apply to the people's court according to Article 58 of the Arbitration Law for setting aside within six months after the service of the re-arbitration award.

Article 24

In cases in which a party applies for setting aside an arbitration award, the people's court shall form a collegial panel to hear the case and to question the parties.

Article 25

After the people's court accepts a party's application for setting aside an arbitration award, where the other party applies for enforcing the same arbitration award, the people's court accepting the application for enforcement shall rule to stay the enforcement after accepting the case.

Article 26

After a party's application for setting aside an arbitration award is overruled, where it also raises, in the enforcement procedure, defense opinions not to enforce the award on the same reasons, such opinions shall not be sustained by the people's court.

Article 27

Where a party did not dispute the validity of the arbitration agreement in the arbitration proceeding, and after the arbitration award is rendered, however, it moves to set aside the arbitration award or puts forward defense opinion not to enforce the arbitration award arguing that the arbitration agreement is invalid, it shall not be supported by the people's court.

Where a party disputed the validity of the arbitration agreement in the arbitration proceeding, and after the arbitration award is rendered, it further moves to set aside the arbitration award or puts forward defense opinion not to enforce the arbitration award relying upon the same reason, after review, if it is in accordance with provisions of Article 58 of the Arbitration Law, Article 217 [renumbered as Article 237] or Article 260 [renumbered as Article 274] of the Civil Procedure Law, it shall be supported by the people's court.

Article 28

Where a party applies for not enforcing a written conciliation statement or an arbitration award rendered based upon the settlement agreement between the parties, it shall not be supported by the people's court.

Article 29

The case in which a party applies for enforcing an arbitration award shall fall into the jurisdiction of the intermediate people's court at the place where the party subject to enforcement domiciles or where the property subject to enforcement locates.

Article 30

Based upon actual needs in hearing cases concerning setting aside and enforcing arbitration awards, the people's court may require statement from arbitration institutions or request to review the case files of relevant arbitration institutions.

The rulings issued by the people's court in conducting cases relating to arbitration may also be sent to relevant arbitration institutions.

Article 31

This Interpretation will be implemented as from the date of promulgation.

Where judicial interpretations previously issued by this Court are inconsistent with this Interpretation, this Interpretation shall prevail.

Index

ad hoc arbitration 7–9; absence of in China's legal system 32; advantages of 8; China's hostility towards, avoiding 94–5; under Chinese law 10–13; inclusion of in Chinese law, reasons for 105–7; omission of in PRC Arbitration Law 99–102; reforming in China 102–4; rejection of ad hoc arbitration agreements under Chinese law 39–41; sovereign states as party to 8; SPC support for arbitration seated in China 56–7; SPC's role in implementing in China 114–19; *see also* Chinese ad hoc arbitrations; enforceability of ad hoc agreements; legitimizing ad hoc arbitration in China
adopting a carefully crafted drafting strategy 81–5
advantages: of ad hoc arbitration 8; of arbitration 4–7; of institutional arbitration 9
ambiguities in Chinese arbitration law 96–8
Ancient Greece, arbitration in 14–15
application for setting aside arbitration award 139–40
appointment of a presiding arbitrator 64
arbitration: ad hoc 7–9; choice-of-law rule on an arbitration agreement's validity 49–52; comparison with litigation 4–7; confidentiality of 6–7; efficiency of 6; foreign arbitration in the PRC 27–9; history of in the Western world 14–15; institutional 7–9; international 94–5; legal transplant 32–8; misconceptions of under Chinese law 95; neutrality of 4–5; New York Convention 4; non-Chinese *lex arbitri*, SPC support of 55–6; in PRC Civil Procedural Law 145–6; private 94, 120; as private dispute resolution mechanism 13; as quasi-public dispute resolution system 31, 37; selection of law governing arbitration agreement 46–7, 52–4; UNCITRAL Arbitration Rules 8, 53–4; universal enforceability of 5–6; *see also* domestic arbitration; foreign arbitration; history of arbitration
Arbitration Law of the People's Republic of China 27
arguments against legitimizing ad hoc arbitration in China 108–9
Arrangement on Mutual Enforcement of Arbitration Awards Between Mainland and Hong Kong Special Administrative Region 43
Arrangement on Mutual Recognition and Enforcement of Arbitration Awards Between Mainland and Macau Special Administrative Region 43–4
Article I(2) of the New York Convention 39, 59
Article V(1)(a) of the New York Convention 59–60, 76–8, 91–2
Article V(1)(e) of the New York Convention 78–80, 92–3
avoiding China's hostility towards ad hoc arbitration 94–5
awards 62; application for setting aside arbitration award 139–40; articles of PRC Arbitration Law regarding 135–9; from Chinese ad hoc arbitration 63; *de facto* set-aside 74–5; enforcement of outside China, increasing chances of 91–3; enforcement of within China, increasing chances of 88–91; from foreign ad hoc arbitration, enforceability of in China 58–62; formal set-aside

proceeding not available 71–4; in institutional arbitration 9; from mediation 113–14; voluntary payment of 63–4; *see also* enforceability of ad hoc arbitration awards in China; unenforceable awards under Chinese law

carefully crafted drafting strategy, adopting 81–5; enforcement of award outside China, increasing chances of 91–3; enforcement of award within China, increasing chances of 88–91
categorizing arbitration 7–9
China Arbitration Association 130, 142
Chinese ad hoc arbitrations 58; appointment of a presiding arbitrator 64; awards 63; *de facto* set-aside of awards 74–5; eliminating obstructions to 85–6, 86–7; enforcement of award outside China, increasing chances of 91–3; enforcement of award within China, increasing chances of 88–91; external obstructions 65–7; good faith principle 69; internal obstructions 64–5; place for hearings, selecting 82; reforming 102–4; successful operation of 63–4; timing of obstructions 67–9; unenforceable awards under Chinese law 69–70; *see also* recommendations for successful ad hoc arbitration in China; successful Chinese ad hoc arbitration
Chinese arbitration law 2; ambiguities in 96–8; hostility towards ad hoc arbitration, avoiding 94–5; legal transplant theories 3; reforming 119–20
choice-of-law rule 49–52; in commercial arbitration 46–7; validity-preferring 52–4
CIETAC (China International Economic and Trade Arbitration Commission) 10, 96–8, 103
Commentaries on Arbitration Laws of China 60–1
commercial dispute resolution: choice-of-law issues 46–7; in the PRC 24–5; selection of law governing arbitration agreement 46–7
Concise Chamber of Commerce Act 19–20
conference minutes 49
confidentiality of arbitration 6–7
Confucianism 17, 110
container contracts, selection of law governing 52–4
contemporary China, mediation during 111–14
cost-effectiveness: of ad hoc arbitration 8; of arbitration *vs.* litigation 6
CPC (Communist Party of China) 23–4, 111
Cultural Revolution 22
"curial law" *see lex arbitri*

de facto set-aside of awards 74–5
dispute resolution: arbitration *vs.* litigation 4–7; reforming in China 102–4; *see also* arbitration
Division of Commercial Arbitration Act 21–2
domestic arbitration in the PRC 23–7
drafting strategy, selecting 81–5; enforcement of award outside China, increasing chances of 91–3; enforcement of award within China, increasing chances of 88–91

economic contracts 23–5
efficiency: of ad hoc arbitration 8; of arbitration 6
Egypt, arbitration in ancient times 14–15
eliminating obstructions to successful Chinese ad hoc arbitrations: external obstructions 85–6; internal obstructions 86–7
enforceability of ad hoc agreements: in Hong Kong and Macau 41–4; under non-Chinese law 45–6; in Taiwan 44–5; *see also* enforceability of ad hoc arbitration awards in China
enforceability of ad hoc arbitration awards in China 58; Article V(1)(a) of the New York Convention 76–8; Article V(1)(e) of the New York Convention 78–80; China's obligation under the New York Convention 58; foreign arbitration 58–62; in Hong Kong and Macau 61–2; increasing chances of 88–91; under New York Convention 75–6; voluntary payment of awards 63–4
external obstructions to successful Chinese ad hoc arbitration 65–7; eliminating 85–6

finality of arbitration 6
flexibility of ad hoc arbitration 8
foreign arbitration: enforceability of in China 58–2; in the PRC 27–9; PRC's treatment of 23; "quasi-foreign"

arbitration 43; *see also* Chinese ad hoc arbitrations; successful Chinese ad hoc arbitration
formal set-aside proceeding, availability of 71–4
formation of arbitration tribunal 134–5
French law 46–7

general provisions of PRC Arbitration Law 127–8
general venue rule of PRC Civil Procedural Law 73–4
good faith principle 69
Greater China Region: Hong Kong and Macau 41–4; Taiwan 44–5
Guangzhou Maritime Court's enforcement of London ad hoc arbitration award 62

hearings, selecting place for 82
historical background of Chinese arbitration law 2
history of arbitration: ancient and Imperial China 16–17; domestic arbitration in the PRC 23–7; impact of history on current Chinese arbitration law 30–2; in the PRC 22–9; during the Qing dynasty 17–20; in the Republic of China 21–2; in the Western world 14–15; during the Zhou dynasty 109–11
HKIAC (Hong Kong International Arbitration Centre) 96–7
Hong Kong: enforceability of ad hoc agreements 41–4; enforceability of ad hoc arbitration awards in 61–2
hostility of Chinese law towards ad hoc arbitration 1, 12–13, 52–3, 122, 123–4; avoiding 94–5; rationale behind 98–102

ICC Arbitration Rules 90, 96–8
impact of history on current Chinese arbitration law 30–2
Imperial China, arbitration in 16–17
inclusion of ad hoc arbitration in Chinese law, reasons for 105–7
increasing chances of award enforcement: within China 88–91; outside China 91–3
institutional arbitration 7–9, 124; advantages of 9; approaches to 96–8
internal obstructions to successful Chinese ad hoc arbitration 64–5; eliminating 86–7
international arbitration 94–5
Interpretation of SPC on the Arbitration Law of the PRC 148–54
Interpretive Revisions 48–9

judicial assistance, PRC Civil Procedural Law 147
judicial interpretations of the SPC 48–9

Kompetenz-Kompetenz doctrine 31, 120

Law on Application of Law in Foreign-related Civil Relations 50
"legal irritants" 34
legal translation 34–5
legal transplant 3, 32–8; Kahn-Freund on 34; Langer on 34–5; Legrand on 34; Orücü on 34–5; Small on 35; Teubner on 34; theories on 33, 122–3; "transplant effect" 35; Watson on 33
legislation: reforming PRC arbitration law 119–20; relating to "arbitration" in the PRC 26
legislative interpretation 48–9
legitimizing ad hoc arbitration in China 124; arguments for and against 108–9
lex arbitri 46–7; non-Chinese, SPC support of 55–6; selecting 87
litigation, comparison with arbitration 4–7
LMAA (London Maritime Arbitrators Association) 96–7
lower cost: of ad hoc arbitration 8; of arbitration *vs.* litigation 6

Macau: enforceability of ad hoc agreements in 41–4; enforceability of ad hoc arbitration awards in 61–2
measures 49, 142
mediation: adoption of during Zhou dynasty 16, 109–11; awards 113–14; in contemporary China 111–14; in the Qing dynasty 20; in traditional China 111
Medieval Period, arbitration in 15
misconceptions of arbitration under Chinese law 95, 120

neutrality of arbitration 4–5
New York Convention 2, 4, 5, 7, 40–1, 61–2, 81, 88, 97; Article I(2) 39, 59; Article V(1)(a) 59–60, 76–8, 91–2; Article V(1)(e) 78–80, 92–3; China's obligation to enforce arbitration awards 58; China's obligation to uphold 11; enforceability of Chinese ad hoc arbitration awards 75–6; international arbitration framework 94–5

non-Chinese law, enforceability of ad hoc agreements 45–6, 87–93
non-Chinese *lex arbitri*, SPC support of 55–6
non-domestic award, enforcement of 88–91
Notices 23, 49
NPC (National People's Congress) 48–9; Commentaries on Arbitration Laws of China 60–1

obstructions to successful Chinese ad hoc arbitration: eliminating 85–6, 86–7; external 65–7; internal 64–5; timing of 67–9
omission of ad hoc arbitration from PRC Arbitration Law 99–102
One Country, Two Systems 42
Opinions 33, 49, 60, 99, 138

place for hearings, selecting 82
PRC (Peoples Republic of China): arbitration in 22–9; commercial dispute resolution 24–5; domestic arbitration in 23–7; Economic Contract Arbitration Commission 25; foreign arbitration in 27–9; Hong Kong and Macau 41–4; Law on Application of Law in Foreign-related Civil Relations 50; legislation relating to "arbitration" 26; mediation in 112–14; treatment of foreign arbitration in 23
PRC Arbitration Law 1, 10–13, 27; application for setting aside arbitration award 139–40; arbitration agreement 130–2; arbitration commissions and the arbitration association 129–30; arbitration proceedings 132–4; Article 58 73; awards from Chinese ad hoc arbitration 63; China's obligation to enforce arbitration awards 58; *de facto* set-aside of awards 74–5; enforceability of foreign ad hoc arbitration awards in China 58–62; enforcement 140; enforcement of award outside China, increasing chances of 91–3; enforcement of award within China, increasing chances of 88–91; external obstructions to successful Chinese ad hoc arbitration 65–7; formal set-aside proceeding not available 71–4; formation of arbitration tribunal 134–5; general provisions 127–8; good faith principle 69; hearing and award 135–9; hostility towards ad hoc arbitration 52–3, 122; impact of history on current Chinese arbitration law 30–2; inclusion of ad hoc arbitration, reasons for 105–7; internal obstructions to successful Chinese ad hoc arbitration 64–5; omission of ad hoc arbitration from 99–102; rationale behind hostility towards ad hoc arbitration 98; reforming 119–20; rejection of ad hoc arbitration agreements under 39–41; special provisions for arbitration involving foreign elements 140–2; supplementary provisions 142–3; timing of obstructions to Chinese ad hoc arbitration 67–9; waiver rules 67–9; *see also* PRC Civil Procedure Law
PRC Civil Procedure Law 59; application for execution and referral 144–5; arbitration 145–6; Article 274 72; general venue rule 73–4; good faith principle 69; judicial assistance 147; provisions on mediation 112–13; *see also* unenforceable awards under Chinese law
private arbitration 94, 120
pro-arbitration stance of SPC 1–2, 11–12, 52–4, 125

Qing dynasty, arbitration during 17–20
"quasi-foreign" status: Hong Kong and Macau 43; Taiwan 44–5

rationale behind China's hostility towards ad hoc arbitration 98–102
recommendations for successful ad hoc arbitration in China: adopting a carefully crafted drafting strategy 81–5; arbitration rules, selecting 82; place for hearings, selecting 82
reform: of arbitration law in China 119–20; of Chinese ad hoc arbitration 102–4; of PRC's legal system 22–3, 125; of Qing dynasty legal system 19
Regulations 48–9, 142
rejection of ad hoc arbitration agreements under Chinese law 39–41
Replies 48–9
Reply letters 49
Republic of China: arbitration during 21–2; mediation during 111–12
Rome, arbitration in ancient times 14–15
rule-of-law in China 2
rules: general venue rule of PRC Civil Procedural Law 73–4; ICC Arbitration

Rules 90; of institutional arbitration 9; selecting for Chinese ad hoc arbitrations 82; of SPC judicial interpretation 48–9; UNCITRAL Arbitration Rules 53–4, 98; validity-preferring 46–7, 52–; waiver rules 67–9

seat of arbitration 31; selection of law governing 52–4, 82; *see also* Chinese ad hoc arbitrations
selection of law governing arbitration agreement 46–7, 52–4, 82
set-aside of awards: *de facto* set-aside possible 74–5; formal set-aside proceeding not available 71–4
sovereign states as party to ad hoc arbitration 8
SPC (Supreme People's Court of China): choice-of-law rule on an arbitration agreement's validity 49–2; decisions regarding ad hoc arbitration 82–5; interpretation on arbitration law of the PRC 148–54; judicial interpretations 48–9; pro-arbitration stance of 1–2, 11–12, 52–4, 125; role in implementing ad hoc arbitration in China 114–19; support of ad hoc arbitration seated in China 56–7; support of non-Chinese *lex arbitri* 55–6
substantive law of the container contract, selecting 52–4
successful Chinese ad hoc arbitration 63–4, adopting a carefully crafted drafting strategy 81–5; arbitration rules, selecting 82; enforcement of award outside China, increasing chances of 91–3; enforcement of award within China, increasing chances of 88–91; external obstructions, eliminating 85–6; internal obstructions, eliminating 86–7; place for hearings, selecting 82
Swiss law, validity-preferring rule 46–7

Taiwan, enforceability of ad hoc agreements in 44–5
theories on legal transplant 33, 122–3; *see also* legal transplant
timing of obstructions to Chinese ad hoc arbitration 67–9
"transplant effect" 35

UNCITRAL Arbitration Rules 8, 53–4, 87, 98, 120
unenforceable awards under Chinese law 69–70; *de facto* set-aside 74–5; formal set-aside proceeding not available 71–4; *see also* awards
United Nations Convention on the Recognition and Enforcement of Foreign Arbitral Awards *see* New York Convention
universal enforceability of arbitration 5–6

validity of arbitration agreements in China 10
validity-preferring rule 46–7, 52–4
voluntary payment of ad hoc arbitration awards 63–4

waiver rules 67–9

Zhou dynasty, adoption of mediation 16, 109–11
Züblin International GmbH v. Wuxi Woco General Engineering Rubber Co. Ltd 89–91

For Product Safety Concerns and Information please contact our EU
representative GPSR@taylorandfrancis.com
Taylor & Francis Verlag GmbH, Kaufingerstraße 24, 80331 München, Germany

www.ingramcontent.com/pod-product-compliance
Ingram Content Group UK Ltd.
Pitfield, Milton Keynes, MK11 3LW, UK
UKHW011017180926
475701UK00004B/801
* 9 7 8 0 3 6 7 5 8 4 5 3 5 *